Communication Issues
in Autism and Asperger Syndrome

also by Olga Bogdashina

Theory of Mind and the Triad of Perspectives on Autism and Asperger Syndrome
A View from the Bridge
Olga Bogdashina
ISBN 1 84310 361 3

Sensory Perceptual Issues in Autism and Asperger Syndrome
Different Sensory Experiences – Different Perceptual Worlds
Olga Bogdashina
Foreword by Wendy Lawson
Foreword by Theo Peeters
ISBN 1 84310 166 1

of related interest

Autistic Thinking – This is the Title
Peter Vermeulen
Foreword by Francesca Happé
ISBN 1 85302 995 5

Autism – The Search for Coherence
Edited by John Richer and Sheila Coates
ISBN 1 85302 888 6

Enabling Communication in Children with Autism
Carol Potter and Chris Whittaker
ISBN 1 85302 956 4

The Development of Autism
A Self-Regulatory Perspective
Thomas L. Whitman
ISBN 1 84310 735 X

Understanding and Working with the Spectrum of Autism
An Insider's View
Wendy Lawson
Foreword by Margot Prior
ISBN 1 85302 971 8

Autism – The Eighth Colour of the Rainbow
Learn to Speak Autistic
Florica Stone
ISBN 1 84310 182 3

Communication Issues
in Autism and Asperger Syndrome

Do we speak the same language?

Olga Bogdashina

Jessica Kingsley Publishers
London and Philadelphia

First published in 2005
by Jessica Kingsley Publishers
116 Pentonville Road
London N1 9JB, UK
and
400 Market Street, Suite 400
Philadelphia, PA 19106, USA

www.jkp.com

Copyright © Olga Bogdashina 2005
Second impression 2005

Library of Congress Cataloging in Publication Data
Bogdashina, Olga.
    Communication issues in autism and Asperger syndrome : do we speak the same language? / Olga Bogdashina.
        p. cm.
Includes bibliographical references and indexes.
    ISBN 1-84310-267-6 (pbk.)
    1. Autistic children--Language. 2. Asperger's syndrome--Patients--Language. 3. Communicative disorders in children. 4. Language acquisition. 5. Interpersonal communication. I. Title.
    RJ506.A9B64 2004
    618.92'855--dc22

                                                                        2004010449

British Library Cataloguing in Publication Data
A CIP catalogue record for this book is available from the British Library

ISBN-13: 978 1 84310 267 0
ISBN-10: 1 84310 267 6

Printed and Bound in Great Britain by
Athenaeum Press, Gateshead, Tyne and Wear

To my children, Alyosha and Olesya

Acknowledgements

I'd like to express my gratitude to the service users of the Thorne House Services for Adults with Autism who very patiently taught me to communicate the 'autistic way' and especially those non-verbal individuals who 'talked' to me about their experiences and concerns.

My warmest thanks go to Ian Wilson who kindly drew the pictures to illustrate some of my ideas.

My special thanks to:

- Eric Jiani Phipps, a very talented artist with ASD, who provided me with his paintings that brilliantly illustrate the creative power of imagination.

- Louis, an extraordinary autistic boy, for his drawings to be used in my book.

- my autistic son, Alyosha, for being my 'language teacher' after seven years of complete silence. Despite all the official predictions that my boy would never talk, Alyosha has proved them wrong. Now he is verbally bilingual (Russian and English) and in addition he 'speaks' several non-verbal languages, his favourite phrase being: 'I'm such a linguist'. You definitely are!

- all the autistic individuals who are willing to share their experiences in order to help us understand what it is like to 'live autistic'.

And I'd love to thank all the staff of the Thorne House Services for Adults with Autism, my friends Julie and Barbara, my husband and my daughter for their support throughout this project.

Contents

List of figures and tables

Introduction

It takes more work to communicate with someone whose native language isn't the same as yours. And autism goes deeper than language and culture; autistic people are 'foreigners' in any society. You're going to have to give up your assumptions about shared meanings. You're going to have to learn to back up to levels more basic than you've probably thought about before, to translate, and to check to make sure your translations are understood. You're going to have to give up the certainty that comes of being on your own familiar territory, of knowing you're in charge, and let your child teach you a little of her language, guide you a little way into his world. (Sinclair 1993, p.2)

There is a general agreement on the diagnosis of the syndrome of autism according to the behavioural symptoms people with autism exhibit. The present diagnostic classifications – the *Diagnostic and Statistical Manual of Mental Disorders* (DSM-IV: APA 1994) of the American Psychiatric Association and the *International Statistical Classification of Diseases and Related Health Problems* (ICD-10: WHO 1992) of the World Health Organization (WHO) – contain the behavioural descriptions of autistic disorders which are based on the Triad of Impairments formulated by Lorna Wing (1992).

Difficulties with language and communication are one of the defining features of autism. Although language and communication impairments have been recognized as essential characteristics of autism (in fact, they are present in all autistic individuals no matter whether the person is verbal or non-verbal), the nature of the language and communication deficits and their role in manifestation of the syndrome remains controversial.

The researchers in the 1970s and 1980s focused on certain questions they tried to answer in their investigation of the role and nature of language idiosyncrasies in autism, the main question being: Are language deficits in autism primary or secondary characteristics of the condition?

Several possible hypotheses have been put forward:

- language deficits in autism are the product of some other primary impairments (Boucher 1976; Waterhouse and Fein 1982)

- language deficits are primary impairments, causing all the other manifestations of autistic symptoms: impairments in social interaction, rigidity of thinking and challenging behaviours (Churchill 1972; Rutter, Bartak and Newman 1971). However, it was found that some children who did develop good grammar and vocabulary still exhibited behaviours specific to autism.

Since the late 1980s, research on language and communication in autism has focused on deficits in the area of pragmatics of the language. Most studies of language development and deficits in autism have been conducted on children with high-functioning autism. This is understandable as these children have some spontaneous speech, which allows researchers to make certain comparisons and conclusions. Some other studies have investigated echolalia. Non-verbal autistic children have been underrepresented in the research of language development.

Traditionally, language is looked upon as a key prognostic factor in autism and the level of language and communicative competence achieved is seen as a measure of outcome. Besides, language development is closely related to the development of social behaviour. There is evidence that so-called bizarre and inappropriate behaviours that are a feature of autism can be significantly reduced with the development of communicative abilities (Carr and Durand 1985). Because of this, most treatments of autism have the development of language and communication skills as their major goal. Different approaches to address this goal have been developed. These approaches vary significantly depending on underlying theories and philosophies. While it is often the practical recommendations that are in demand, it is necessary to make sure that each particular approach has a sound theoretical framework/foundation in order to explain why some methods work with some children but not with others. If we do not understand *why* this particular approach works (or does not work) with this particular child, any progress becomes doubtful. A sound theory can provide a strong conceptual foundation for the understanding of communication problems in autism and for improving the efficiency of strategies to develop communication skills.

Since the 1980s there has been a shift of attention from language to communication impairments as the fundamental problem. The argument is that both verbal and non-verbal forms of communication are affected and, even if structural language ability is good (in cases of individuals with high-functioning autism and those with Asperger syndrome), communication and the social use of language remain impaired. This approach to communication problems rather than language *per se* seems quite justifiable. However, in this book I try to combine both approaches and consider the tools of communication and cognition in autism. I would like to return to language difficulties in autism from different perspectives by answering the questions:

- What language are we discussing?

- Is the verbal language the only language possible?

The main assumption in this book (to which we will return over and over again) is that the 'triadic' impairments of social interaction, communication and imagination are better described as qualitatively different ways to interact, communicate and process information which do not coincide with conventional ones.

It is like learning to speak a foreign language. When we find ourselves among foreigners, we do not assume that they have nothing to say or that they cannot communicate. If we want to understand them and to establish communication with them, we have to learn their language or find an interpreter.

Now that we do realize how fundamentally different autistic people are, it is worth acquiring knowledge about the culture of these 'dyscultural' (Richer 2001) people in order to make the 'culturalization process' less painful for them.

> To acquire such knowledge one must put aside all theories, pertaining to developmental psychology and actually try to gain an understanding of how people with autism think and feel. The best way of doing that is, of course, to listen to and read accounts by young people and adults with the disability. (Gerland 1998, p.32)

Imagine the situation. You have to go on a business trip to a foreign country, say, to China. Do you bother to learn the Chinese language and culture? I doubt it. Does it stop you from going there? No way. You expect that the

Chinese know your language (at least a few hundred words), so you can communicate with them. The same is our approach to autistic people. We expect *them* to know our language and our culture (and we are always happy to help them learn it), but we are not bothered to learn even a few words of theirs. It is unfair. Let us meet them halfway. Let us learn their communication systems and teach them to translate from ours to theirs. It will enable both sides to communicate with each other.

Let us learn their language(s). If they try to interpret our way of functioning, why can't we do the same? Since imagination is one of the areas in which people with autism have difficulty, it should be easier for us to imagine what it is like to experience the world in an 'autistic way' than the other way round. Then we could help autistic people use their natural mechanisms to learn and develop their potential. We could help them develop strategies to deal with their difficulties, such as sensory hypersensitivities and information overload. We could help them cope with behavioural and emotional problems. And, what is very important, we could learn their communication systems and teach them translation skills in order to make communication easier for both us and them.

As we know that autistic people have differences in their brain structure or/and chemistry (for whatever reasons this might be) we must assume that their development is different and they follow different stages (or the same stages but in a different order). So, in this book the comparison of their development with that of the non-autistic population is undertaken only in order to explain about their differences and not to find ways to 'correct' or 'repair' their development.

In **Part 1** we identify the theoretical foundation and the main concepts that will be used throughout the book. First we define communication, language and speech, and examine a range of communicative functions and different means of communication (Chapter 1) in order to create a framework for the discussion. In Chapter 2 there is an overview of theories of language acquisition in normal development and a brief discussion of factors that may cause problems in this domain. We will further consider how sensory perceptual differences affect cognitive processes and are reflected in the differences of thinking, language and communication development (Chapters 3 and 4), and then move on to the discussion of the 'autistic languages' and a controversial issue of 'autistic culture' (Chapters 5 and 6).

Part 2 is devoted to language characteristics, learning styles and language development (Chapters 7 to 9) and 'fluent speakers'' problems (Chapter 10).

Part 3 contains the information on assessment and intervention issues, with practical recommendations for selecting the appropriate methods and techniques to enhance communication based on the specific mode of communication a person uses. It gives some clues as to where to look and what to do in order to help autistic people use their natural mechanisms to learn and develop social and communicative skills.

Now that more and more personal accounts written by autistic individuals have become available, we have a unique opportunity to learn about their own explanations of some phenomena and to get an idea about their inside perspective. For at least 30 years autistic people have been publishing information, trying to communicate the existence of the misinterpretations of their differences, without much professional notice. They are trying to explain something that most of us have *never* experienced. That effort alone can be complex; in addition, they are trying to speak in the language form of typical non-autistics, not in their own language. Many of them have had to learn to translate between the languages. Besides, the ideas are *unconventional* to most of their audience.

The 'What they say' section at the end of each chapter helps the reader to 'see through the eyes' of people with autism and to 'listen to' their problems and experiences first hand.

The 'What we can do to help' sections contain practical recommendations on what to do in order to help autistic individuals in certain areas of functioning.

Throughout the book examples are offered to illustrate different phenomena of autistic perception, thinking, language and communication.

The use of 'he' or 'she' should be taken to imply both genders.

Part 1

Definitions, Theories and Hypotheses

Chapter 1

Communication – Language – Speech

– Que?
– What?
– Si.
– Si? Que-si. What are you trying to say?
– Non, non, non. 'Que' – 'what'.
– Que what?
– Si.
– Si que what? Who is Si-Que-What? What are you talking about, you, silly little man? (*Fawlty Towers: Communication Problems*)

Before we start to discuss our subject matter, we must clearly define and distinguish among the terms we are going to use: communication, language and speech.

Communication

Communication is the transmission and reception of information. According to this definition we may identify the elements necessary for communication to take place as being:

- a sender, i.e. someone who transmits information

- a receiver, i.e. someone who receives information

- something to transmit/communicate about, i.e. an awareness of one's needs, ideas, etc.

- communicative intent, i.e. desire/necessity to affect the receiver's behaviour, emotions, ideas, etc.

- a medium of transmission, i.e. a means of communication shared by both participants.

Many individuals with autism will lack one or more of these pre-requisites to communication. (The possible causes and consequences will be discussed further in Chapters 3 and 4.)

There can be different means of communication (media for transmitting information) – linguistic and non-linguistic ones.

Non-linguistic means of communication include:

- body language

- facial expressions

- gestures

- pictures/symbols (photographs, drawings, cartoons, Makaton system, etc.).

Linguistic means of communication are:

- sign language

- spoken/written language.

A range of communicative functions can be distinguished and grouped into three major categories:

- instrumental ('non-social' – Wetherby 1986), in other words they affect the behaviours of others in order to achieve desirable ends; for example, request for object or action, rejection

- social, in other words they affect mental states; for example, attracting or directing attention to self, object or action

- expressive, in other words they express one's own mental states, emotions; for example, to comment.

Let us investigate how successfully we are able to communicate different messages (instrumental, social, expressive) using only non-linguistic means of communication. Try to communicate the following three messages using either body language or facial expressions, or gestures or pictures/symbols (choose the means of communication you think is most appropriate for the task or use several of them):

1.   Will you give me your pen, please? (instrumental)

2.   The weather forecast for tomorrow is not very good, I am afraid. (social)

3.   'I wandered lonely as a cloud/ That floats on high o'er vales and hills.' (expressive)

What difficulties did you experience in transmitting information by nonverbal means? What did this experience tell you about the use of language in communication?

Language is the best of all other means of communication because of its flexibility, expressiveness and efficiency. Unlike other forms of communication, language permits us to transmit an infinite number of messages (Moulton 1970). Only language can be used for all the messages that we want to transmit. But what is language?

Language

Language is typically defined as a structured symbolic form of communication, consisting of the use of words in agreed way. Another definition of 'language' is a system of symbols (words) and methods (rules) of combination of these symbols (words) used by a section or group of people (as a nation, community, etc.).

Thus, the main characteristics of language are as follows:

1.   *Language is a system of signs, or a code,* whereby ideas about the world are represented through a conventional system of arbitrary signals for communication (Bloom and Lahey 1978). Sounds form words and words form sentences according to a system of rules. These rules determine which sounds can be combined. For instance, in English it is atypical to find the words with more than two consonant sounds combined together, whereas in the Polish language four or five consonant sound combinations are very common. As a code, language is a way to represent one thing with another without reproducing the original stimuli. In order to represent information in a message we have to *encode* this information, i.e. combine the code's elements using the rules and methods used by the people speaking this language. In order to extract the information from a message, the receiver has to *decode* it, i.e. recognize the code's elements.

2.   *Language is a convention.* The members of a particular community have agreed on the usage of words. Language represents shared knowledge (Bloom and Lahey 1978). This conventional characteristic means that each language contains distinctive elements of the culture of people who speak it.

Language can be *receptive* (the language we understand) and *expressive* (the language we use).

Moulton (1970) defines language as an *abstract structure* connected at two ends with concrete reality: at one end there is a sound/letter, at the other end are the receiver's experiences. Outside language (i.e. at either end, sound or experience) there is no linguistic structure. Inside language, however, there is a structure.

The smallest units of language structure are *phonemes*. Standing alone, phonemes usually have no meaning. We get meaning out of a sequence of phonemes arranged in a particular order. We can understand the meaning of these sequences of phonemes only if we know the language of the speaker, as different languages structure sound in different ways. The smallest unit of language to have meaning is the *morpheme*. Morphemes consist of phonemes.

Syntax or *grammar* represents the combination of morphemes into meaningful sentences.

At the other end, language connects with the cognitive reconstruction of the reality based on the experiences of the receiver. Moulton (1970) states that there are major differences between the concrete realities at either end of language. The number of meaningful units at the experience end is much larger than the number of phonemes.

We can only speculate how structured sound is translated into meaningful units. Given the diversity of experiential background of, for example, a child and an adult, and the diversity of cognitive processes of, for instance, autistic and non-autistic people, the exact meaning of the language units will be different.

Speech

Language (an abstract structure) finds its reflection in speech. *Speech* is defined as the faculty or art of speaking. As speech is the form of language existence (realization) it can be external (to perform a communicative function of language) and internal (to reflect a cognitive function). External speech is subdivided into spoken and written.

Box 1.1 Components of the structure of language

Bloom and Lahey (1978) distinguish three major components of the structure of language: content, form and use. The relationship among content or meaning, form or coding, and use or purpose provides a rationale for describing language development and understanding language disorders.

The *content* of language is the topics represented in a message and the relationships among these topics. Bloom and Lahey single out three main categories of language content: object knowledge, relations between objects and relations between events. *Semantics*, the content of language, is the linguistic representation of what persons know about the world of objects, events and relations (Bloom and Lahey 1978).

The *form* of language is represented by the units of sound (*phonology*), the units of meaning (*morphology*), and the rules of combination of these meaningful units (*syntax*).

The *use* of language has two components: *purpose* (the reason people speak) and *context* (the conditions of communication). Both purpose and context influence the form and content of the message.

The integration of content, form and use represents the speaker's language competence.

Different types of speech reflect different ways or mechanisms of expressing or formulating the thought. Thus, thinking is reflected in the formulation of the thought in the form of internal speech. Speaking is the expression of the thought in the form of external speech.

Thus, language is an abstract structure that can be filled in with symbols (representing particular language) in accordance with the rules of this language. So, given this definition, what other forms of communication could be considered language?

Other forms of language

Sign language is a complex visual–spatial language that meets all the requirements of a true language. It is linguistically complete with its own phonetics (rules for handshapes), morphology (rules for forming the words), and syntax (creating sentences). Though sign languages are onomatopoeic, like spoken (verbal) words the signs are arbitrary. For instance, each Australian sign 'dialect' uses quite different signs for familiar animals.

Sign language is not just a 'gestural' version of spoken language as it possesses the potential to express multiple things at the same time. (In contrast, spoken language is linear – a stream of phonemes combined in words and sentences one at a time.) Although a 'sign language word' (kinaesthetic and visual) is quite different from a spoken word they are cognitively equivalent in terms of the subject–referent relationship. The only difference between these two domains is in the modality of expression (Bates *et al.* 1979; Petitto *et al.* 2000). Deaf children acquire their manual–visual language as rapidly as hearing children acquire speech. The semantic relations expressed in sign language develop in the same sequence that has been reported for hearing children (Bates *et al.* 1979) and according to the same time schedule (Petitto and Marentette 1991). It is significant that formal sign language is processed in the language areas of the brain (left hemisphere), while gestures are dealt with in other regions of the brain (Carter 1998). Sociolinguistic studies show that, like spoken languages, sign languages change over time, demonstrating the same types of historical change that are seen in spoken languages (Petitto 1994; Woodward 1976); for example, signs borrowed from other sign languages (Battison 1978). Another important implication of these findings is that speech (spoken language), *per se*, is not critical to the language acquisition. Whether the language comes as speech, as sign language, or in some other way does not appear to matter to the brain (Petitto *et al.* 2001).

Sign language is 'spoken' by particular communities; for instance, deaf people. There is a great diversity of sign languages (American Sign Language, British Sign Language, Langue des Signes Quebecoise, etc.) that are not gestural forms of the spoken languages. There is even 'international sign language' – Gestuno – developed by the World Federation of the Deaf. Gestuno is not a natural language but a language system to be used with those who 'speak' different signs. It serves the function of Esperanto for 'signing–speaking' communities. Pidgin Sign English is often used when signing to a hearing person.

Box 1.2 The brain: language areas

In approximately 95 per cent of people, the language areas are situated in the left hemisphere of the brain, in the temporal and frontal lobes. The two main areas associated with language have been known as Wernicke's and Broca's. Wernicke's area is believed to be responsible for speech comprehension, and Broca's area for speech production. The same brain activity was shown in deaf individuals 'speaking' sign language. This supports the idea of specific areas of the brain devoted to language. Brain-imaging studies, however, have revealed that other areas are also involved, and each main language area is probably split into many different sub-areas each of which is responsible for its own type of processing and production of speech. For instance, there are regions where only consonants are processed. Damage to different regions of the brain can result in a wide range of very specific language problems.

The specific functions of these sub-areas are identified by studying people with different language disorders caused by brain injuries. For example, damage to the connections between the auditory cortex and Wernicke's area results in a specific language disorder, called *word deafness*. People with word deafness cannot understand spoken language, though they are able to speak, read and write normally.

People with damage to Broca's area, on the contrary, can understand spoken speech but are unable to produce meaningful sentences. Although they know what they want to say, they are unable to produce any intelligible verbal speech.

In addition to Broca's and Wernicke's areas, other regions of the brain are involved in language function; for instance, motor control areas. Furthermore, the language areas of the brain differ slightly from one person to the next, and even from one language to another in people who are multilingual (Ojemann 1991). (See an extensive review of the brain basis of language and speech in Damasio and Damasio 1992.)

Different sign communities show regional accents in their signing, and different choices of 'words' depending on their socio-economic background (Battison 1978).

Language serves several functions. The main functions of language are considered to be communicative (to be a means of communication) and cognitive (a means of formulating and expressing thoughts). The *communicative* function of language takes the speaker's idea, encodes it and transmits the message. The aim is to bring the speaker's original idea in the mind of the receiver.

Let us consider the *cognitive* function of language – transmitting information between thoughts, and formulating and expressing thoughts – and its reflection in speech (both internal and external). How do we think? Do we think in a continuous stream of internal speech that unfolds itself in external speech?

The following experiment will help us to make some conclusions. Read the following short passage of several sentences and then close your eyes and repeat the passage:

> Many autistic people affectionately, humorously refer to themselves as aliens. They feel displaced on a vast planet, which has a code of life, and understanding they can't ever quite subscribe to. If they are welcomed, however, and cherished as the individuals they are, then there wouldn't be as much dissension on both sides. Aliens can become more comfortable and less paralyzed in fear, while still remaining who they are. Their essence stays the same. Then they don't have to despise their alien status, as if it were forced upon them. Instead, they can enjoy their uniqueness, just as others enjoy theirs. (O'Neill 1999, p.119)

Did you repeat the passage word by word or just convey the gist of it? How can we explain this phenomenon?

The possible explanation is that we transform the language of this passage into meaning, represented in abstract form, and then transform this meaning back into the external speech which is different in form (not in meaning) because of this double transformation.

We may single out several cognitive abilities necessary to 'acquire' mental language:

1.   The ability to make mental images (representations) that represent perceivable objects, people, events – *mental semantics.*

2.   The ability to semantically link sounds/letters or other symbols/signs to these mental representations. These links are symbolic and arbitrary (established by convention). Arbitrariness is seen very clearly in verbal languages: different languages have

different words for the same concepts. In non-verbal languages, they are more literal, though there might be discrepancies between non-verbal languages in different cultural environments.

3.   The ability to establish relations, interactions, causal links, etc. between these representations – *mental syntax*.

Both abilities (linking external representations to mental ones and establishing links between them) are found in animals as well, though the level of categorization and generalization is considerably lower.

What type of language do we think in?

There are several theories on the medium of thoughts. They can be classified into four groups:

1.   Thought involves a non-linguistic medium. This theory reflects the Lockean indirect theory of perception stating that our primary perceptual experiences are of perceptual (for example, imagistic) representations. Peacocke (1992) calls them 'non-conceptualized experiences'.

2.   There are different media used in communication and cognition. Spoken languages serve to communicate meanings that are primarily expressed in an innate language of thought, viz. 'mentalese' (Fodor 1975).

3.   The cognitive conception of language attributes linguistic aspects to the way we think. According to this theory, our thoughts unfold in our native, spoken languages (Carruthers 1996). However, if our thoughts are purely linguistic, do babies (who have no linguistic representational abilities) think? With no linguistic concepts of perceptual experiences, babies do have thoughts (perceptual representations), although they are much less sophisticated than those of adults. The 'linguistic thought' is acquired later in development (Kaye 1995).

4.   Different 'mental languages' coexist. Qualitative thoughts may be conscious without being linguistically represented, although much human conscious thought occurs in spoken language because that is the dominant medium for thinking in humans (Kaye 1995).

The latter interpretation of the 'cognitive languages' seems more reasonable as it recognizes the existence of qualitatively different cognitive media. In fact, there is no evidence that verbal language is the only means of cognitive operations in adults. There have been found other types of cognitive processes as well; for instance, perceptual memory or visual thinking. Merlin Donald (1991) argues that thinking 'without language' is not necessarily primitive and can be remarkably sophisticated. To support his claim, Donald gives two examples of non-linguistic ('non-verbal') thinking. The first one is the capabilities of congenitally deaf individuals who (for whatever reasons) have not yet acquired *any* language. The second is the case of a French-Canadian monk, Brother John, who suffers from frequent epileptic fits that leave him totally aphasic for hours. Although during these periods Brother John can neither comprehend nor produce words (i.e. has no language, either external or internal), he can still record the episodes of his life, assess events, assign meanings and thematic roles to agents in various situations, acquire and execute complex skills, learn and remember how to behave in a variety of settings (Donald 1991).

The following example, described by Temple Grandin, a woman with high-functioning autism, is a brilliant illustration of the use of 'non-linguistic thoughts' in making conscious decisions:

> The near-accident occurred in fairly light traffic on a sunny day while I was driving to the airport… Cruising along at 70 miles per hour in the southbound lane, I suddenly saw a huge bull elk running full speed across the northbound lanes. I knew I had to react quickly to avoid hitting him. Instantly, three pictures appeared in my mind. Each picture represented the end result of an option available to me. The first picture was of a car rear-ending my car. I knew from experience that slamming on the brakes could cause this. The next picture was the elk smashing through my windshield. From my understanding of animal behavior, I knew that swerving or any sudden movement of my car might cause the elk to stop or slow down. The third picture was of the elk passing harmlessly in front of my car. In this picture I saw what would happen if I gently applied the brakes to slow down. These pictures were like the picture menus one can click on an Internet web page. They appeared in my mind one at a time, but all within one second. This was enough time for me to selectively compare the options and choose the slow down gradually picture. I immediately calculated the elk's trajectory and speed coming across the highway, and my speed and position in the southbound lane, and began to slowly apply the brakes. This choice prevented me from being rear-ended, or having the elk crash through my windshield. The conscious choice was a visual process without the use of internal verbal dialog. (Grandin 1998)

(We will discuss 'non-verbal' thinking in Chapter 4.)

Research (Farah 1989; Zeki 1992) shows that verbal thought and visual thinking work via different brain systems. Could it mean that people using non-verbal cognitive mechanisms (for whatever reasons this may be) think in and 'speak' a different language?

Let us conduct a simple memory test often used in research of autistic children's cognitive abilities – try and recall as much as possible of the following strings of words:

1. SUMMER – HOME – WHERE – AGAIN – PEN – MY – IS

2. WHERE – IS – MY – PEN – HOME – AGAIN – SUMMER

3. IN – SUMMER – WE – OFTEN – GO – TO – THE – COUNTRY – SIDE – TO – SEE – OUR – RELATIVES

Similar experiments were conducted with autistic children, intellectually disabled and normal children. The researchers (Frith 1989; Happé 1994) describe the results of these experiments as follows: autistic children were consistent in that they always remembered the end of the string, regardless of what kind of string it was. In contrast, non-autistic children only did this when the word string was entirely random (string 1 in our case). However, when half of the string was a proper sentence (string 2 – 'where – is – my – pen') the non-autistic children repeated the sentence wherever it was and lost the rest, whereas the autistic children repeated the last few words just as they always did. When confronted with a string of a super-long sentence (3), which would be beyond the memory span if it had been a string of random words, normal children managed to repeat it (Frith 1989). The author concludes that the ability of autistic children to remember unconnected words almost as well as meaningful sentences can be explained by weak coherence, a lack of preference for coherent over incoherent stimuli (Frith 1989). In contrast, non-autistic children exhibit strong central coherence, i.e. a tendency to process incoming information in context for gist.

However, let us look at these results from a different perspective, that is, language understanding. Another experiment will help us to formulate the hypothesis. The task is the same: try and recall as much as possible of the following strings of words:

1. KNIGA – STOL – OKNO – LODKA – SOBAKA – ZVON

2. ZIMA – VESNA – LETO – OSEN – VREMENA – GODA

Did you repeat the last/first few seemingly meaningless words in both strings? If you did, does it mean you also manifest weak central coherence? These 'words' seem meaningless to you but for Russian-speaking people they make sense. Try again with the translations:

1. BOOK – TABLE – WINDOW – BOAT – DOG – BELL

2. WINTER – SPRING – SUMMER – AUTUMN – ARE – SEASONS

Are the results better now?

We may hypothesize that autistic children (or at least some of them) 'speak' (even those who are mute) a different language. Verbal language is a sort of foreign language for them. And as they do not learn it naturally earlier in their lives, we have to help them master their second language with the support of their 'first language' if we want to share a means of communication with them.

So, what language do autistic people speak? And can we talk about any language at all in the case of non-verbal people? The answer is affirmative. Non-verbal people do possess their own language system, external and internal speech. Before we can teach them a 'foreign language' we have to learn theirs first in order to get the ability to 'interpret/translate' their messages at the initial stages of our communication with them.

Let us return to the definition of language. 'Language' is a system of signs that serves as a means of communication and a means of formulating and expressing thoughts. It is conventional to identify signs in this definition as words. The error of mistaking the acoustic/written manifestation of language (reflected in speech) for language itself leads to the misconception that the language is necessarily verbal. However, although they are conventional, verbal (linguistic) words are not the only signs that satisfy the criteria of language (cf., for example, sign language). It is logical, therefore, to distinguish two types of language: verbal (consisting of words) and non-verbal (consisting of non-verbal symbols). From this perspective, the assumption (expressed by some professionals) that non-verbal children 'lack inner language' would be incorrect.

Box 1.3 Language and intelligence

– 'Are you brainless? You almost got us killed!'

The creature looked offended:

– 'Brainless? I can speak!'

– 'The ability to speak does not make you intelligent!'

Qui-Gon was having none of it. (*Star Wars. Episode 1: The Phantom Menace*, Brooks 1999, p.43)

In the case of autism, level of language competence is often considered to be a precursor of positive outcome. But is it always the case? And what is the connection between language and intelligence?

There are some conditions that bring doubts as to whether there is any direct link between the level of communicative/language development and the person's IQ, and whether language can be an indicator of a good prognosis. For instance, Williams syndrome is a syndrome of infantile hyper-calcaemia, heart abnormalities and a characteristic facial appearance. It is believed to be caused by a genetic mutation that produces considerable mental retardation (the average IQ of people with Williams syndrome is between 50 and 70) and yet very remarkable linguistic skills, empathy and intuition. People with this condition seem very articulate and can talk fluently and very expressively; however, they use language not for conveying information but for its own sake – they enjoy talking without saying anything.

On the other hand, sometimes patients have lost their speech, both internal and external, as a result of a specific brain injury; however, there is no evidence that the loss of speech has brought cognitive deficits. In his book *The Origins of the Modern Mind* (1991), Merlin Donald compares the loss of language in these patients to the loss of a sensory system: they have lost a tool that simplifies their functioning but, as in the case of a blind or deaf person, this loss is not accompanied by diminished intellect or consciousness.

Autistic individuals emphasize that all autistic people have a form of inner language even if they cannot communicate through conventional systems such as typing, writing or signing (O'Neill 1999; Williams 1996).

What they say

Although words are symbols, it would be misleading to say that I didn't understand symbols. I had a whole system of relating which I considered 'my language'. It was other people who did not understand the symbolism I used, and there was no way I could or was going to tell them what I meant. I developed a language of my own. Everything I did, from holding two fingers together to scrunching up my toes, had a meaning... Sometimes it had to do with telling people how I felt, but it was so subtle it was often unnoticed or simply to be some new quirk that 'mad Donna' had thought up. (Williams 1999b, pp.30–1)

I would be denied the ability to think by scientists who maintain that language is essential for thinking... My experience as a visual thinker with autism makes it clear to me that thought does not have to be verbal...to be real. I considered my thoughts to be real long before I learned that there was a difference between visual and verbal thinkers. I am not saying that animals and normal humans and autistics think alike. But I do believe that recognizing different capacities and kinds of thought and expression can lead to greater connectedness and understanding. (Grandin 1996a, pp.159, 164)

Chapter 2

Language Acquisition – The Theories

> *Poirot:* What have I always told you? Everything must be taken into account. If the fact will not fit the theory – let the theory go. (*The Mysterious Affair at Styles,* Christie 2000, p.77)

A number of theories of language development have been proposed. The major ones are:

- a behavioural theory
- a biological theory
- a cognitive theory
- a psycholinguistic theory
- a pragmatic/social-interactive theory.

A behavioural theory

A *behaviouristic* explanation focuses on language as a learned skill and speech as a form of human behaviour, viz. verbal behaviour. There are two schools of thought on the nature and development of language: the traditional behaviouristic school, represented by Skinner (1957), and the neo-behaviouristic one (Mowrer 1960; Osgood 1962).

Skinner excludes from his inquiry everything that cannot be observed (e.g. cognitive processes) and concentrates only on the observable in verbal behaviour, i.e. the physical manifestations of language. He considers the verbal behaviour as that consisting of stimulus–response associations which should be reinforced by another organism. The reinforcement may come also through a kind of sub-vocal conversation, i.e. the individual may reinforce his own behaviour (Skinner 1957). According to Skinner, children acquire language when sounds they utter are selectively reinforced and shaped by the environment. In other words, parents (or other adults) must just wait until an adequate response is uttered and reinforce it.

A number of scientists have considered this behaviourist position too rigid and unrealistic as there is more to verbal behaviour than there is to other forms of behaviour. The works of I. Pavlov, L.S. Vygotsky and A.R. Luria have shown that the classical conditioning principle cannot be applied to the verbal behaviour; moreover, it is speech that has a directive effect on other forms of behaviour and transforms them (Tikhomirov 1959). Some studies (Brown and Hanlon, 1970; Demetras, Post and Snow 1986; Hirsh-Pasek, Treiman and Schneiderman 1984) showed that the behaviourist explanation was unreliable: for instance, they did not find any correlation between parents' responses to their child's utterances (both grammatical and ungrammatical) and the child's progress in language acquisition.

To avoid the flaws of Skinner's theory, neo-behaviourists focus on inferred mediating processes in language acquisition. Osgood (1962) originated mediation theory and introduced this formula: stimulus – mediating response – self-stimulus within the organism – response.

A stimulus, representing a number of stimuli associated with the object, arouses reactions of the organism. When these stimuli reappear later, in the absence of the original object, they continue to elicit part of the total reactions to the object, thus becoming *signs* of the original stimulus-object. According to Osgood, there is a meaning ('a representational mediation process') in verbal behaviour. This mediating 'meaning' is a distinctive part of the total reaction to an object that becomes conditioned to the word for that object. These mediating reactions may be aroused by the object itself, or by stimuli associated with the object (words or signs).

Mowrer (1960) takes the theory of mediation one step further. He believes that the 'representational mediation process' in the verbal behaviour is that part of the total reaction to an object that has become conditioned to emotions – fear or disappointment (secondary motivation) and hope or relief (secondary reinforcement). On the basis of his observations with children, Mowrer (1960) originated his *autism* or *self-satisfaction theory* of language acquisition – the child learns his first words from his mother for whom he feels warm emotions; in order to recreate the same feelings he repeats these words over and over again, reinforcing the verbal behaviour in the absence of the mother, and thus learning the language. According to this theory, emotions are key factors in learning one's mother tongue: the emotions of fear and hope, and their counterparts relief and disappointment, are mediating reactions which become conditioned to stimuli associated with some actions which result in reward or punishment.

Some researchers (for example Miller 1951; Lewis 1957) support Mowrer's autism theory and emphasize the important role of emotions in a child's acquisition of language. Lewis points out that:

> nothing could be less 'neutral' for the child. The word comes to him charged with emotion, as much a part of his experience of his mother at this moment as her physical presence... So that when...the phonetic pattern of the word comes to stand out for him in this experience, it carries for him a richness of emotional experience. (Lewis 1957, p.73)

Mowrer (1960) distinguishes several elements in 'meaning' (of a word): emotional or evaluative and cognitive or denotative. The proportion of these elements will vary from individual to individual. A certain stability of meaning for most words can be explained by common experiences, whereas the particular experiences of the individual will always be present as a certain distinctive mediating reaction.

This approach accounts for the fact that different words (synonyms) can bring very similar responses as they are conditioned to the same mediating process or 'mediated equivalence of cues' (Mowrer 1960). On the other hand, objects which appear very similar to others may arouse different responses from the individual as they might have acquired specific meaning for her ('mediated discrimination of cues'; Mowrer 1960). This may explain why there can be misunderstandings in communication even among people speaking the same language and accounts for the development of specific personal responses and individual vocabulary.

Mowrer (1960) believes that during communication we do not transfer meaning to another person but, by associating and combining the meanings he has already acquired, we give him new information, i.e. while communicating we transfer meanings from sign to sign within that person.

Both behaviouristic and neo-behaviouristic explanations of language development consider environmental variables as the major factors, with a child as a passive learner in the process.

A biological theory

A *biological* interpretation of language acquisition focuses on innate language mechanisms that automatically unfold with the development of a child.

Eric Lenneberg (1967), a prominent researcher in the field, believes that language development is genetically programmed alongside with motor and cognitive development. Language appears at a certain age and develops at a certain pace. Language development begins slowly (by 18 months of age a child learns between 3 and 50 words) and then suddenly accelerates – the so-called 'language explosion' takes place (by the end of the third year a child's expressive speech contains about 1000 words, and her receptive vocabulary is about 3000 words) and by the age of four she has acquired the grammar of her mother tongue. According to this theory, the child does not 'learn language'. With the development the genetic programme for language unrolls. 'Learning' consists of adapting this programme, revising it and adjusting it to fit the realities of the cultural language the child happens to encounter. Without such a programme, the simplest of cultural languages would be quite unlearnable (Bickerton 1981). This programme would merely require triggering by some form of linguistic activity from others (that is why wolf children, who share our biological inheritance, cannot speak). A normally developing child can acquire any language without difficulty if he is placed in any linguistic community at the right age (Kess 1976). Lenneberg (1967) emphasizes that environmental variables, such as conditioning, reinforcement, imitation, etc., are a poor explanation of the phenomenon, and suggests that language development follows a biological programme which starts unfolding at a certain age and continues until completion (about 12 or 13 years of age). After puberty, the ability to acquire language considerably decreases. The process corresponds to the critical periods of brain development.

A cognitive theory

Cognitive theories of language development consider language as part of cognitive abilities. The most famous of these theories is that of Piaget who links language development to the development of cognitive abilities and shows that language function differs at each of the four cognitive levels.

Piaget (1926) distinguishes two major speech categories:

- *Egocentric speech*: children do not care to whom they speak or whether anyone is listening to them. Egocentric speech is subdivided into three types:

  1. repetition (devoid of social character; children repeat words and phrases for the mere pleasure of talking – talking for its own sake)

  2. monologue (children talk to themselves – thinking aloud)

  3. collective monologue (other children are present but not listening to the speaker – speech is not addressed to anybody in particular).

- *Socialized speech*: children ask questions, answer questions, exchange views, criticize one another. Piaget (1926) believes that children's understanding of other people and their ability to communicate thought does not appear before the age of seven or seven and a half. Piaget draws the parallel between verbal and cognitive abilities, and emphasizes that verbal ability reflects the development of cognitive structures.

A psycholinguistic theory

A *psycholinguistic* interpretation of language acquisition assumes that children are born with an innate knowledge of language – the language acquisition device. The theoretical foundation of this explanation is based on transformational grammar originated by Noam Chomsky (1957). The main assumptions of transformational grammar are:

- All languages share the deep properties of organization and structure.

- These deep structures are innate rather than acquired.

- These structures provide the basis for perception and production of sentences.

Chomsky developed a model of language perception and learning: a physical stimulus (a speech signal) is filtered through a series of beliefs, strategies and memory and transforms into a *percept* (the representation of the original signal and its interpretation by the receiver). Thus, the percept becomes the structural description of the speech signal (containing phonetic, syntactic and semantic information). To illustrate the idea Chomsky uses three sentences:

1.   I told John to leave.

2.   I expected John to leave.

3.   I persuaded John to leave.

On the surface (surface structures) the sentences contain the same elements and structure: subject – *I*, object – *John*, predicate phrase – *to leave*. However, the meanings of the sentences (deep structures, reflected in the percept) are different.

The surface structure is related to the phonetic and grammatical forms, while the deep structure is linked to the semantic interpretation and is not directly connected to the physical signal.

This theory can also account for the identical meaning of different sentences (Aitchison 1976). For instance:

Large brown cows have eaten up the grass	=	The grass has been eaten up by large brown cows

On the one hand, these sentences are different (surface structure); on the other hand, they are the same (deep structure).

Chomsky assumes that children automatically know that language has two levels (surface and deep structures) linked by 'transformations'. Children gradually recognize speech regularities and make assumptions about the rules of their mother tongue, thus constructing internalized grammatical structures. No matter what their native language is, children acquire a set of rules for forming speech patterns and sentences that they have never heard before, because they possess innate language knowledge with pre-programmed language universals that can fit any language. According to Aitchison, children's assumptions are actually guesses or hypotheses, which develop and become more sophisticated with age. It means they must possess an innate hypothesis-making device plus language universals (Aitchison 1976). Because of this innate device children intuitively know how to use their native language in whatever environment they are born.

In opposition to this approach, some authors (Vaneechoutte and Skoyles 1998) argue that language acquisition depends upon a music acquisition device, which has been doubled into a language acquisition device through memetic evolution: children learn spoken language by means of an innate melody recognition capacity. Intonation provides cues to how words are structured in sentences (Morgan 1996) and helps to identify word beginnings. Vaneechoutte and Skoyles (1998) hypothesize that children start off experiencing language as a kind of music, with parents responding to this sensitivity by making their language more musical – so-called 'motherese'.

A pragmatic/social-interactive theory

Unlike psycholinguistic and cognitive interpretations of language acquisition that consider a child to be an active hypothesis-maker who 'discovers' language in the interaction with the environment without any instructions or environmental influences, *pragmatic* theory (Bates 1976) or *social-interactive* theory (Duchan 1984) emphasizes the important role of social experiences in language acquisition.

The main emphasis of these theories is put on the role of social interaction in the development of language and communication. Only through social experience do children learn language and develop communicative skills. It means that both 'parties' (the child and environment) are active in the process. The major concepts of pragmatic/social interaction theories are:

- *Communicative intent and function*: people communicate for a purpose, to get things done (Halliday 1975), to influence others. Children learn how to communicate intentionally by observing others reacting to their behaviour as if it were intentionally communicative (Harding 1984). Gradually, children learn to use more sophisticated means to communicate.

- *Discourse and conversational behaviour*: through social interaction with others children learn to take turns, initiate, respond, maintain or terminate conversation, etc.

- *Language adjustment and social-linguistic sensitivity*: through their social experience children learn to make judgements, adapt to different communicative situations, adjust their language and style in accordance with particular social interactions, etc.

The proponents of these theories justifiably emphasize the active role of both the child and the environment in the acquisition of language.

Problems in language acquisition

All these theories have their strengths and limitations. However, no matter how useful they might seem in explaining the development of language, these theories do not account for the problems some children develop with language acquisition. If we can manipulate the environmental variables to teach children verbal language (as in behavioural theory) then mute and language-disabled children are the product of bad teachers. Or, if we all possess the innate language acquisition device (according to the psycho-linguistic explanation), why does it fail to work for some children? If language is the reflection of cognitive structures (the cognitive interpretation), does it mean that mute children do not think? Or if language is acquired via active social interaction, does it mean that children with language impairments have been ignored by their 'communication partners'?

Why do some children develop problems in language acquisition?

Bloom and Lahey (1978) have identified a list of elements necessary for a child to acquire a language:

1.   An intact peripheral sensory system.

2.   An intact central nervous system.

3.   Adequate mental abilities.

4.   Emotional stability.

5.   Exposure to the language.

Deficits in these categories may cause various impairments and disabilities which, in turn, may produce different language/communication disorders.

It is important to remember that language does not appear from 'nowhere' and does not develop in isolation from other aspects of functioning. In normal development, there are strong interrelationships among cognitive function-ing, social interaction and language/communication development; in other words, all these developmental systems are in close synchrony with one another (Tager-Flusberg 1989). Tager-Flusberg (1988) argues that developmental disorders are characterized in part by the breakdown in these developmental synchronies. There are different profiles of asynchrony in different disorders that provide distinct developmental profiles leading to specific differences in language development; for instance, in Down syndrome there is a different profile of asynchrony from that of autism (Tager-Flusberg 1989).

Bates *et al.* (1979) view language as a new machine created out of various cognitive and social components that initially serve completely different functions. They suggest that the development of the symbolic function (language) emerges out of 'old parts', cognitive and communicative developments that are only indirectly related to language. Because some of these components are 'pre-adapted' to serve non-linguistic and perhaps non-communicative functions, their role in language development may not be obvious. However, if one of the old components is disturbed or delayed, the new (linguistic) system may fail to appear. They conclude that at least some forms of language deficiency may result from a deficit in one or more of the non-linguistic components that underlie the capacity of symbols (Bates *et al.* 1979).

In the next two chapters (3 and 4) we will discuss the 'non-linguistic factors' that could influence the language acquisition and development:

- information processing
- conceptual development.

Chapter 3

From Sensations to Concepts – Via Different Routes

Without being taught, we'd still absorb the sensory patterns of the world around us from which we'd later form more and more complex patterns of interpretation which gets called 'thought'. (Williams 1998, p.73)

Let us start with the definitions and interpretations of the main notions in order to create the framework of our discussion.

Perception is the process by which an organism collects, interprets and comprehends information from the outside world by means of the senses. *Cognition* refers to mental operations such as thinking, conceiving, reasoning, symbolizing, expectancy, complex rule use, problem-solving, imagery, belief and intention (Reber 1995): all the processes by which the sensory input is transformed, reduced, stored, recovered and used. Cognitive processes appear as early as the first days of life (for example, attention) and change throughout our lives, following a discernible pattern (Piaget 1926). In this chapter we will discuss the process of perception and then (in Chapter 4) move on to cognitive mechanisms and strategies.

Stages of perception

The process of perception has several stages. It starts with sensation, when we perceive (see, hear, feel, etc.) the object; then the incoming information passes through special areas in the brain and the sensory perceptions are interpreted (percept, or mental image is created) and then joined with appropriate cognitive associations (concept — idea of a class of objects/general notion — is formed).

We sense (see/hear/touch, etc.), interpret and then get the idea of what we see/hear/touch, etc. and what we can do about it.

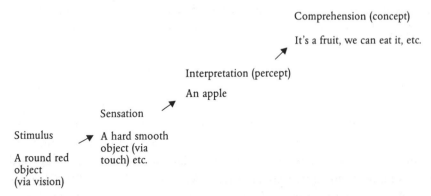

Comprehension (concept)

It's a fruit, we can eat it, etc.

Interpretation (percept)

An apple

Sensation

Stimulus   A hard smooth object (via touch) etc.

A round red object (via vision)

The first stage of perception, when we experience sensation without interpretation and attaching meaning to it, may be called 'literal perception'.

Our earliest experiences are sensory. They begin with sensations, both internal and external. In order to get the sensation (primary information about the object), we need our senses. The senses provide us with the ability to receive sights (vision), sounds (hearing), touch (tactility), smell (olfaction), etc. We are not born with ready-made strategies to interpret and comprehend the world around us. Through interaction with the environment we develop our visual and auditory processing skills, learn how to discriminate different stimuli from a chaos of sounds, shapes, colours, patterns and movements, and learn how to connect sensory images with meaning.

Babies are flooded with sensations which are fragmented through all their sensory modalities. With development and maturation, and by interacting with the environment, babies learn to 'sort out' incoming information and stop 'experiencing sensory flooding' (Williams 2003a). Sensory experiences become linked with one another and become patterned. These are so-called non-verbal (or pre-verbal) ways of knowing about the self and environment. They may be seen as 'sensory abstractions' ('non-verbal thoughts') which are still not sufficiently understood or appreciated. According to Winnicott (1960), this is the basis of 'true self' experience, which derives directly from the world-as-experienced and has its origins in the earliest sensations.

'Sensory knowing' starts with the recognition of patterns and they are less accessible to conscious, verbal, rational thought (Charles 1999; Stern 1994).

Memories of very early experiences (before the appearance of language) become stored and expressed as *sensations* rather than in highly elaborated form (Innes-Smith 1987). These early experiences are remembered and yet not easily accessible. Affective memories appear to exist prior to, and to some extent separate from, cognitive memories; they influence secondary processes whether or not this influence becomes conscious (Bucci 1997; Krystal 1988).

With development, sensory experience becomes transformed into verbal thought, and verbal thought becomes realized through this primary experience, in their ongoing interplay as alternately container and contained (Bion 1963). Sometimes pre-verbal experiences are described as 'primitive'; however, they might be more usefully conceptualized as 'primary' modes of experience because, although verbal/rational ways of knowing become more dominant over time, they do not take the place of, nor are they necessarily more complex than, more implicit ways of knowing (Charles 2001). Here we may distinguish two types of consciousness: thought consciousness and sensory consciousness – where the central issue is not thinking but feeling – 'of being alive and living in the presence of sensation' (Humphrey 2002, p.368).

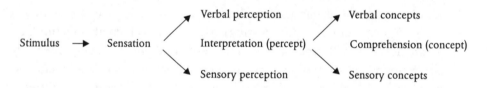

Although verbal capacities develop from the non-verbal ones, the two ways of knowing do not represent a continuum and they are not in opposition with one another; they develop alongside each other as two interactive systems, according to different sets of rules (Matte-Blanco 1975).

Processes of generalization and abstraction are often seen as distinguishing features of verbal rather than non-verbal domains. The concrete is the basis for any real understanding, whereas abstraction has the effect, by removing the concrete and particular, of eliminating aspects that obscure the relationship of one element to another (Bion 1963). However, abstraction is not necessarily always a function of verbal meanings, but rather pertains to semantic relations that may or may not be verbal in form (Johnson-Laird 1989).

The interplay between these two levels of experience is not so different from physiological processes that go on without our awareness, and yet can be affected by both conscious and unconscious thoughts. What analysis offers us is a way to understand and communicate semantic relations that had been unknown in the verbal domain. A lack of appreciation of the nonverbal channels leaves our thinking insubstantial and trivialized, cut off from its roots. Life at either extreme obviously has its drawbacks, but our culture seems to elevate the verbal channels to a point where meaning is diminished... An appreciation of the intertwining and interweaving of the verbal and nonverbal domains of experience may help us to value each without pathologizing either. (Charles 2001)

Although we possess both capacities of interpretation and comprehension of the world all our lives, one of them becomes dominant in very early childhood and develops rapidly. In normal development the dominant side of interpretation (and later on, communication and thinking) is a verbal (symbolic) one, whereas in autism we may observe sensory-based thinking or, at least, a later transition of dominance from sensory to (verbal) symbolic plane of comprehension. Very few individuals remain 'fluent' in both 'languages'. For instance, Donna Williams, a woman with high-functioning autism, has become 'bilingual' in acquiring and becoming reasonably able to use both systems:

In my case, I remember this transition from the system of sensing into the system of interpretation began to happen not in the first days or weeks of life as usual but at around three years old. It was not until around the age of ten that the system of interpretation (with much begrudgement) eventually came to be relied upon rather than merely put up with or tuned out. Even then, it was taken on, not as a first and primary 'language' but as a secondary one and much later as one of two equal but different 'primary' systems. (Williams 1998, p.79)

Some autistic individuals acquire a system of symbols later in life as a secondary (not dominant/primary) language. Some remain 'monolingual' with a sensory-based system; this is in contrast with monolingualism in non-autistic individuals, which is based on verbal (symbolic) system of functioning.

We learn to form concepts. The information that does not fit the concepts is screened out as irrelevant. With the appearance of language and the development of vocabulary the conceptual system changes. Children learn to get meaning from things, people and events, and to go beyond what is perceptually available. They move from non-verbal (and less conscious) to verbal forms of perception, thinking and communication:

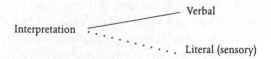

They learn to form categories and generalize. They unite things (not identical but serving the same function, for example) under the same label. Thus 'a cat' becomes a representation of a small soft-furred four-legged domesticated animal, no matter what colour or breed an individual may be (Figure 3.1).

Figure 3.1 A cat, by Ian Wilson

They store concepts (not perceptual images and experiences). These concepts become filters through which all sensory experiences are filtered and organized into classes, groups, types. All sensory information seems to be forced fit into the most likely interpretation based on our prior knowledge (Snyder and Barlow 1988).

Concepts bring order. They help to put 'bits and pieces' of information together to form a cohesive picture. For instance, apparently randomly distributed black spots can be transformed into a meaningful unit when given a name (Figure 3.2).

Figure 3.2 Black spots or a Dalmation dog?

The outside world becomes conceptualized and represented and expressed in words that can be easily operated to create new ideas. Cognitive processes become more efficient and rapid as we 'jump' from a very few perceptual details to conceptual conclusions: we do not need to process all the details to get an idea of what we see. A few details are enough to create expectations and easily fit into their mental representations.

Snyder and Thomas (1997) hypothesize that the brain has mental representations that embody the salient or ecologically significant aspects of the environment that allow for automatic complex actions. The process of interpretation (formulation of the percept) is accelerated by incorporating expectations about familiar or important objects (Snyder and Thomas 1997).

In this context two important issues arise:

1.   the amount of information we actually deal with at a time (see 'Using a short-cut' below), and

2.   the role of attention (see 'Attention' in Chapter 4).

Using a 'short-cut'

How much do we see? In fact, we *see* very little, just a few things our attention happens to focus on. Every time we look at something we just pick up a few features (ignoring irrelevant ones) and 'recognize' the whole picture from our past experiences and memories. When we enter a familiar room, for example, we do not have to examine every item there to recognize it. We just know what and where everything is located. A quick glance is enough. So do we actually *see* the environment or do we just *know* what is there? In fact, our perceptual reconstruction (or what we *think* we see) comes from two opposite directions – from outside (environmental stimuli) and inside (mental images we have stored in the brain). The more familiar the environment or situation, the less we actually perceive it. The brain does not need to process *all* the stimuli; it just 'fills in the gaps' and predicts the final picture. We move through the process

Stimulus ➝ Sensation ➝ Interpretation (percept) ➝ Comprehension (concept)

very quickly. We 'jump' (using a 'short-cut') to the conclusion.

That is why we are easily fooled by visual illusions. It is the object labels (concepts) that are of ultimate importance, as they give us the idea of what is there without any need to be aware of all the details (a few are enough to identify the object). We are blinded by our 'mental paradigms' or mindsets (Snyder 1996a).

This can be illustrated by children's drawings. They draw what they can verbally identify, i.e. they draw not what they see but what they know is there, their own 'internalised schema for objects' (Snyder and Thomas 1997, p.94). Their pictures reflect their mental concepts. For example, they draw a person, an animal, etc. primitively, devoid of details. In contrast, autistic artists (having no mental 'restraints') draw their pictures with minute details, without filtering significant from insignificant information (Figure 3.3). They do not

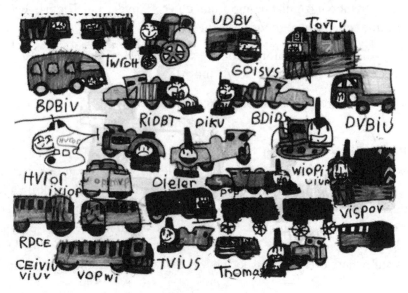

Figure 3.3 Drawing by Louis

impose either linguistic concepts or expectations on their work and consequently, to them, every detail is of equal importance (Snyder 1996a). Their perception is more accurate because the interpretation does not interfere with or distort what is perceived.

Another example of 'seeing from inside' – 'seeing something that does not exist' – is illustrated by a well-known illusion of the Kanizsa triangle (shown in Figure 3.4). Non-autistic individuals report they *see* a triangle. But the triangle does not exist. It is our mind that makes the blank space meaningful. We cannot look at things without interpretation. We impose our concepts on them. Those autistic individuals who have acquired certain conceptual knowledge also succumb to these illusions (see Garner and Hamilton 2001), while those who are at the stage of literal perception do not see the triangle.

Figure 3.4 The Kanizsa triangle

Our interpretation of the world depends on our memories and experiences. We often see what we expect to see or what is closer to our mental representations ('mindsets' – Snyder 1996a). For example, clouds may be seen differently by different people. Somebody will see a garden; someone else, a castle, etc. What a person perceives often reflects that person's past experiences and present beliefs and state of mind. For instance, a Conservative and a Labour MP who listen to the same speech will 'hear' different things and will make different conclusions.

In a way, we are limited in our perception. On the other hand, as Snyder (1996a) puts it, a mind without paradigms is more conscious and hence potentially aware of alternative interpretations. However, there are disadvantages to this 'superability':

- Such a mind would have difficulty in coping with the flood of information and would need routines and structure to make sense of the world, because every detail has to be examined anew each time it is perceived and with equal importance to every other detail.

- There would be lack of (or delay in) development of symbolic systems, such as communication, language and verbal thought (Snyder 1996a).

Snyder hypothesizes that autism may be considered as 'a retarded acquisition of mental paradigms'. At the low-functioning end of the autism spectrum we may find a lack of paradigms across various domains; and at the other end (high-functioning autism and/or Asperger syndrome) individuals can be deficient in only 'the most elaborate mindsets, such as those necessary for subtle social interaction' (Snyder 1996a).

Literal perception

Let us consider possible scenarios (outcomes) of each stage of perception if something goes wrong.

If one (or several) of the senses are lost (for example, sight or hearing), the other senses develop to compensate and restore the balance. Blindness or deafness creates different perceptual images. However, the end product – concept formation – is the same (if a person's blindness or deafness is not complicated by other impairments).

With autism the situation is very confusing. It is not that the senses of autistic people work or do not work; it is that they work differently. What aggravates the issue even more is that these differences (and difficulties) are 'invisible' to outsiders, and the matter is further complicated because no two autistic people appear to have the exactly same patterns of sensory-perceptual experiences.

Many autistic authors describe sensory processing problems as one of the main difficulties they experience. It has been suggested that there is a continuum of sensory processing problems in autism, which goes from perceiving only fractured, disjointed images at one end to a slight abnormality at the other (Grandin 1996b).

Many autistic individuals stop at the first stage of perception, 'literal perception', much longer than non-autistic babies. People with 'low-functioning' autism may remain at this stage well into adulthood and store experiences on the level of sensation:

> Those who appear not to seek to make sense of their environment may not necessarily be 'retarded', disturbed, crazy or sensorily impaired, but may, in spite of not using the same system everyone else uses, still have one of their own. They may, in spite of apparent delayed development, actually continue to use a system that others have left behind very much earlier. (Williams 1998, p.53)

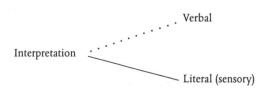

For those who are at the stage of literal perception words have no meanings. They are meaningless sound-patterns and may serve as 'auditory toys' to play with. This leads to literal interpretation. When a child, Tito did not realize that words had any meaning. For him, they were just patterns of wonderful sounds. When his mother was reciting poems, Tito used to play with words in his mind, creating his own rhymes with sound-patterns (Mukhopadhyay 2000).

At the stage of literal interpretation they do not connect verbal labels with sensory experiences. Instead, they have their own 'words' for things, based on sensory patterns. They construct and store sensory perceptual mental images. Autistic 'perceptual words' at the level of interpretation are very concrete and specific. They recognize (interpret) things using these sensory impressions they stored in the memory. For example:

> Most words do not relate in any direct way to sensory experiences. The word 'cat' says nothing of the sound that comes from the thing when stroked, the noise it makes or the tactile sensation felt when stroking it. I had developed two words for the sensory experience of 'cat'. One was 'foosh' which defined it by the sound made by your hand over the fur when stroking the creature. The other was 'brook' (with a rolled 'r') which defined it by the noise which came out of the creature when it was stroked. (Williams 1998, p.80)

> In my early to mid childhood, I would hold what was otherwise a comb but perceive a flat, solid form that could be scraped with teeth and into which a very fine indentation could sometimes be made. I would

perceive it not by its functional purpose but by its sensory one. It was a 'rih-rih' sounding instrument that would make this sound when run across my teeth. (Williams 1998, p.15)

The sensory impressions they store in their long-term memory become templates for recognition and identification. It is at this stage that they develop their 'non-verbal languages', as 'the level of the literal is enough to be able to use much of the language of interpretation on all levels: the language of touch, visual language and auditory language' (Williams 1998, p.104).

Non-autistic children learn socially and culturally accepted notions and have no problems to unite for instance, different breeds of dogs under one label, or accept that one and the same thing may be referred to differently (e.g. coat, anorak or jacket). Autistics either stick to the 'one name – one object' scenario (Example 1), or categorize things and events by their 'sensory feel' ('perceptually-based generalizations') (Example 2).

Example 1: One word – one object

I vividly remember my teacher announcing, 'Children, find your mats and take your nap.' I refused. Again, the teacher called my parents...

'Liane, why won't you take your nap?' my parents wondered of me...'Because I don't have a mat.'

'You most certainly do have a mat. There it is in your cubby', the teacher replied.

'I don't have a mat.'

'You see what I mean?... She is an obstinate child.'

'Why do you say you don't have a mat?' the folks asked, not giving up on me.

'That is not a mat. That is a rug,' I honestly and accurately replied.

'So it is,' said my father. 'Will you take a nap on your rug?'

'If she tells me to,' I said matter-of-factly.

'Tell her to take a nap on her rug,' my father said as my parents turned to take me home... I wasn't trying to be difficult, I was trying to do the right thing. The trouble was, the teacher assumed I understood language like other children did. I did not. (Willey 1999, pp.19–20)

Example 2

Instead of uniting objects under one 'word-umbrella' in accordance with their meaning – purpose, function, form, shape, etc. (for instance, cats, dogs, horses are animals) – some autistic people unite them using sensory-perceptual impressions, thus forming very unconventional (for verbal language) 'synonyms':

> So many things were 'degoitz'. 'Degoitz' was a sound pattern that became associated within emotional sensation triggered by certain sensory-buzz experiences... Instead of objects being labelled by their functional use, I'd label them by their shared sensory-emotional impact and these things, though functionally quite different, even perceptually quite different, were all the same on a sensory-emotional level. They were all 'degoitz'... 'So, describe this (clear deep red) glass will you Donna.' 'Degoitz.' The natural assumption of someone who used only the system of interpretation would have been that either I wasn't listening, was being silly or was showing some kind of disturbed response... (The origin of degoitz was degoitz-degoitz and probably came from associating the emotional sensation that went with tickling with the misheard words tickle-tickle.) (Williams 1998, p.100)

With development and maturation many autistic individuals learn how to 'proceed to the next stage of processing information' – interpretation; while persons with 'low-functioning' autism may be stuck at the stage of sensation much longer. However, in the state of sensory overload, even people with high-functioning autism sometimes lose their ability to interpret things and are thrown back to sensory agnosia.

It is not unusual for one and the same object to have different 'sensory names' in different sensory modalities or in different environments, for instance:

> Going back to the door before it is known in terms of function; before it is, in fact, 'door' (which is a function concept), it may have no word at all. Later, as one moves from non-physical sensing of what happens to be a door to physical-based sensing of what happens to be a door, its sound-concept is very unlikely to be 'door'. If you tapped the door, it may (depending on the door) tell you its name is 'took'. If it made a noise when it gave way under impact, it might say its name is 'rerr' if it drags on the carpet or 'ii-er' depending on the sound of the hinges. It may have no sound concept at all or sound concept relating to the experience of door might come from the emotional experience of a sensory buzz associated with that door. So taking the example of the swinging

door fascination, if this buzz experience brought out a little suppressed squeal (hard to write such a suppressed buzz squeal in letters), for me, the sound concept associated with the experience of door may well become this stored and later triggered sound. In someone in whom the buzz experience brought out an emotionally connected body expression movement such as the sudden staccato contraction of the fingers into outward-facing fists that jerk suddenly back towards the torso, this may become stored as something akin to a language sign associated with the buzz experience brought on by the swinging door. (Williams 1998, pp.99–100)

What they say

In the bathroom were things that were white, cold, smooth, with curved edges, all had metal fixtures (with quite contrastive sensory experiences) and which made the same sound when tapped and same chinking sensation when bitten. They also had running water. On a sensory level, nature comes first, pattern comes second and function comes last. On a sensory level all had a comparably similar sensory nature. On a pattern level, you could sit upon the edge of any of these and let water come out of your body and run downwards into the 'bellybutton' of these objects and all could be 'flushed' with running water as per pattern. On a functional level, what the hell if these were thought of as basin, bath and toilet with specific assigned social purposes for each. (Williams 1998, p.99)

In order to see why autistic people take a 'different path' in the direction of concept formation, we have to return to the stage of sensation and consider possible differences in experiencing it.

Qualitative differences in experiencing sensations/receiving information

What I do realise is that I do not see the world as others do. Most people take the routines of life and day-to-day connections for granted. The fact they can see, hear, smell, touch and relate to others is 'normal'. For me, these things are often painfully overwhelming, non-existent or just confusing. (Lawson 1998, pp.2–3)

The qualitative nature of sensory experience should be taken into account. Do people with autism experience sensations the way we do or are their experiences qualitatively different? If they are, what are these differences?

Gestalt perception

There is much evidence that one of the problems many autistic people experience is their inability to distinguish between foreground and background stimuli (inability to filter foreground and background information). They often are unable to discriminate relevant and irrelevant stimuli. What is background to others may be equally foreground to them; they perceive everything without filtration or selection. This results in a paradoxical phenomenon: sensory information is received in infinite detail and holistically at the same time. It can be described as 'gestalt perception' – perception of the whole scene as a single entity with all the details perceived (not processed!) simultaneously. Autistic people may be aware of the information others miss, but the processing of 'holistic situations' can be overwhelming. As there is too much information coming in, it is hard to know which stimuli to attend to. It is often difficult for the autistic person to 'break' the whole picture into meaningful entities, to 'group together' and to 'draw the boundaries' around plenty of tiny sensory pieces to make them meaningful units (Bogdashina 2003).

In contrast to the non-autistic's *guessing* 'what is there' from their experience and memory instead of actually *seeing* it, autistic children seem to be unable to filter the incoming information and tend to perceive all the stimuli around them. Instead of 'inventing' the world as others do, they actually *perceive* it. Such 'acute perception' brings overwhelming information the brain cannot cope with.

Autistic children are bombarded with sensory stimuli. They often feel 'drowned' in the 'sea of background noise/colours/smells'. In crowded places their brains seem to try to process all the stimuli around them – what each person is saying, and what other noises and sounds coming from all directions mean.

> *In the supermarket Alex seems to follow all the conversations around him. He is actively involved in the discussion of 'having enough of these economy things' taking place in the next aisle, while keeping 'updated' as to what his mum is saying about the washing-up liquid to his dad. All of a sudden a baby starts crying, and Alex kicks a box of*

soap on the floor. He is 'losing his battle' with this overwhelming storm of sounds around him.

Autistic people may experience gestalt perception in any sensory modality. A person with auditory gestalt perception (like Alex) seems to pick up all sounds around him with equal intensity. Any auditory stimulus he wants to attend to comes as a package with all the environmental noises: fans working, doors opening, somebody coughing, cars passing, other people talking, etc.

Children with visual gestalt perception experience all visual stimuli (details) around them simultaneously. They can see (not process) changes that happen in milliseconds where non-autistics are 'blind' to them. For instance, some autistic individuals visually experience (see) the flickering of fluorescent lights, making the environment around them visually unstable.

On the conceptual level, gestalt perception leads to rigidity of thinking and lack of generalization. Autistic children can perform in exactly the same situation with the exactly same prompts but fail to apply the skill if anything in the environment, routine or prompt has been even slightly changed. For example, a child can perform the task if she is being touched on the shoulder and fails if she is not. These children need sameness and predictability to feel safe in their environment (Bogdashina 2003).

For individuals with gestalt perception, each and every situation is unique. They can learn what to do in one situation but be lost if the slightest detail is different. For example, Alex could successfully select the right pictures to complete a story while he was wearing a blue T-shirt and sitting on the settee with his mother in the living-room, but was bewildered when he was asked to do the same task while wearing his jumper and sitting in the play-room with his sister.

Autistic children might be baffled when things change or go differently. Even the slightest changes may confuse and upset them. For instance, if the door to the kitchen is usually shut between meal times, and they happen to find it open after lunch, they do not know what to do in this situation.

Another confusing (and frightening) thing for autistic children may be when something emerges in the situation that does not belong to it. For example, once Tito was playing on the grass in their garden, when he heard the voice of their neighbour. The matter was, the voice used to come from over the fence. It should not be in the garden, but that day it was there! The boy was frightened because he did not recognize the situation and did not know what to do. The only solution available to him, was to scream. And he did (Mukhopadhyay 2000)!

Children with autism make their own connections (cause and effects) and create new gestalts. Thus, Tito connected his screaming with the place he was in when it happened (on the grass in the garden) and refused to walk on the grass for years.

To feel safe they create gestalt behaviours – rituals and routines. These ritualistic behaviours bring reassurance and order in daily life which is otherwise unpredictable and threatening. These rituals may be long and complicated. For instance, in 'a bed-time ritual', a child may start with going round his father's chair twice; he then touches the wall behind it, taps three times at the dressing table and only after that goes upstairs to his bedroom to launch the next phase, the 'undressing ritual', and then going to bed. For outsiders these behaviours seem bizarre and complicated. However, for an autistic person it is *one* act of meaningful experience, and if any part of it is missing (for example, the child is prevented from tapping at the dressing table) the whole experience becomes incomplete, unfamiliar and frightening.

For autistic individuals, these gestalt behaviours are 'safety belts' on a roller coaster they have no control of.

What they say

As a little girl I was coping in a world where other people effectively realised nothing of that. I reacted to all this bombardment and confusion with those physical movements, silence and strange sounds which are generally lumped together as 'autistic behaviours'. (Blackman 2001, p.19)

It is thought that the medical basis lies in the inability to adequately filter out information received through each of the senses. I think of my brain at such times of confusion as being like a freeway crowded with reckless and non-law-abiding drivers, causing massive traffic jams. Why, mail trucks would have difficulty getting through in such a case, and so do my conscious thoughts.

In a crowded store, for instance, my brain seems to want to process what each person is saying, causing my mind to become dazed. In autistic children, this cognitive confusion often leads to use of poor judgment, aggression, echolalia, inappropriate laughter, social awkwardness, choppy sentences, and inattentiveness. (Hawthorne 2002)

Sensory information seems to come to the autistic individual in infinite detail and holistically, that is all at once. It is often hard for the autistic person to integrate what they are experiencing into separate and unique entities. Also, they are very sensitive to many stimuli that most people ignore. Autistic children become aware of this fact at a very young age. Since their parents are usually not autistic, they are often of little help to the autistic child in sorting out sensory information and making sense of their world. This is the first step that begins the loneliness that most autistic people feel for much of their life. (Joan and Rich 1999, p.2)

I would learn how to tackle a given situation in one context but be lost when confronted by the same situation in another context. Things just didn't translate. If I learned something while I was standing with a woman in a kitchen and it was summer and it was daytime, the lesson wouldn't be triggered in a similar situation if I was standing with a man in another room and it was winter and it was nighttime. Things were stored but the compulsive overcategorization of them was so refined that events had to be close to identical to be considered comparable. (Williams 1999c, p.58)

Moments with their own uniqueness challenged me so much that I began to fear all those unknown paths, clothes, food, shoes, chairs and strange human voices. Each one challenged me by putting in front of me a new situation for me to face and understand. (Mukhopadhyay 2000)

All ritualistic behaviour is for reassurance and creating order in daily life. Autistic people count on their routines. They give structure to the day. Specific rituals involving getting dressed each morning, or preparing for a task, may be quite long and complicated. Often, eating also becomes a ritual. Certain foods are eaten in certain ways, using the same progressive steps. Rituals are soothing and they do feel nice. They define areas of living. (O'Neill 1999, p.117)

What we can do to help them 'sort out' sensory information

- We should find out which modality does not filter information and make the environment visually/auditorily, etc. simple. The next step would be to teach the person to break the visual/auditory, etc. picture into meaningful units, i.e. teach the child to recognize relevant features of objects and situations while ignoring irrelevant ones.

- Structure and routine make understanding of everyday activities easier and provide feelings of safety and trust.

- It is important to always communicate to the child beforehand, in a way he can understand (for instance, using verbal, visual or tactile means) what will be changed and why. Changes should be gradual, with his active participation.

- Let the child have a 'safety object' (a toy, a piece of string) when she goes to an unfamiliar place or faces an unfamiliar situation.

Thus, we do not need to interpret *all* the stimuli around us. We pick up only the stimuli relevant to the situation, while ignoring the rest. Autistic individuals, on the other hand, find it very difficult to filter irrelevant information and struggle to interpret what they perceive with equal intensity. They cannot cope with the rate of incoming information. Without filtering they are flooded with sensory stimuli. The overflow of sensory information that cannot be filtered and/or processed simultaneously brings sensory overload. There are several possible consequences:

- fragmented perception

- delayed perception

- hypersensitivity and/or hyposensitivity

- inconsistency of perception (fluctuation).

Fragmented perception

> I had always known that the world was fragmented. (Williams 1999b, p.11)

Gestalt perception often results in fragmented processing. We may distinguish at least two types of fragmentation:

Fragmentation 'inside' modality

This is also known as 'binding problem' (Sejnowski 2003). It is to do with how information that belongs together stays together. For example, if you have a red cup, the redness of the cup and the shape of the cup are bound together. For some people the binding process does not come naturally. They have to 'paste' together in their mind different characteristics of one and the same object, in order to get a full picture of what they are seeing/hearing/feeling, etc. For Tito, for example, the shapes come first and then the colour. If it moves, he has to start all over again.

We can only imagine what it is like for people like Tito to mentally paste different aspects of one and the same image together in order to understand what they are seeing.

What they say

I don't think that what I see is what you see. That is unless what you see are vague clouds and shadows of substance... I am really pretty good at deciphering what I am looking at now after practice but sometimes I do still have troubles, especially with colors. It is not that I don't see colors, it is that I see wrong colors. The worst ones are colors made of two other colors because instead of seeing one color I see a mix of the two other colors and I have to figure out exactly what color I am looking at. An example of this...is if I look at purple I see swirling reds and blues. This doesn't bother my eyes (in fact sometimes it looks pretty kewl) but it does bother my brain when I am trying to see the one single color. (McKean 1999)

Fragmentation while processing gestalt (in one modality if monotropic)

When too much information needs to be processed simultaneously, very often people with autism are not able to 'break down' the whole picture into meaningful units and to interpret objects, people and surroundings as constituents of a whole situation. Instead, they process 'bits' that happen to get their attention (Bogdashina 2003). Where non-autistics may see a room, an autistic person sees a door handle, a leg of the table, a ball under the chair, etc.

Autistic people often select for attention minor aspects of objects in the environment instead of the whole scene or person. They may look at the person and see his eye, then they shift their attention and see his ear, then his nose, his hand. The person seems to be bits of jigsaw that do not make sense. For example:

> I picked up his hand and looked at it closely. I traced it with my eyes from the fingers to the shoulder, from the shoulder to the eyes, down to the nose and mouth. Ian was a jigsaw of bits that my mind was in no state to make sense of as a whole. (Williams 1999a, p.21)

Fragmentation may be felt in all sensory modalities.

As autistic children perceive their surroundings and people they encounter in 'bits and pieces', they 'store' their individual (and idiosyncratic – from the non-autistic point of view) impressions of their experiences, which they use later to recognize and define places, things and people. If the 'sensory word or definition' of their mother, for instance, is a particular earring (visual modality) or particular perfume (smell), then if the mother changes her earrings or perfume, the child may not recognize her. One needs to know the child very well in order to identify the 'sensory concepts' this child uses to function in his environment. It is no wonder that autistic children exhibit a maintenance of sameness and resistance to change as they try to make sense of the ever-changing world around them.

> *Alex is afraid of hands that seem to be unconnected to the people. He hates it when somebody points at things to attract his attention, as a suddenly appearing hand 'from nowhere' in front of him can scare him and trigger aggression – a protective reaction (from his point of view). Processing fragmented information means that Alex defines places and people by the 'bits' he stored in his memory. That is why any changes in the environment or person's appearance make them unrecognizable to him. He does not recognize his classmates if they wear different clothes or have changed their hairstyle. He cannot 'read' facial expressions and body language.*
>
> *Alex instinctively tries to calm himself down during the times of anxiety. He flaps his hands in front of his eyes; it helps him to ignore many 'offending' and confusing stimuli (pieces of people, things, etc.) around him.*
>
> *The feeling of safety in times of sensory overload can be achieved by any object in the environment (the item Alex has chosen as a recognizable 'bit' of the environment/event/situation). If this item has been unintentionally removed, it can lead to a panic attack as he cannot identify the place or situation and everything becomes unpredictable (= dangerous).*

What they say

You may observe the same autistic person rubbing sandpaper on his bare arm, or banging his knuckles sharply into a solid wooden dresser, then peering at them as if to say, 'Oh, hello, hand. So you do belong to me, then'. Sometimes the body feels fragmented, also, so it appears to be suspended or floating in pieces. This can be an eerie but neat sensation. A lot of self-stimulations, including rocking the body, swaying, flapping the hands, rubbing the skin, and countless others, are pleasurable, soothing connections with senses. They help ground the autistic person, provide rhythm and order, calm, and simply feel good! (O'Neill 1999, p.33)

I had a fragmented perception of things at the best of times, seeing eyes or a nose or whiskers or a mouth but mostly putting the bits together in my head. (Williams 1999a, p.162)

...because things that were meant to be tuned out weren't, these things were all competing for processing when they shouldn't have been. I was jumping between processing the white of the page as well as the print, the flicker of light and shadow as well as the objects themselves, the sounds of the people moving about in between syllables of words being said at the time, the rustle of clothing and the sound of my own voice. (Williams 1996, p.92)

My ability to interpret what I saw was impaired because I took each fragment in without understanding its meaning in the context of its surroundings. I'd see the nostril but lose the concept of nose, see the nose but lose the face, see the fingernail but lose the finger. My ability to interpret from what I heard was equally impaired. I heard the intonation but lost the meaning of the words, got a few of the words but lost the sentences. I couldn't consistently process the meaning of my own body messages if I was focusing in on something with my eyes or ears. (Williams 1998, p.33)

This autistic sensitivity for parts in the perception instead of wholes is common knowledge and is denominated as 'overselectivity'. It seems as though autistic people reacting upon parts of the objects as being complete entities in themselves... For instance, when they perceive an object from a certain point of view, they perceive probably a total different object when confronted with a nearby point of view produced by a small rotational movement. For me the same mechanism of unrelated points-of-view is working when I approach a familiar street by accident from an unusual direction in which I do not recognize my homely environment. (VanDalen 1995, p.12)

What we can do to help the child to identify the 'right pieces of the jigsaw' and put them into the right places to get a clear picture of his or her environment

- Structure and routines make the environment predictable and easier to control. Routine and rituals help to facilitate understanding of what is going on and what is going to happen.

- Introduce any change very slowly and always explain beforehand what is going to happen differently and why.

Autistic persons may experience not only fragmentation but also all sorts of distortions in their perception. Distortions are reported to become worse when the person is in a state of nervous overarousal and information overload. For instance:

> My weird sound environment, and my enchanted world of light and sudden gaps into which people and objects moved, affected the way that I processed my fellow human beings, and may have been part of the reason I could not interact...

> No one guessed that my eyes picked up different signals from the light, shade, colour and movement that passed into the retina and thence to my brain. I basically emphasised folds and depths... So I perceived people, especially their faces, but also their bodies, as slightly distorted. This was not only in shape, but also in the composition of the components of their bodies in my visual imagination.

> I seem to have lived in a world where depth was not a factor. I now realise that my sense of perspective did not develop properly. If something moved from one point in space or time to another, I sometimes did not realise why it was no longer visible in one spot and then suddenly was in position in another. As a corollary people did not move through space. They arrived in a certain point within their own space which supplanted the space that was already there. I think that is why I still draw figures which seem to have a long veil which flows from above where their head would be, to somewhere approximating their elbows. (Blackman 2001, pp.26–7)

Do we live in the same time zone?

There are children in my class who respond to my verbal instructions and questions with some delay. John, Helen and Vicky need at least a few minutes to understand and answer my questions as if they were far away and it took the sound waves some time to reach them. Alex sometimes gives responses even a few days later. You must be a detective to connect his 'announcements' with the question he was asked a week before. For an outsider, his responses, unconnected to the present situation, seem weird. Does time seem faster for them while we think these kids are 'slow', I wonder? (author's unpublished notes)

As a consequence of fragmented perception autistic people may experience delayed processing.

Perception by parts requires a great amount of time and effort to interpret the whole. Many autistic individuals emphasize that they need a great amount of 'thinking' to make sense of the world.

The experience of 'delayed hearing' happens when the question has been sensed and recorded without interpretation until the second (internalized) hearing (i.e. the processing of the received message). They may be able to repeat back what has been said without comprehension: that will come later. In less extreme cases, to process something takes seconds or minutes. Sometimes it takes days, weeks, months. In the most extreme cases, it can take years to process what has been said. The words, phrases, sentences, sometimes the whole situations are stored and they can be triggered at any time.

> *In the middle of the night the mother rushed to her son's bedroom. The boy was screaming at the top of his voice. The mother eventually calmed him down and started her usual interrogation in order to try and prevent it happening again.*
> *– What's happened, sweetheart?*
> *– Echo has come.*
> *– Echo? And what did it say?*
> *– 'Come here! We are getting ready to go for a walk.' (These were mother's words uttered the day before.)*
> *Isn't it frightening for a small boy to 'hear' 'Come here!' in the middle of the night?*

There are several consequences to delayed processing for people with autism:

- They are often unable to start the action immediately as they need time to interpret and comprehend the situation.

- When they finally reach 'comprehension', the situation has changed. This means that they 'experience meaning' out of the context in which it should have been experienced. That is why experiences, no matter how similar to previous ones, are perceived as new, unfamiliar and unpredictable, and responses to them are poor regardless of the number of times the person has experienced the same thing (Williams 1996).

- The amount of time needed to process any experience often remains slow (or delayed) regardless of whether the person has had similar experiences in the past; things do not get easier with time or learning (Williams 1996).

What they say

As a child…it appeared as though I didn't feel pain or discomfort, didn't want help, didn't know what I was saying, didn't listen or didn't watch. By the time some of these sensations, responses or comprehensions were decoded and processed for meaning and personal significance, and I'd accessed the means of responding, I was fifteen minutes, one day, a week, a month, even a year away from the context in which the experiences happened. (Williams 1996, p.90)

Some people think I am not paying attention when I'm asked a question, because of the pause I often need to process the question and my response, and the blank look I often have when concentrating on such processing. When people try to get my attention, they actually just distract me, slow me down, and annoy me horribly with their impatience. (Blackburn 1999)

Before taking proper action, autistic people must go through a number of separate stages in perception by making 'decisions'. It is very important to realize that, if this long decision-chain is interrupted by the outside world, the autistic person must start all over again because overselectivity has changed the scene completely. In other words, an interruption effectively wipes away any intermediate result confronting the autistic person literally 'for the first time' with the [object of his inspection]… The long autistical process towards meaning-generation of the complex situation restarts from scratch and when someone else, seeing the delay in action, wanted to assist by placing well-intended functional remark then the autist is forced back to the point of departure again. (VanDalen 1995, p.15)

What we can do to help

Give people with autism time to take in your question/instruction and to work out their response. Be aware that autistic individuals often require more time than others to shift their attention between stimuli of different modalities and they find it extremely difficult to follow rapidly changing social interactions.

Intensity with which the senses work

Other common sensory problems autistic people experience are their hyper- or hyposensitivities to sensory stimuli. Their senses seem to be too acute (in the case of *hypersensitivity*) or not working at all (in the case of *hyposensitivity*).

Hypersensitivity

Hypervision means that one's vision is too acute. For example, hypervisual people notice the tiniest pieces of fluff on the carpet, complain about 'moths (air particles) flying', dislike bright lights, look down most of the time, are frightened by sharp flashes of light, etc.

Children with *hyperhearing* are generally very light sleepers, are frightened by sudden unpredictable sounds (telephone ringing, baby crying), dislike thunderstorms and crowds, are terrified by haircuts, etc. They often cover their ears when the noise is painful for them, though others in the same room may be unaware of any disturbing sounds at all. Sometimes hyperauditory kids make repetitive noises to block out other disturbing sounds.

Some autistic individuals with *olfactory hypersensitivities* cannot tolerate how people or objects smell, although non-autistics can be unaware of any smell at all. They run from smells, move away from people and insist on wearing the same clothes all the time. For some, the smell or taste of any food is too strong, and they reject it no matter how hungry they are. They are usually poor eaters, gag or vomit easily, and eat only certain foods.

Some autistic children are *hypertactile*; they pull away when people try to hug them, because they fear being touched. Because of their hypertactility resulting in overwhelming sensations, even the slightest touch can send them to a panic attack. Small scratches that most people ignore can feel very painful to them. Parents often report that washing their child's hair or cutting nails turns into an ordeal demanding several people to complete it. Many children refuse to wear certain clothes, as they cannot tolerate the texture on their skin. Some children with hypertactility overreact to heat/cold, avoid wearing shoes, avoid getting 'messy' or dislike food of a certain texture.

People with *vestibular hypersensitivity* experience difficulty changing directions and walking or crawling on uneven or unstable surfaces. They are poor at sports. They feel disoriented after spinning, jumping or running and often express fear and anxiety over having their feet leave the ground.

Individuals with *proprioceptive hypersensitivity* hold their bodies in odd positions, have difficulty manipulating small objects and sometimes do not feel their body at all.

As each individual is unique in their sensory profile, it is very difficult to adapt the environment for each individual's sensitivities. Often it is not the stimulus itself that can trigger what we call difficult behaviours, but rather the inability to control or predict it. An understanding of each individual child's sensitivities is vital for those around her, or any intervention becomes a nightmare for both the child and those who work with her.

> *Chris is an eight-year-old boy with autism. He gets easily frustrated when he tries to do something in a noisy, crowded room. He often covers his ears, even if the staff and other children are not aware of any disturbing sounds at all. Chris's hearing is hypersensitive. He cannot tolerate certain sounds, especially if he does not know the source of these noises and he cannot control them. Not only certain sounds but also any sudden unpredictable sounds (for example, the fire alarm, a telephone ringing) seem to be painful for him. In order to block the sounds over which he has no control, the boy may rock and make loud repetitive noises. In the classroom he sits in the corner, with a spare table between him and the other children.*
>
> *One afternoon during break time, Chris is sitting in the playroom, covering his ears with his hands and rocking. There are five other children with ASD and two members of staff there. One of the children, Jamie (an eight-year-old boy with Asperger syndrome) has brought a toy mobile phone and is happily explaining to his classmates how it works. He presses the buttons and all sorts of sounds and verbal messages can be heard.*

Chris shows the first signs of frustration and starts producing repetitive loud noises ('ah-ah', 'uh-uh'). Jamie wants to involve Chris in his game and proudly shows him his toy phone: 'Look, Chris, what I've got. Do you want to phone me? Press this button and leave your message.' The toy phone produces ringing tones. Chris covers his ears and shouts 'Come on. You like it.' Jamie is encouraged to show Chris all the functions of his new toy. He approaches Chris with 'Look, you can send me a text message as well. You have to press...' However, he is unable to finish his sentence as Chris grabs the toy from his hand and hits Jamie with it.

Jamie bursts into tears, and retreats behind the support assistant. She tries to comfort him while talking to Chris: 'Chris, you shouldn't hit people, it is not nice. Look, Jamie is crying. You've hurt him. Say "sorry" to Jamie.'

Chris starts screaming and hitting his head with his hand. The other support assistant tries to calm him down: 'Come on, Chris, let's have a biscuit and a drink.' She tries to escort him out of the room. Chris bites her hand and grabs the toy again. He throws it against the wall, then falls on the floor, screaming. With 'He's broken my mobile!' Jamie attacks Chris. Two support assistants physically restrain Jamie while the teacher (who has heard the screaming and rushed into the play-room) comforts Chris. The other children in the room cover their ears because Chris is screaming at the top of his voice now. Some children start crying.

In ten minutes Chris returns to the classroom with a biscuit in his hand. He has calmed down and quietly sits at his desk. The children are ready for their last lesson (drawing) with the support staff handing out paper and crayons. The teacher enters the classroom with the 'offending' object (toy phone) in her hand. Chris begins to rock repeating 'Come on. You like it.' The teacher sees his frustration and explains: 'Chris, I am going to put it away. Don't worry. It won't disturb you any more.' She puts the toy on the shelf among other 'unwanted items', unintentionally moving a box of dominoes so one-third of it is now off the shelf, balanced in the air. Chris's attention is moved to the box and he seems to be unable to shift his eyes from it. He does not see anything else and seems oblivious of what is going on in the classroom. The box of dominoes becomes his only concern. If it fell down it would produce a loud noise. The boy wants to be prepared for the 'bomb to explode'.

The teacher calls his name to attract his attention and get him to do his work. However, there is no response. It is very unusual because drawing is one of the boy's favourite subjects. The teacher tries to establish eye contact but Chris seems to look through her. She insists and the boy hits her.

Challenging behaviour? Yes (from the teacher's point of view) and no (from Chris's). The fear of a stimulus that 'hurts' is often the cause of Chris's tantrums and aggressive outbursts. In some cases, the antecedents cannot be easily identified, as they are 'possible future antecedents' (the box may fall or it may not). If the child who is trying to protect himself (i.e. watching the 'dangerous' object to be prepared for a possible 'explosion') is forced to do something else, he is very likely to exhibit 'challenging' behaviour.

What they say

There are certain things I touch that hurt my hands. I have heard of (and, unfortunately, seen) cases where children with autism will adamantly refuse to wear clothes because of a pervasive sense of pain encompassing the entire body. Perhaps I am blessed in that in my case, only the palms of my hands and soles of my feet are affected. One example of this is in the air around us. There are times when I walk and the air brushing past my hands is a source of pain. (McKean 1999)

I still dislike places with many different noises, such as shopping centers and sport arenas. High-pitched continuous noise such as bathroom vent fans or hair dryers are annoying. I can shut down my hearing and withdraw from most noise, but certain frequencies cannot be shut out. It is impossible for an autistic child to concentrate in a classroom if he or she is bombarded with noises that blast through his or her brain like a jet engine…

The fear of a noise that hurts the ears is often the cause of many bad behaviors and tantrums. Some autistic children will attempt to break the telephone because they are afraid it will ring. Many bad behaviors are triggered due to anticipation of being subjected to a painful noise. The bad behaviors can occur hours before the noise. Common noises that cause discomfort in many autistic individuals are school bells, fire alarms, score board buzzers in the gym, squealing microphone feedback and chairs scraping on the floor. (Grandin 1996b, pp.1–2)

Visual sensitivity to fluorescent lights can make them appear like strobe lights to a person with autism, creating an unsuitable environment for learning. An elementary-school child in this situation may very well get out their seat to shut off this source of sensory overload that, in addition to being a distraction, may cause physical pain. I have seen the eyes of people of those with sensory sensitivities vibrate in synchrony with the 60 Hz. cycling of fluorescent lighting. The teacher, unaware of the student's condition may interpret this 'out of seat' activity as an avoidance behavior. However, in reality, this behavior is an attempt to eliminate a sensory assault that interferes with functioning in class. Alternatively, a child, more severely affected by autism, who is nonverbal and less aware of the source of her sensory overload, may simply have a tantrum. (Shore undated)

I appear to have very sensitive ears, eyes and skin. Certain noises very definitely 'hurt' my ears and certain lights 'hurt' my eyes. Strip lighting is one of the worst, and lights that flash. If the strip lights have a grid covering them then I cope with them better. I have an insatiable appetite for touch and love to feel the roof of my mouth, especially when I am either insecure or very secure! I love soft material and soft skin but I hate to feel my own skin against myself. This means that I need to wear pyjamas in bed or put the sheet between my legs so that they do not come into direct contact with each other. (Lawson 2001, p.119)

Hyposensitivity

Sometimes the senses of people with autism are in 'hypo' and they do not really see, hear or feel anything. To stimulate their senses they might wave their hands around or rock forth and back or make strange noises.

Autistic people with *hypovision* may experience trouble figuring out where objects are, as they see just outlines; then they may walk around objects running their hands around the edges so they can recognize what it is. These children are attracted to lights; they may stare at the sun or a bright light bulb. They are fascinated with reflections and brightly coloured objects. Having entered an unfamiliar room they have to walk around it touching everything before they settle down. Often they sit for hours moving fingers or objects in front of their eyes.

Hypohearing children may 'seek sounds' (leaning their ears against electric equipment or enjoying crowds, sirens, etc.). They like kitchens and bathrooms – the 'noisiest' places in the house. They often create sounds themselves to stimulate their hearing – banging doors, tapping things, tearing or crumpling paper in their hands, making loud rhythmic sounds.

Children with *hypotaste* or *hyposmell* chew and smell everything they can get – grass, play dough, etc. They sniff and lick objects, play with faeces, eat mixed food (for instance, sweet and sour), regurgitate.

Those with *hypotactility* seem not to feel pain or changes in temperature. They may not notice a wound caused by a sharp object or they seem unaware of a broken bone. They are prone to self-injuries and may bite their hands or bang their heads against the wall, just to feel they are alive. They like pressure, tight clothes; they often crawl under heavy objects. They hug tightly and enjoy rough and tumble play.

People with *vestibular hyposensitivity* enjoy and seek all sorts of movement and can spin or swing for a long time without being dizzy or nauseated. Autistic people with vestibular hyposensitivity often rock forth and back or move in circles while rocking their bodies.

Those with *proprioceptive hyposensitivity* have difficulty knowing where their bodies are in space and are often unaware of their own body sensations; for example, they do not feel hunger. A child with a hypoproprioceptive system appears floppy, and often leans against people, furniture and walls. He bumps into objects and people, stumbles frequently, and has a tendency to fall. He has a weak grasp and drops things. For instance, Tito had no body awareness. To check that he did exist he used…his shadow: he flapped his hands and watched the shadow flapping its hands. It seemed he existed because of his shadow (Mukhopadhyay 2000).

What they say

My senses would sometimes become dull to the point that I could not clearly see or hear, and the world around me would seemingly cease to exist. The sensory flow would seem to become confused as well. Oftentimes, I would be aware that my body hurt somewhere, but I would be unable to pinpoint what was hurting, even to the point of being unable to distinguish between whether the distress is kinesthetic or aural in nature. (Hawthorne 2002)

There has been a lot of talk and writing about children…with autism having tactile defensiveness… What is not well documented is the subsection of people with autism who are in the opposite situation. People have told me in the past that I have 'tactile offensiveness' and I suppose it may be true. I have never really been comfortable unless I have had tactile feedback. Without that, I feel part of me is missing, or that I am incomplete, and so I feel a constant, low-intensity pain. (McKean 1999)

I never knew my relative position in the surrounding or situation. ...It is necessary to mention that I had no concept of my body. So I never paid attention to it. And I never enjoyed experiencing it. My hands were mere objects which I used to pick and throw. (Mukhopadhyay 2000, p.18)

What we can do to help

Hypersensitivities:

- Identify which stimuli the child finds disturbing and either reduce or eliminate them (for example, use natural lighting instead of fluorescent lights) or, if impossible, provide the child with 'sensory aids' (tinted glasses, earplugs, etc.).

- Depending on the sensitivity, desensitize the child's ability to tolerate the stimuli via a sensory diet.

- Monitor a number of simultaneous stimuli and reduce all irrelevant stimuli.

- If possible, warn the child about fire alarms, bells, etc.

Hyposensitivities:

- Provide extra stimulation through those of the child's channels that work in 'hypo' (bright lights, shiny objects – for hypovision; strong smells – for hyposmell, etc.).

Inconsistency of perception

Although we could address hyper- and hyposensitivities by desensitizing a child and/or providing the aids to help him cope (in the case of hypersensitivity), and by providing more stimulation to 'open' the affected channel (in the case of hyposensitivity), these methods do not often lead to the solution of the problem. The matter is, the volume of the child's perception is not stable, it fluctuates between hyper- and hypo-, or between hyper-/hypo- and normal. The fluctuation depends on many factors, such as the developmental level, physical state, the severity of the autism, the degree of familiarity with the environment and situations, and will vary with the age and circumstances of each person.

What they say

...I was often tossed in a sensory maelstrom, so that skin sensation was so unbearable one minute and yet completely unfelt the next... When I was little, the fluctuation of sound was continual. The distant noises on the main road that ran about sixty metres from our house were always present. They sloshed against the day-to-day sounds of my own home in a sort of wave-on-the-shore effect. I could feel the sensation of cars and a heavy-laden truck pass, and also feel my own physical response to the noises that the vehicle made from its tyres, its engine and the wind of its passing... Other people learn to make social decisions from ongoing and consistent stimuli. I have not been able to make instinctive social judgements based on prior experience in a reliable way, because the incoming signals were switched often enough that I did not learn to untangle those shadowed moving faces and their inconsistent voices. Real and extraordinary fluctuations in all sensation were a part of daily life. (Blackman 2001, pp.18, 35)

It is well documented that there are certain textures and patterns that are painful or displeasing to the touch of the person with autism. This is true from my own experience, but I am not able to tell you what they are because they are always changing. Day to day, hour to hour, sometimes even minute to minute. This can be very frustrating. (McKean 1999)

Even now, I still have problems with tuning out. I will be listening to a favourite song on the radio, and then realize I missed half of it. My hearing just shuts off. In college, I had to constantly keep taking notes to prevent tuning out. The young man from Portugal also wrote that carrying on a conversation was very difficult. The other person's voice faded in and out like a distant radio station. (White and White 1987, p.226)

Vulnerability to sensory overload

Many autistic people are very vulnerable to sensory overload. They may become overloaded in situations that would not bother other people. The overload comes when they have taken in more than they can keep up with. The causes of information overload can be:

- the inability to filter out irrelevant, or excessive information

- hypersensitivity

- delayed processing

- a distorted or fragmented perception.

The overload can lead to several different routes they can (or are forced) to take and may result in:

- systems shutdowns that can give them a break and let them 'recover'

- hypersensitivity or/and fragmentation, if they continue to try to process all the information coming in, despite their inability to keep up with it. This eventually brings anxiety, confusion, frustration and stress that, in turn, leads to tantrums and difficult behaviour.

The threshold for processing sensory stimuli varies among autistic persons, at different ages and in different environments.

Alex could cope with shopping trips if he was wearing his tinted glasses to reduce his visual hypersensitivity. However, to take him pre-Christmas shopping in a large supermarket was a big mistake that his mother was soon aware of. Their usual 'shopping adventure' turned into a nightmare.

There were THOUSANDS of people in the supermarket, bright Christmas lights, music, sales announcements, babies crying, people talking, laughing and moving in all directions, long queues... In 15 minutes Alex's mother could see that the overload was setting in. Her boy was literally 'attacked'. She could see he was in pain. The last straw was when a lady tried to reach the shelf from behind while they were standing in a queue. Alex lashed out and hit her. His mother tried to get him out as soon as possible but all the aisles were blocked by trolleys and people. Those around them were staring (and it did not help as Alex could not tolerate any direct perception). While his mother was dragging him out of the shop, he was kicking the trolleys, pushing people...

Outside the boy was crying, trying to explain: 'It was a panic attack. My eyes hurt. I did not want to hurt anyone. I won't do it again. I will fight "my panic"…' His mother knew he was doing his best and told him that she did understand what had happened, that it was not his fault, that she loved him…

It was too much for the boy and his mother. Eventually she was crying too. She could not explain this to the people around them, who had no idea why a handsome teenager was screaming like a baby and being aggressive to others.

Each individual may cope with overwhelming stimuli in different ways: monoprocessing, avoiding direct perception, withdrawal, stereotypies, etc.

What they say

My lack of interest and involvement in the outside world did not protect my mind from the flood of unwanted information that continually assaulted my senses. The unmodulated sensory input often overwhelmed me, causing me mental torture, and I would begin feeling mentally confused and sluggish. My head would feel fogged so that I could not think. My vision would blur, and the speech of those around me would become gibberish. My whole body buzzed. The slight tremor that always plagued me would worsen. My hands would feel detached from my body, as if they were foreign objects. I would be paralyzed, unable to comprehend my own movements unless I could see them. I could not tell where my hand started and the table ended, or what shape the table was, or even if it was rough or smooth. I felt like I was in a cartoon world. Indeed, I often felt more in common with the furniture around me than I did with other people. I felt lifeless, dazed, and had difficulty refocusing on anything. (Hawthorne 2002)

When hearing becomes acute, sounds that are normally inaudible can be as audible as usual sounds. Because too much information is already coming in for the brain to keep up with its connections, the perception of these additional sounds can make them intensely unbearable…

The same thing can happen with touch. When I have been taking in a lot of visual or sound information, my sense of touch can be overly sensitive, sharp as a pin and to be touched can be 'shocking' as though being jolted. The problem, however, is not with touch, the problem is that I remained too long attending to information I could not process efficiently at the pace it was coming in... Before having special lenses to correct the overload of visual information the same was true of my vision which would make many types of bright light physically uncomfortable and distressing. (Williams 1996, p.202)

If things became really bad and I suffer what I call a sensory overload, then I close out all the sounds and noises of the world. I could sit somewhere quietly or put my hands over my ears... Somehow to just sit and close off gives me space and time to recover from being anxious. It helps me to calm down. If I cannot find the room to do this, then the overload can build to an explosion! (Lawson 1998, pp.100–1)

What we can do to help

Learning to recognize sensory overload is very important. It is better to prevent it than to 'deal with the consequences'. A child may need a quiet place where he can go to 'recharge his batteries' from time to time. A 'first aid kit' (for sensory overload) should be always at hand. Possible contents might include sunglasses, ear plugs, squeezy toys, favourite toys, 'I need help' card, etc.

As soon as you notice early signs of a coming sensory overload (which are different for different children), stop any activity in which the child is involved and provide time and space for her to recover; for example, invite the child to get into a quiet place or outside. It is useful to teach the child how to recognize the internal signs of the overload and ask for help or use different strategies (for instance, relaxation) to prevent the problem.

Perceptual styles

Unreliable, and sometimes painful, perception may lead to a range of defensive strategies and voluntary and involuntary adaptations and compensations the person with autism acquires very early in life.

These adaptations and compensations become perceptual styles. The most commonly reported perceptual styles in autism are:

- monoprocessing
- peripheral perception (avoidance of direct perception).

Monoprocessing

According to the number of senses working at a time, they can be classified into 'multitrack' *versus* 'monoprocessing' (Williams 1996) or 'being singly channeled' (Lawson 1999). The ability to receive and process information via multiple sources can also be referred to as 'polytropism', in contrast to 'monotropism' (using one channel at a time) (Lawson 2001; Murray 1992).

Most people use their senses simultaneously. When they are hearing something, they are still aware of what they see and feel emotionally and physically, because they are able to process information from several sensory channels simultaneously. This parallel processing lets them form 'multi-sensory concepts', for example:

> APPLE = visual (red/yellow/green, round) + auditory (the sound it produces when bitten) + tactile (hard, smooth) + smell/taste (sour/sweet) + written/heard word 'apple'

This helps us recognize 'apple' if we are exposed to only one sensory image (a picture of an apple, for instance).

In monoprocessing, concepts are often 'one-sensory', for example, if an apple was yellow when you first saw it, you cannot identify it if it is red.

To avoid an overload of sensory information, many autistic individuals use only one modality to process information consciously. Monoprocessing means that a person focuses on one sense, for example sight, and might see every minute detail of the object. However, while his vision is 'on', the person might lose the conscious awareness of any information coming through other senses. Thus, while the person sees something, he does not understand what he is being told and does not feel touch. When the visual stimulus fades out, the sound can be processed, but then the sound is the only information the person is dealing with (disconnected from sight). As the person focuses on only one modality at a time, the sound may be experienced as louder (hypersensitivity) because it is all the person focuses on (Bogdashina 2003).

The individuals with autism define this monoprocessing (monotropism) as one of their involuntary adaptations to avoid sensory overload or hypersensitivity. For example, when their vision is overwhelmed (has become hypersensitive, distorted and/or painful), they might touch something and 'send the information through a different sensory channel', thus 'getting a break' for their eyes. Switching between the channels gives them an opportunity to be aware, though partially, of what is going on around them, through the sensory modality available to them at the moment.

What they say

I have noticed that when I am using a particular channel to address a task, if I attempt to introduce another channel, then I lose my place in the completion of the task and need to begin again. This is very frustrating! For example, you might notice that when a child with ASD is using the channel of 'touch' to dress themselves, if an adult then says 'look at what you are doing' (introducing a second channel, vision) the child may stop the task altogether and react with aggression, self-injury or by giving up on the task completely. (Lawson 2001, pp.141–2)

Many times, sensory stimuli are perceived in fragments. The child focuses on one sense, such as sight. Whilst he is examining something with his vision, he sees every minute detail and colours are vibrant, perhaps radiatingly brilliant like the jewel tones of a modern painting. As he brings in the visual stimulus, however, he loses track of his other senses. So he doesn't make much sense of sounds in the background. Also his body seems suspended, floating, as he loses knowledge of feeling touch. (O'Neill 1999, pp.24–5)

I wasn't able to filter incoming information properly so I was being sensorily flooded by it…this led to a range of involuntary adaptations, one of which I call being 'mono'. What being mono meant was that even though I'd progressed beyond mere mergence with things in my environment, I still had big restrictions in being able to process information produced from the outside and the inside at the same time. This meant that I could feel the texture of the wood, for example, but in taking the action physically to do so I would have no sense of my own hand. I could also switch channels and feel my own hand but would lose sensation of what my hand was in contact with. This also applied to my own body parts. If I touched my own face with my hand, I could feel the texture of my face *or* the effect upon my hand, but not both at the same time. I was either in a constant state of jolting perceptual shifts or I remained on one sensory channel or the other. (Williams 1998, pp.55–6)

What we can do to help

- A child who monoprocesses may have problems with multiple stimuli. Find out which channel 'is open' at any one moment and reduce all 'irrelevant stimuli'.

- Always present information in the child's preferred modality. If you are not sure what it is or which channel is 'on' at the moment (in the case of fluctuation), use a multisensory presentation and watch which modality 'works'. Remember, though, that the child could switch channels.

Peripheral perception

Direct perception in autism is often hyper. It can cause sensory overload resulting in switching to 'mono'. Some autistic individuals actually hear (= understand) you better when they are not looking at you!

Some autistic people seem to be hypersensitive when they are approached directly by other people. Some, if they are looked at directly, feel the look as 'a touch', a sort of 'distance touching' with actual tactile experience.

Autistic children often seem to look past things and are completely 'absent' from the scene. This could be their attempt to avoid experiencing visual or auditory stimuli directly. This strategy gives them the ability to take in sensory information with meaning. Avoiding direct perception is another involuntary adaptation they use that helps them to survive in a sensory-distorted world by avoiding (or, at least, decreasing) information overload.

They can often understand things better if they attend to them indirectly; for example, by looking or listening peripherally (such as out of the corner of the eye or by looking at or listening to something else). In this case it is a kind of indirectly confrontational approach in contrast to a 'normal' directly confrontational one (Williams 1998). The same is true for other senses if they are hypersensitive: the indirect perception of smell or touch are often defensive mechanisms to avoid overload.

However, some people can use only central vision because their peripheral vision is impaired. For example:

> I have almost no peripheral vision and when I see something it is only close to my line of sight, straight on. If I want to see something on the side, then I turn my head. I cannot just use my eyes to follow outside of my visual field. (Grant 2000, p.10)

What they say

Autistic people often glance out of the sides of their eyes at objects or other people. They have very acute peripheral vision and a memory for details that others miss. Gazing directly at people or animals is many times too over-whelming for the autistic one. Eyes are very intense and show emotions. It can feel creepy to be searched with the eyes. Some autistic people don't even look at the eyes of actors or news reporters on television. (O'Neill 1999, p.26)

Like many of my autistic peers, I also had far more impact from peripheral vision than most people. This gave a sort of 'wide screen' effect, rather than a narrower and deeper comprehension of the world that I scanned... My childhood use of peripheral vision, together with its corresponding loss of detail when I seemed to look in front of me, had given me a world view that shaped all my social responses. This may have been a result of my inability to process anything too close to the centre of my vision, or it may have caused the problem. Whatever the reason, I felt instantly unwell and sometimes terrified if I were face-to-face with a person, or even a thing like a wall or a chair. I would sit and be aware of my father's presence, marked by shoes or bare feet resting on the carpet, near where I sat. I identified him by the smell of his cigarette, his voice and his glasses. (Blackman 2001, pp.27, 28)

What we can do to help

- Never force eye contact.

- Do not approach the child directly in his hypersensitive modalities. When the hypersensitivity of the affected sensory channel is addressed and lessened, the direct perception becomes easier.

Sensory agnosia and systems shutdowns

'Sensory agnosia' (or difficulty interpreting a sense) is sort of 'literal perception'; for example, people with autism may *see* things without interpretation and understanding (literal vision), *hear* sounds without comprehension (literal hearing), etc. The difference between 'literal perception' and 'sensory agnosia' is about permanence and temporality. In this book we use 'literal perception' to describe individuals with 'low-functioning' autism who have not yet 'moved' from this stage to the stage of conceptualization, while the term 'sensory agnosia' refers to a temporary state of literal perception caused by sensory overload. In the state of this sensory agnosia, the interpretation of any sense can be lost. Although autistic people can see and hear, etc. adequately, they may often have only limited comprehension of what is being seen or heard, etc. For instance, they may be able to recognize the location of pieces of furniture in space to avoid bumping into them, but may not be able to identify what these objects are unless some cues (verbal or otherwise) are provided. Sometimes they cannot even identify people as people and may be startled by unexpected movements of 'noisy objects'. In this case they often act as if they were really blind, deaf, numb, sometimes 'dead'. It is a very frightening experience. In the state of sensory agnosia they need similar aids to those of visually or auditorily impaired people. Each individual develops his own strategies to cope with it.

Too much sensory overload may result in systems shutdowns, in which the person loses some or all of the normal functioning. The difference between sensory agnosia and shutdown is the first is involuntary, the latter is more conscious (voluntary). If it is used early in life it leads to self-imposed sensory deprivation.

When the person cannot cope with sensory information, he may shut down some or even all sensory channels. Many autistic children are suspected to be deaf as they sometimes do not react to sounds. Their hearing, however, is often even more acute than that of an average person, but they learn to shut it down when they experience information overload. To shut down the painful channel they may engage in stereotypic behaviours, or deliberately distract themselves through other channels (for instance, touching objects when their hearing is overwhelming) or to withdraw all together.

What they say

Everything became sort of free-floating in the cognitive disconnectedness that resulted from...visual overload. The words for things failed me and were defined instead by their size, shape, textures, sounds, and materials – or by their use or relationship to other things or people around them. The glasses on the interviewer became shiny, metal, round, 'ping-ping' things. The pen became a long thin thing for writing. The shadows and shine on every object in the room cut the room and its objects and people up into angles and shapes. The interviewer's hand was now conceptually disconnected from his body in all but theory and seemed merely tacked onto the end of his sleeve, rather than protruding from it. His head and neck looked plonked onto his shirt collar in the same way, as though he were a statue, disassembled and reassembled again into some bizarre work of art. Visually Ian didn't mean so much now. In his place was a bundle of associated, but only vaguely connected, bits that I knew theoretically was him. The lights were too bright and the rainbows reflecting in the light fittings themselves were starting to sensorily hurt. I had enough and was starting to shake. I was feeling alienated from my surroundings again. (Williams 1999a, p.211)

Compensating for an unreliable sense with other senses

Because of hypersensitivity, fragmented, distorted perception, delayed processing and sensory agnosia, one sense is never enough for autistic people to make sense of their environment. For instance, when they have visual problems, they use their ears, nose, tongue or hand to 'see' – they compensate for their temporary 'blindness' through other senses. Thus, a child may tap an object to produce the sound and recognize what it is, because her visual recognition may be fragmented and meaningless. Some children smell people and objects to identify them.

To many autistic people the senses of touch and smell are reported to be more reliable. Many autistic children touch and smell things, some constantly tap everything to figure out where the boundaries are in their environment.

It is important to let the children use the sensory modality they prefer to 'check' their perception. However, the 'compensating sense' may become easily overloaded as it does two or three 'jobs' simultaneously. For example, touch may compensate vision (if distorted) and hearing (if overloaded or hypersensitive and eventually shut down) and continue to serve as a tactile channel.

With appropriate treatment and environmental adjustments to decrease hypersensitivities they gradually learn to use their sense organs properly – eyes to see, ears to listen, etc.

> *Alex smells and touches objects or food to check his visual perception of them. Sometimes he shuts down his vision completely and uses his ears to 'see' his environments. He can recognize the objects by the sounds they produce much better than their visual images. The disadvantage of this 'auditory seeing' is that when his hearing becomes overloaded and cannot cope with auditory and 'visual' information, it may either become hypersensitive (and painful) or shut down altogether. Then he finds his 'world' unusually quiet ('The spoon has grown quiet') and dangerous. It leads to panic attacks.*
>
> *Alex has difficulty sleeping because 'sound pictures' in his environment make it hard for him to relax. All these experiences cause anxiety, stress and panic attacks.*

What they say

I began to become afraid. I tried to name the things around me. I could not. The shapes and patterns and colors could not be interpreted. I began to get more frightened...

I hit the hard surface under my hand. *Splat*, said the surface. 'Bricks,' I said in reply. I hit another surface, commanding my mind to bring interpretation back. *Thud*, said the surface. 'Wood,' I said in reply. 'Yes, wood,' said Ian. 'Stone,' I said, stomping upon *clack-clack* cobblestones. 'A laneway,' I said, looking around and finally getting a whole picture of where I was. (Williams 1999c, p.196)

The sensory differences in autism are often overlooked. Here it is important to emphasize that sensory differences are not necessarily problems/difficulties.

Differences in perception lead to a different perceptual world, which inevitably is interpreted differently. We have to be aware of these and help autistic people to cope with painful sensitivities and develop their strengths ('perceptual superabilities'), which are often unnoticed or ignored by non-autistic people.

The real world and the perceived world (i.e., our mental image of the world) differ. Although we live in the same physical world and deal with the same 'raw material', differences in sensory functioning create invisible walls between autistic and non-autistic people. The metaphorical descriptions of children and adults with autism – such as 'aliens', 'Martians' – become factual! They do live in a different world! The same stimuli look, sound, feel, smell differently for them. When we want to show our love and affection by hugging the autistic child, she pulls away as the pain from the touch is unbearable. So what is our interpretation? – 'She doesn't love me.'

We are often 'deaf' to the sounds our child cannot tolerate (for instance, sounds of fans working, kettle boiling). We are 'blind' to a 60-cycle flickering of fluorescent lights that makes the room pulsate on and off. Just because we are deaf, blind and dumb to the stimuli our little 'aliens' perceive with extreme acuteness, we describe their behaviours as bizarre, odd, inappropriate. However, as their systems work differently, their responses to sensory stimuli are 'normal' (from an autistic point of view), although different and unconventional for us, living in a parallel world.

Just as we never find it strange or bizarre if a blind child touches things to recognize them, the behaviour of a child whose sensory-perceptual problems are not straightforwardly visible should be tolerated. We should not demand that he 'behave himself' and 'stop mouthing and smelling objects' (when he tries to recognize things).

As these children literally live in a parallel (differently reconstructed) world and are misunderstood (= mistreated), they are likely to display behavioural problems, such as self-stimulation, self-injury, aggression, avoidance, rigidity, high anxiety, panic attacks, etc.

> *Matthew is a 15-year-old boy with Asperger syndrome. He attends a mainstream school with three hours' support a week. He has very good academic records. However, because of his challenging behaviours (aggression towards peers and teachers when he is frustrated and non-compliance with the school rules), Matthew has been expelled from the school for different periods of time.*
>
> *There are 25 other students in Matthew's class. His classmates know about Matthew's difficulties and are very supportive. However, sometimes they are scared by his uncontrollable 'outbursts'. Matthew's English teacher is very confident about 'managing' Matthew, as she has had some experience of working with a child with Asperger syndrome ('And there were no problems at all! He was very quiet and eager to please.') Well, Matthew is different. The teacher believes in rules, discipline and the ABC approach of managing challenging behaviours.*
>
> *One morning, at the English literature lesson, the teacher tells the students about Shakespeare's comedies. She writes key words (titles, names) on the blackboard. The students take notes. The teacher notices that Matthew neither looks at her nor takes notes in his book:*
>
> *'Matthew, stop staring at the wall. There is nothing written there. Don't you know you are supposed to listen to the teacher at the lesson?'*
>
> *Matthew is startled: 'But I am listening!'*
>
> *The teacher continues about the comedies and then gives the students the topic of their essay they have to write now.*
>
> *'Matthew, you are not listening!'*
>
> *'I am listening!'*
>
> *The students start writing. Matthew takes his pen and carefully writes the title of his essay in the middle of the line. Several students ask*

the teacher questions about the length of the essay, subheadings, etc. The teacher explains while moving from one desk to the other, watching the students working. Matthew writes a few words but is unable to finish the sentence as two girls behind him are arguing about the spelling of the word 'Venice'. Matthew turns round and joins in the discussion. A very loud 'Matthew!' from the teacher startles him. The teacher comes up to his desk and looks at what he has managed to write. She is not happy with what she sees: 'Matthew, how many times have I told you that you were not listening at the lesson? That is why you do not know what you are supposed to do now. Get on with your work! We will talk about your behaviour after the lesson.'

The teacher returns to her table to make notes in Matthew's home–school book. The students are working. Five minutes before the bell, Matthew loudly announces: 'Two!'

The teacher is taken aback: 'Too? Too what?'

Matthew's answer does not shed much light to the situation: 'Two times.'

'Two times what?'

'You have told me two times that I was not listening at the lesson!'

Some of the students roar with laughter. The teacher has had enough. She makes another note in his home–school book and with 'I-won't-tolerate-a-clown-at-my-lesson' sends Matthew out of the classroom. Matthew kicks his chair, swears at the teacher and slams the door behind him.

So what has gone wrong here?

To avoid sensory overload or hypersensitivity, Matthew is able to attend to one sensory input at a time (monoprocessing). He cannot take notes at the lesson because he either listens or writes, but does not do both simultaneously. It is as though either his eyes work or his ears do but not at the same time. His teacher thinks he is being lazy or inattentive when Matthew is sitting at her lesson with a blank look on his face. He does not seem to be listening.

Matthew has difficulty concentrating on someone's voice as it is all of a piece with the environmental noises. His ears pick up all sounds around him with equal intensity. He is easily distracted if there is more than one person talking.

> *His responses are often delayed ('Two!') as it takes him some time to process the question and prepare the answer.*
>
> *Matthew did exhibit inappropriate behaviour, but was it his fault?*

It is crucial to understand how the qualitative differences of sensory perception associated with autism affect each particular child. Teachers and other professionals who work with autistic children need to recognize sensory differences in autism in order to select appropriate methods and plan intervention for these children. As all the senses are integrated, the deficiency in one may lead to disturbances in the other(s). It is, therefore, necessary to find out which sense(s) are deficient and to what extent, and which senses can 'be relied on'.

The sensory-perceptual profile of a child could be a starting point for selection of methods and, probably, working out new ones, in order to address the individual needs of each particular child. (For one of the possible ways to develop a sensory-perceptual profile of an autistic child see Bogdashina 2003.)

Chapter 4

Cognitive Styles
and Functions in Autism

Autistics are always thinking, thinking, thinking. They are often described as being far from intellectual. But actually, being immersed in their inner kingdoms, their minds are constantly actively doing many things: trying to synchronize their built-in rhythms, striving to keep themselves feeling safe, dissecting the meanings of endless stimuli, soaking up interesting information, reliving pleasurable events. It's difficult for them to settle down mentally. (O'Neill 1999, p.59)

In the previous chapter we dealt with the ways to get the information from the outside world via sensory channels and considered possible qualitative differences of perception in autism. In this chapter, we move on to information-processing problems and differences in autism considering different cognitive styles and ways to select the information (attention), process it (conceptualization), store and retrieve it (memory) and manipulate the received information units (thinking).

Autistic children learn very early in life to control their environment and the amount of information coming in. The timing of the beginning of sensory problems can often explain the different routes of language, communication, social and emotional development. If sensory problems (such as gestalt, fragmentation, delayed processing, hyper- and hyposensitivities – all leading to overload) start early and the child learns to shut the systems down (in order to protect himself from painful and scary experiences), he creates a self-imposed sensory deprivation. It means he literally isolates himself from the environment (and people) around him. It prevents him from learning via imitation and social interaction. The autism-specific perceptual styles children acquire (monoprocessing, peripheral perception) lead to different experiences which cannot be shared with non-autistics.

If the capacity to perceive and interpret information is impaired, no verbal conceptualization is achieved spontaneously. If the sensory perception is inconsistent, fragmented, distorted and unreliable, the next stages of the process will not go smoothly. Autistic people often have difficulty moving from sensory patterns (literal interpretation) to understanding of functions and forming concepts.

We can draw a scheme of information processing leading to cognitive functioning, which is simplistic but useful for the purpose of our discussion.

- attention

- processing for meaning and conceptualization

- storing and retrieving – memory

- manipulating – thinking, imagination, intellectual functioning.

Attention

We are surrounded by thousands of stimuli. However, we are limited in our ability to process all the stimuli simultaneously. At every moment we have to filter the information and select which stimuli to attend to, thus placing them into our focus of attention. The situation is changing every moment, and we have to shift our attention from one stimulus to another. If we interact with somebody we have to establish and sustain joint attention to certain stimuli.

For the purpose of our discussion, we distinguish the following characteristics of attention:

- The selection of relevant stimuli while ignoring irrelevant ones – the ability to recognize relevancy of stimuli.

- The focusing of attention, or 'attentional spotlight' (Posner 1980), also known as the 'zoom lens' (Eriksen and Yeh 1985) – the distribution of attention across present stimuli with certain concentration on the relevant stimuli – which can be too broad, optimal or too narrow.

- Attention span – the ability to concentrate on certain stimuli long enough to complete the task.

- The flexibility to contract and expand an attentional focus on demand and the ability to shift attention quickly enough from one stimulus to another in order to 'keep updated' with the situation.

- Directed attention.

- Joint attention (if not alone).

Impairments of one or more of these attentional abilities can lead to different disorders of attention.

Some researchers (for instance, Burack and Enns 1997; Ornitz 1989) suggest that impaired attentional functioning may be central to many social and cognitive deficits observed in persons with autism, as efficient attending is essential to the development of all aspects of functioning. The attentional difficulties experienced by autistic individuals appear to originate at a more primitive level of information processing, commensurate with the related notions of early selection deficits and inefficient attention lens (Burack and Enns 1997).

The inability to filter out the information (gestalt perception) and distinguish the relevant from the irrelevant; to distribute different amounts of attention across present stimuli, depending on their significance and to sustain attention results in increased distraction, overloads and impairs cognitive functioning. Involuntary responses to irrelevant stimuli interfere with the processing of relevant information. Without efficient filtering and differentiation of relevant and irrelevant stimuli (selectivity) the child cannot make sense of the environment.

Autistic children appear to ignore relevant stimuli in favour of apparently meaningless stimuli in their environment. We should remember, however, that the decision which stimuli are relevant and which are meaningless depends on the child's experiences and knowledge. Autistic individuals might attend to what *they* find important and meaningful in each particular situation, but it is not necessarily what non-autistic people find relevant. We describe this as an 'idiosyncratic focus of attention'. However, it might be lack of shared experiences that brings different preferences in choosing which stimulus to attend to.

One of the disorders of attentional mechanism is Attention Deficit/ Hyperactivity Disorder (ADHD). According to the diagnostic criteria of

DSM-IV (APA 1994) and ICD-10 (WHO 1992), ADHD is reflected in the three major categories of symptoms: inattention, hyperactivity and impairments in social, academic and occupational functioning. Now we know that autism and ADHD can often overlap. What is called the 'short attention span' in ADHD can be one of possible attentional patterns in autism as well. A short attention span means that a child is easily distracted and cannot concentrate on the task too long. Even if she tries to pay attention, she cannot. Her attention is very easily shifted (in contrast to narrow-focused attention). She has no control over her attentional mechanism. It is not the child who 'pays attention' to something, but rather different stimuli around her 'demand' her attention – they 'jump out' at her. Her attentional focus is too broad and her attention is too 'thinly spread' among many stimuli. Often stimuli are seen/heard/smelt/felt, etc. without the child intending to see/hear/smell/feel, etc. The child is too aware of everything around her, cannot 'keep on track' for too long and is unable to finish whatever she is doing/thinking because there are too many things to attend to.

> *Mark tries to listen to the teacher but gets distracted by the sound of the microwave in the kitchen two rooms away. As a result, he hears a few words, then the buzzing sound of the microwave, then another word, then… Mark becomes frustrated with himself at not being able to pay attention but he cannot help it.*
>
> *Des goes to the toilet but before he can reach it his attention is grabbed by a light switch on the wall. It 'demands' that he switch it off. He is being reminded of the point of his destination by the teacher and makes a few steps in the direction of the loo, but his eyes are 'caught' by the ruler on the table and he turns to grasp it. Without 'an escort' Des might wander around the school for hours forgetting where he is going to.*

In order to avoid sensory information overload, some autistic people acquire voluntary and involuntary strategies and compensations; like mono-processing, when they focus their attention to one single channel; or 'tunnel attention', when they concentrate on a detail instead of a whole. In contrast to those who have a 'broad attentional focus' (for example, children with ADHD), they have very narrow-focused attention. Autistic individuals often compare this attentional pattern with having 'a mind like a flashlight', 'a laser pointer' or 'a laser beam' that highlights only a single dot (an area of high focus) that they see very clearly while everything around it is grey and fuzzy (Blackburn 1999; O'Neill 1999). Murray (1992) refers to this phenomenon in monotropism as 'attention tunneling'. In this case, only certain stimuli are perceived as going together, all the stimuli outside the attention focus being ignored.

What they say

...for children on the autism spectrum, the zone of attention can be a very limited 'bubble'. One of the goals in working with children on the autism spectrum is to expand this environmental awareness. My lack of body-to-environmental awareness probably explains why I seemed to ignore my mother's calling me into the house for lunch. I never heard her. She would have to actually touch me to make me aware of her presence. (Shore 2003, p.87)

Autistic children are often unable to divide their attention between the object they want and the person they are supposed to ask for it. In this case they may concentrate on the object of their desire and either do not perceive the person as a person or even notice the person at all. In this case they may appear to ignore people or use them as 'tools' to get what they want. Another problem autistic children with narrow attentional focus experience is difficulty in switching attention. For many of them shifting attention from one stimulus to the other is a relatively slow process that results in a sort of pause or delay of reaction. This 'too-slow attention switching' process may be caused by delayed processing of each stimulus. The research (Courchesne *et al.* 1994) has provided some evidence that autistic individuals have problems in shifting rapidly their mental focus of attention between visual and auditory stimuli, and this simple delay in attention switching might account for many developmental problems associated with autism.

Some children find it difficult to have their attention directed by others. One of the reasons may be that they are 'blind' to the conventional gestures used to direct someone's attention such as pointing, holding objects up for inspection, etc. For children with perceptual fragmentation, pointing may even seem threatening – a hand, unconnected to anything, suddenly appearing in front of them.

> *Alex becomes aggressive when somebody points at something to attract his attention. As he perceives an 'unidentified object' (a hand) as a threat, he hits back shouting 'Don't point!'*

The most common attentional problem in autism is the failure of autistic people to establish and maintain joint attention, in other words, the ability to attend to the same stimuli as another person. That leads to the failure to share experiences. As a joint attention task involves a divided attention task, when the person should attend to both the object of the joint attention and the person with whom the experience should be shared, an autistic individual often fails to monitor both of these (if he works in 'mono' or has 'tunnel attention') and fails either to attend to the object of joint attention or to the other person's shifts of attention. This results in the failure to comprehend the meaning of the interaction and hinder social and cultural development.

What they say

A deficit in joint attention could result from impaired attention shifting, limited capacity, inability to read signals cueing joint attention, or an innate inability to recognize human beings (as different from inanimate objects). (Blackburn 1999, p.13)

When one considers the notion of monotropism and expert focusing, one might conclude that the issue is not one of attention deficit but rather one of attentional difference! I think that this is much more the case. (Lawson 2001, p.143)

For learning the language, joint attention is essential. A child connects a new word with the object of joint attention. A deficit in joint attention affects the way autistic children learn new concepts. They may hear the word and remember it in connection with a part of the object they are attending to at the moment, or the whole object (different from the object of joint attention but at the focus of their attention, their 'flashlight'), or even the whole scene (gestalt perception) or sensation they are experiencing at the moment. The main thing is not to assume that autistic children will always share our attentional focus, even when they look in the same direction.

During a science lesson, the teacher shows a picture of a plant and explains what different parts of the plant do: 'The root holds the plant in the soil and takes in water; the petal attracts insects...' Johnny, a boy with autism, seems to stare at her and listen to the explanations. However, his attention at the moment is directed to the play of light on the teacher's earring; the colour changes each time the teacher moves her head.

A few days after the lesson, Johnny goes for a walk with his father. After the rain, the air is fresh and the sun shines through the leaves on the trees. The father shows Johnny the rainbow: 'Look, Johnny, isn't the rainbow beautiful?' Johnny looks at the rainbow and happily announces, 'The petal attracts insects'. The lesson has been learned.

What we can do to help

- Create a 'shared attentional focus'. Be sure that the object of joint attention is in the child's 'flashlight'. Give all the instructions explicitly ('Look at what I am looking/what I am holding, etc.'). If he looks in the same direction as you do, it does not necessarily mean he sees the same thing. Always try to 'see' from the child's perspective (considering his perceptual and cognitive patterns).

- Give the child enough time to switch attention from what she is doing to you, and then to the object you are talking about.

- In the case of 'one sensory modality focus', there is no way that the child can make a connection between the verbal label of an object and the object in question, even if the speaker holds the object near her lips. The child with 'single channel narrow attentional focus' either does not hear the label or does not see the object. In this case, the teacher has to find out the child's attentional focus, 'enter' it in the same sensory modality (e.g., visual, auditory, tactile, etc.) and either introduce the object of would-be joint attention into this focus or help the child to 'move' (shift) his attention to it.

Conceptual *vs* perceptual memory

> My mind…has been stretched and stretching since the moment of
> my conception. My capacity for learning, storing, accessing, and
> utilizing information and ideas seems infinite beyond belief. I have
> even referred to myself as 'a human sponge' and compared my
> brain to a finely organized computer. (Kochmeister 1995, p.10)

Memory may take many forms. Some people tend to remember concepts,
ideas, abstract information. This is 'conceptual memory'. Conceptual
memories contain vast amounts of thought and information in a highly
abstract, logically ordered form (Sacks 1995). Perceptual memory is characterized by little or no conceptual capacity; it contains 'sensory experiences'.
Some people exhibit good conceptual memory. Many autistic people seem to
possess remarkable perceptual memory. Some people may have different
combinations of both.

'Items' of conceptual memory are not fixed. They are constantly
changing, becoming modified with new experiences we have every day or
when we think about them. Everything is continually updated, being
re-categorized and re-generalized. When we retell a story we always bring
some tiny changes into it. Conceptual memory is very flexible.

'Items' of perceptual memory are without 'names'. For instance, Tito (at
the age of three) knew numbers in increasing and decreasing sequence, not as
values but as designs (the way they look):

> The numbers [on the calendar] looked so enchanting to me that I
> wondered standing in front of them whether they were little strings
> folded to take such shapes. I mentally memorised them in order,
> without even knowing what they were called. I did not want to know
> … They looked like patterns to me. (Mukhopadhyay 2000, p.9)

The main characteristics of 'autistic perceptual memory' are literalness and
gestalt.

Gestalt memory

In gestalt memory the 'items' (whole episodes of the situations) are not 'con-
densed' (i.e. are not filtered, not categorized, not summarized for a gist). They
are remembered as the whole chunks of events and situations, including all the
irrelevant (from the non-autistic perspective) stimuli. That is why, while

retrieving information (whether to answer a question or prepare a response) people with this type of memory have to 'play' the whole piece in their memory to 'find' the right 'word' (image, situation, etc.), for instance:

> ...if I try consciously and voluntarily to remember what was said to me, it may all be floating about and I may remember a few keywords but may have little idea how they are linked or what the significance of that linking is. If a mental replay of a serial memory relating to a certain time or place is triggered, however, I will re-experience the placement of people in different parts of the room and replay a kind of mental audio-tape of what was said as it related to where people were in relation to the objects around them when they said things. (Williams 1996, p.148)

Gestalt memory (in whichever modality – visual, auditory, tactile, proprioceptive) is characterized by undistinguished equality of all the stimuli – the large and small, the relevant and irrelevant get the same prominence.

> There is little disposition to generalize from these particulars or to inte-grate them with each other, causally or historically, or with the self. In such a memory there tends to be an immovable connection of scene and time, of content and context (a so-called concrete-situational or episodic memory) – hence the astounding powers of literal recall so common in autistic savants, along with difficulty extracting the salient features from these particular memories, in order to build a general sense and memory... Such a memory structure is profoundly different from the normal and has both extraordinary strengths and extraordi-nary weaknesses. (Sacks 1995, p.190)

A very interesting theory of memory and sensory perception was put forward by Bergson, who claimed that each person was at each moment capable of remembering all that happened to him and the function of the brain and nervous system was to protect us from being overwhelmed and confused by this mass of largely useless and irrelevant information. The brain shuts out most of what we should otherwise perceive and remember at any moment, and leaving only that very small and special selection which is likely to be practically useful (Huxley 1954).

Literalness

'Perceptual words' are stored in the memory as unprocessed, uninterpreted, unrevised and unedited images. These images are fixed and do not change with time. Sacks (1995) hypothesizes that pure perceptual memory, with little or no conceptual disposition or capacity, may be characteristic of some autistic savants. These memories remain unchanged for years and there is always some element of fixation, fossilization or petrification at work, as if they are cut off from the normal processes of re-categorization and revision (Sacks 1995).

The best examples of this type of memory are the feats of autistic savants who can remember books, sceneries, dialogues and musical pieces and reproduce them with ease.

What is it like to remember 'perceptions'? It means that, while remembering, people with autism actually experience the sensations they had when they first remembered the object, event or situation: they see, hear, feel, smell or taste it (in their mind). The thought about something produces the real experiences they had when encountered this thing or event for the first time. They store their visual, auditory, olfactory, gustatory, tactile memories, which are very real.

Drawings by autistic savants give us a revealing glimpse into the autistic mind. Their pictures show naturalism and realism of the individual animal or object. Louise's drawings, for example, exhibit no conceptualization but rather an immediate representation of his thoughts. He draws in detail scenes he has seen, sequentially presenting the movement of the main characters (see Figures 4.1 to 4.4).

Figure 4.1 Drawing 1, by Louis

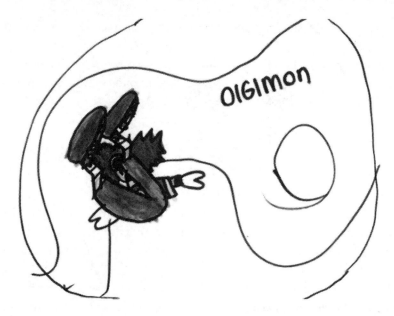

Figure 4.2 Drawing 2, by Louis

Figure 4.3 Drawing 3, by Louis

Figure 4.4 Drawing 4, by Louis

A lack of or impaired verbal language and remarkable drawing abilities often occur together. Nadia, by the age of six, still had no spoken language, but at the age of three, she had exhibited an extraordinary drawing ability. Selfe (1977) hypothesized that it was Nadia's failure to develop verbal language that was the key. Nadia could match different items with the same perceptual quality, but she failed to match items belonging to the same conceptual class. For instance, she could match a picture of an object to a picture of its silhouette, but she failed to match pictures of an armchair and a deckchair as objects of the same conceptual class (Selfe 1985).

Rigidity of thought and behaviour is often attributed to autism. This may be the consequences of problems with generalization – either a lack of generalization or an excess of it (overgeneralization). Both a lack of generalization and overgeneralization are, in fact, two sides of one and the same coin. Gestalt and literal perception bring lack of generalization, and fragmentation leads to overgeneralization.

As the interpretation of 'sensory concepts' remains literal, each item stored in the memory may remain separate. It results in autistic hyperselectivity and a lack of generalization: the item to be recognized must be exactly the same as the one that was stored the first time.

'Verbal concepts' are different. Any word generalizes. It is like a folder that contains all the information about a class of objects, events, situations.

These 'folders' categorize the world, bringing order and providing the person with easily accessible 'slots' into which they can sort the incoming information. For those who have difficulty easily forming these 'verbal concepts' the world consists of unconnected and incomprehensible experiences. For example:

> [In an art gallery] I was buzzing on an array of free-floating coloured forms against a big white background. The forms had different edges and curves, seeming almost to swim among the white. Then Mary Kay remarked, 'Oh, you like the painting of the lion,' and something freaky happened. The shapes stopped being just shapes. The whiteness stopped being a big square whiteness. I saw a lion, a lion on a white canvas. I was absolutely shocked, as though she had done magic. It was then that I had my first conversation about the power of labels to trigger the concepts that would cause visual cohesion to happen. It taught me many things. It taught me I could control overload in a new way, by looking away, tuning out, and struggling for an umbrella term, a folder, for a fragmented experience. (Williams 2003a, pp.77–8)

Remembering 'literally' means that everything is 'the' something. For instance, different breeds, colours, sizes of cats make each of these pets different 'sensory concepts' as they are perceptually different (see Figure 4.5).

Figure 4.5 The cat, by Ian Wilson

As a child, Wendy was shown fuzzy felt animals on the fuzzy felt board to prepare her for a visit to a farm. She noticed that the fuzzy felt pig was pink, half the size of her hand and was still. In the farm Wendy was allowed to get close to and stroke the farm animals. And surprise, surprise – the 'live' pig was not like the fuzzy felt pig on the fuzzy felt board! Therefore, maybe the 'live' farm pig was not a pig at all! (Lawson 2001). Wendy Lawson calls this literalness 'thinking in closed pictures' – not connecting ideas or concepts – in contrast to 'thinking in open pictures' – the common style of conceptual thinkers.

Concerning behaviour, a lack of generalization occurs if a previously learned behaviour cannot be applied to similar situations. The difficulty may be caused by gestalt perception, when the slightest change may create a 'new gestalt' that has not been stored in the memory and, consequently, all 'old behaviours' become 'non-applicable'. Overgeneralization occurs if the response from the memory is triggered by a certain detail (fragmentation). If the detail is present the person responds to it as they did in the past, regardless of whether the situation is similar or completely different.

So, if their memory is so good (actually, sometimes it is very difficult – if not impossible – for them to forget), why can't autistic children answer the simplest questions, such as: 'What did you do at school today?'

The answer may lie in the difficulty they have searching their own memory and retrieving the information they want. Jordan and Powell (1995) highlight how the individual with ASD can have a good rote memory and recall of detail alongside an inability to give the gist of a story of an event and a failure to remember what happened even a moment before. However, is it a surprise that they are often unable to give a gist of the story, if they have the whole chunks (gestalt) stored in their memory as single entities?

Jordan and Powell (1995) consider the main memory difficulty in autism is the failure to develop a personal memory for episodes; in other words, the failure to experience the self as a part of events that leads to a difficulty in developing personal memories. They can remember things but they may fail to remember these things happening to *them*. In order to recall they need to be prompted with specific cues. Events can trigger in a child with autism whole chunks of memory recalled as complete episodes, but when asked to search his memory for particular incidents that same child may have extreme difficulty (Jordan and Powell 1995).

However, if they remember 'perceptions' we have to use their 'language' while asking them questions. The memories of verbal thinkers are triggered by words; those of non-verbal thinkers are triggered by 'non-verbal words'. It means that we speak 'different languages'. If we asked them, using 'their language', they might have no problem with remembering; for example:

> By having a key point...triggered, I can 'let the scene run' and I might find a string of things said in a certain order in relation to the order of other things done. I may even be able to repeat these strings, even if I hadn't processed them for meaning. This was how I impressed my primary school teachers that I had understood what they said. If I was asked what they said, in their attempt to prove I 'wasn't listening', I could play back the audiotape, speaking it as them. Those last words are the keywords here. It wasn't that I'd taken this information on as me, with the interpretation and understanding of significance that this entails, I had taken it on as the sources of this information... I have also been able to trigger serial memories by mentally replaying a physical movement or physical impact on me. (Williams 1996, p.148)

Autistic children are dependent on the 'right triggers'. The smell, taste, movement, noise and pattern may help them to remember what has happened and answer the question. In contrast to people with low-functioning autism, autistic savants may have 'privileged access' (Snyder and Mitchell 1999) to their memory which allows them to produce outstanding results in art, music, calculation, etc.

Memories according to preferred modalities

Although visual memory seems to be quite a common feature of autism, it is by no means the only one. Depending on the modality that is most reliable for each autistic individual, he may have auditory, kinaesthetic or tactile memories. People with a very good auditory memory ('sound memory') seem to have 'audiotapes' in their memory with detailed 'sound pictures' of objects, people and events. Some autistic people store 'smell images' in their memory; others, who have a kinaesthetic memory, store 'proprioceptive pictures'.

> *Alex, who has a remarkable 'sound memory' and who often uses his hearing to 'see' (because of his unreliable visual perception) once asked his mother: 'What is 'nightmare'?*
> *Mother: 'It is a frightening dream.'*
> *Alex: 'I know now, "nightmare" is silence. It is when I see silence in my dream.'*

Autistic memory is often described as 'associative memory' (Grandin 1996a).
Temple Grandin (2000) compares this type of memory with a Web browser. A
Web browser finds specific words; by analogy, autistic people look for
memories (visual, auditory, kinaesthetic, etc.) that are associated with the
'stimuli words' they 'hear'. For instance, touching the picture on the wall may
trigger the memory of touching the same picture in the same room another
time and the events that happened after this.

Sometimes a word, combination of sounds, certain patterns or movements
may trigger the child to remember the situation that has been stored. If these
triggers are connected with something unpleasant or painful, a child may
throw a violent tantrum which would be interpreted as 'out of the blue'. The
best-trained therapist in the Applied Behaviour Analysis (ABA) approach
would not be able to find the triggers ('antecedents') as these are 'past
antecedents' brought into the present by an unintended trigger.

> *As soon as Jamie enters the classroom, Matthew lashes out at him. The
> teacher intervenes: 'Matthew, why did you hit Jamie? He hasn't done
> anything to you.'*
>
> *Matthew provides the explanation: 'He is wearing the same shirt
> he wore when he threw my homework into the rubbish bin last
> November.'*

On the other hand, the same type of memory (an associative memory) may be
of advantage to a person with autism. They may use it as a compensation for
their inability to process information quickly (delayed processing). If they
cannot process information at the time it happens, they often respond to the
situation 'from memory' when something remembered is triggered.

> *Mark, an autistic adult, is approached in the street for directions. He
> replies straight away, 'Sorry, I don't know. I am a stranger here' (the
> phrase he remembered from a film).*

However, sometimes it is 'inappropriate':

> *Alex (a teenager with autism) has broken an expensive vase. He knows
> that his mother liked it very much. When she enters the room he recites,
> 'Oh, Alex. What have you done?'*

Someone with autism often cannot keep track of conversation as, in the short break between two halves of a sentence, a huge number of tracks may have been triggered, leading to tracks, leading to tracks (Williams 1996). They just cannot stop endless associations (Grandin 1996a) and often use songs, commercials, etc. to respond, or use idiosyncratic routinized responses.

> Mother: *'Alex, get ready. We are going to Sainsbury's.'*
> Alex: *'Sainbury's making life taste better [from the commercial].'*

What they say

The memories I easily recall are all based on facts I am interested in or situational events that happened in my past. For some reason, I cannot seem to recall how to act as easily as I can recall how I did act. It is as if when I look backwards I see a photo album filled with vivid images and shapes, but when I try to look forward I cannot recall to mind one reliable picture to guide me along. Instead, I spend a great deal of time imagining how things should happen, rehearsing possible scenarios over and over, contriving lines I might say, and directing how others should act and how I would react to their reactions. I will play this game until I feel I have exhausted every possible scenario, and then I will typically obsess over which scene is most likely to happen in real life. But, of course, things rarely turn out exactly as I had rehearsed and so I suppose it will never be possible for me to always know how to act. The human saga is just not reliable enough for me to predict. (Willey 1999, p.67)

If I was presented with a situation that triggered some sense of significance, it is very likely that something stored in a serial way will be triggered, not to make sense of the situation, but to offer up ways of automatically responding to it. This has often happened, in particular with songs and commercials, and I am constantly finding these triggered by someone using a related product, saying a keyword, using a key-rhythm or a key-pattern.

Although I have outgrown the use of these as language (songs and commercials can be used to give a rough impression of what you want or to acknowledge you've understood someone's topic), I still use many of these phrases to make my speech more fluent at times. (Williams 1996, p.149)

What we can do to help

- Identify the preferred channel which will be your 'gate' to reach the child.

- Create 'daily diaries-dictionaries' describing the day's events, with key words representing 'mental images' in the preferred sensory modality – pictures or photographs of main events of the day (visual), objects or parts of objects to smell (olfactory) or touch (tactile), etc. – that can trigger remembering and help discuss what has happened during the day. These diaries may become weekly or monthly magazines, and then annuals which can be gone through from time to time in order to create the connection between the stored memories and perceptual experiences.

- Teach the child a range of strategies for memorizing and retrieving information, such as making stronger connections between 'sensory words' and 'verbal labels'.

Perceptual thinking

> I struggled to use 'the world' language to describe a way of thinking and being and experiencing for which this world gives you no words or concepts… (Williams 1999c, p.77)

Perceptual thinking is quite common in autism. It is literal, in whatever modality it is realized. Thoughts bring real sensations.

Let us briefly discuss different modes of cognitive processes in autism which have been documented in the research literature and personal accounts.

One of the characteristics of autism is the remarkable ability of many (maybe the majority of) autistic people to excel at visual–spatial skills while performing very poorly at verbal skills.

For visual thinkers, the ideas are expressed as images that provide a concrete basis for understanding (O'Neill 1999). Every thought they have 'is represented by a picture' (Grandin 1999b). We may say that 'visual thinkers' actually see their thoughts. For them, words are like a second language. In order to understand verbal information (both oral and written) they have to translate it into images (pictures). Temple Grandin, probably the most famous 'visual thinker' in the world, reveals that she has to translate both spoken and written words into full-colour movies, complete with sound, which run 'like a VCR tape' in her head (Grandin 1996a).

Visualized thinking patterns vary from one person to the other. Some 'visualizers' can easily search the memory pictures as if they were searching through slides and are able to control the rate at which pictures 'flash' through their imagination. Others have a great difficulty in controlling the rate and may end up overloaded, with too many images coming all at once. Still others are slow to interpret the information in their 'visual mode': they may have problems with visualizing quickly what is said, or mentally holding visual images together. Besides, the 'quality' of visual thinking may depend on the state the person is in, and even the time of the day. For example, for Temple Grandin (2000), pictures are clearer and with the most detailed images when she is drifting off to sleep; her language part of the brain is completely shut off at night.

However, it is important to remember that not all autistic individuals are 'visual' in their thought-production process. Some autistic persons may use a different modality (language); for example, Tito, mostly thinks 'auditorily'.

'Kinaesthetic thoughts' seem to be quite common:

> I mentally built my own staircases, on which I tried climbing mentally. … I got fascinated by them when I was still a small boy … I can feel a very *thrilling sensation* when I climb on something even today. The sensation is *a totally physical experience* of feeling my legs better as it works against gravity. Perhaps that feeling got stabilised in my memory and led me to do the climbing in my own mind. (Mukhopadhyay 2000, p.8)

These 'thoughts' might become obsessive. The person cannot stop thinking them. Where they originally brought calmness, they may turn into frustrations. When a person is left to his own devices and seems to do nothing, in fact, his obsessive thinking may be 'on', whether it is visual, auditory or kinaesthetic. The ABC (antecedent – behaviour – consequences) approach cannot alleviate this because the antecedent, thinking, is 'invisible'.

> Frustrations … I did not know how to stop climbing although the monotonous climbing made me mentally tired. I did not know how to suppress my frustrations … And I knew nothing other than scream. (Mukhopadhyay 2000, p.8)

> *Alex is sitting in the corner of the room, talking to himself (actually, he is 'replaying' his conversation with his mother over and over again).*

His sister enters the room: 'Alex, let us play dominoes...' With a cry of
'Mummy's disappeared!' Alex lashes out at her. He has 'lost' the echo
of his mummy's voice and panicked.

What they say

I also have to deal with memories as sensory input – mostly well-preserved scenes of failed interactions with other people. They are crystal-clear even after several decades, and I experience them as strongly as I would experience bright lights or loud sounds. Thoughts – especially repetitive, obsessive ones – seem like sensory input to me as well. At times I may become overloaded with them and 'shut down' as [I] would from other stimuli. (Spicer 1998, p.2)

Sometimes events that are stored in my long-term memory (and this is probably so for others with ASD) present not as parts of the past but as very present issues. Time, therefore, appears to always be in the present. (Lawson 2001, p.40)

These songs and jingles can also be very annoying because they often can't be cut off halfway through, so they continue to run mentally, even if I try to ignore my mind's occupation with them. (Williams 1996, p.149)

Sequential and spatial thinking

Another way to classify thinking patterns is in accordance with the way thoughts unfold, i.e. sequential (usually verbal) and spatial thinking.

The *sequential* system involves analysis, the progression from simple to complex, organizing information and linear deductive reasoning. It is influenced by hearing and language and an awareness of time. Temporal, sequential and analytical functions are thought to be associated with the left hemisphere of the brain. In contrast, *spatial* thinking involves a synthesis, an intuitive grasp of complex systems (often missing the steps), simultaneous processing of concepts, inductive reasoning (from the whole to the parts), use of imagination and generations of ideas by combining existing facts in new ways (creative thinking). It is influenced by visualization and images and an awareness of space. Spatial, holistic and synthetic functions are thought to be associated with the right hemisphere of the brain (West 1991).

The main characteristics of these two types of thinking are summarized in Table 4.1.

Table 4.1 Sequential and spatial thinking

Sequential thinking	Spatial thinking
Verbal: Using words	Non-verbal: Using 'sensory-based images'
Symbolic: Using a symbol to stand for something	Concrete: Literal
Temporal	Non-temporal
Linear	Spatial

Perceptual thinking may be both fast and slow. It is fast because it is not sequential. When people who think perceptually remember things, they remember the whole gestalt of the situation and do not have to wait for each word unfolding into a string of words. On the other hand, it may be slow as it takes time 'to play the video- or audiotape' to find the 'right word' to answer a question or to initiate a request.

In all the cases, a whole or gestalt is visualized or heard, and the details are added in a non-sequential manner. For example, when Temple Grandin designs equipment, she often has a general outline of the system, and then each section of it becomes clear as she adds details (Grandin 2000).

Unlike most people who think from general to specific, 'visual thinkers' move from video-like, specific images to generalization and concepts, for example:

> ...many people see a generalized generic church rather than specific churches and steeples when they read or hear the word 'steeple'. Their thought patterns move from a generic concept to specific examples. I used to become very frustrated when a verbal thinker could not understand something I was trying to express because he or she couldn't see the picture that was cristal clear to me. (Grandin 1996a, p.27)

There are both advantages and disadvantages to perceptual thinking.

The advantage is that it gives an unbiased approach to any problem. People who think perceptually are not restricted by traditional conventions. For example, Temple Grandin has become one of the most successful designers of livestock equipment thanks to her ability to 'see' from a very different perspective.

The disadvantage is that they often have difficulty with language as, in order to communicate their thoughts, they first have to 'select' particular images and place them in order, then they have to 'translate' these images (i.e. find appropriate words to describe them). It is very important, at this stage, to be able to hold the images together in the memory while verbalizing them.

The same is true, the other way round; in other words, when they have to respond to verbal instructions. As they have poor auditory short-term memory, they have difficulty in remembering instructions consisting of three or more steps. That is why 'visual thinkers', for instance, often have difficulty with long verbal information and prefer written texts or to be given the instructions in 'visual steps' – pictures, photographs, etc. In this case, it is much easier for them to 'translate' the message from 'auditory' into 'visual' code.

Perceptual thinkers have trouble with words that cannot be constructed into a mental picture and often have problems learning abstract things that cannot be thought about in 'mental images'. To understand abstract concepts they use, for example, visual images:

> The words 'know' and 'feel' were like 'it' and 'of' and 'by' – you couldn't see them or touch them, so the meaning wasn't significant. People cannot show you a 'know' and you cannot see what 'feel' looks like. I learned to use the words 'know' and 'feel' like a blind person uses the word 'see' and a deaf person uses the word 'hear'. Sometimes I could grasp these unseeable, untouchable concepts, but without inner pictures they would drift away again like wispy clouds. (Williams 1999c, p.61)

Social experiences present an even greater challenge as they cannot be represented with 'sensory-based mental images' and 'because the social experience itself is not an entity that is there to be sensorily tested out again in any comparable way' (Williams 1996, p.147).

On the other hand, the ways people who think perceptually develop to overcome these particular problems bring certain advantages and can explain a seeming paradox: that such concrete thinkers may develop a highly poetic language, full of beautiful metaphors and similes. The reason for this is that, in order to 'translate' abstract ideas into mental images, they have to employ the 'vocabulary' available to them, i.e. concrete notions, for example, a dove or an Indian peace pipe for 'peace', placing one's hand on the Bible in court for 'honesty', etc. (Grandin 1996a).

When these concrete notions are used to describe abstract ideas they turn into the original metaphorical and poetic expressions so typical of autistic writers.

Contrary to the common assumption that autistic people 'lack understanding emotions', their thought processes (memories) may be 'emotionally charged':

> Each time I begin to write, my brain becomes filled with images. I think visually – my emotions show colour and texture against my mind's eye like a projector. (O'Neill 2000)

> In my own case the strongest visual images are of things that evoked strong emotions, such as important big jobs. These memories never fade and they remain accurate. However, I was unable to recall visual images of the houses on a frequently traveled road until I made an effort to attend to them. A strong visual image contains all details, and it can be rotated and made to move like a movie. Weaker images are like slightly out-of-focus pictures or may have details missing. For example, in a meat-packing plant I can accurately visualize the piece of equipment I designed but I am unable to remember things I do not attend to, such as the ceiling over the equipment, bathrooms, stairways, offices, and other areas of little or no interest. Memories of items of moderate interest grow hazy with time. (Grandin undated)

Perceptual thinkers are often acutely aware of everything in their environment (due to hypersensitivities, gestalt perception, etc.) and they are often over-whelmed by the effort of functioning in the environment. This 'superability' can be seen in the classroom as a learning disability or/and challenging behaviour.

What they say

Teachers who work with autistic children need to understand associative thought patterns. An autistic child will often use a word in an inappropriate manner. Sometimes these uses have a logical associative meaning and other times they don't. For example, an autistic child might say the word 'dog' when he wants to go outside. (Grandin 1996a, p.32)

...my mind was constantly active, trying to learn from my own observations. For a while it looked like this. People studying me and I studying people. People inferring the possible reasons as to why I flapped my hands. While I [was] wondering why on earth their shadows did not flap and then realising that no one had such a friendly shadow as I had. I flapped more trying to show each shadow how to flap and make friendship. (Mukhopadhyay 2000, p.14)

What we can do to help

- Autistic children learn better with concrete information, whether it is visual, auditory, tactile, etc.

- Let children use their ways to explore the world. In many ways 'autistic perception' is superior to that of non-autistics. Autistic individuals with their heightened senses often can appreciate colours, sounds, textures, smells and tastes to a much higher degree than people around them. Their gifts and talents should be nurtured and not ridiculed, as is often the case.

- In the case of 'obsessive thoughts', it is important to distract them from their 'internal mental exercises', through external activities.

- Now that we know that autistic individuals have problems with information presented verbally, there is a great emphasis on using pictures to help them comprehend information. However, not all autistic people are 'visual thinkers'. That is why it is important to choose the methods of instruction to match the child's 'mental language'; for instance, tactile aids for 'tactile thinkers', audiotapes for 'auditory thinkers'.

Imagination

One of the diagnostic characteristics of autism is a lack or impairment of imagination. However, what we call the impairment of imagination in autism takes the form of extreme literalness caused by difficulty to form verbal concepts. In fact, as we have seen, literalness may be seen not as an impairment but rather as another form of mental processing, viz. perceptual thinking, which processes images (visual, auditory, kinaesthetic, tactile) rather than ideas.

The experimental studies of creativity and imagination in autism and Asperger syndrome (see, for example, Craig and Baron-Cohen 1999) show that children with autism produced less varied patterns in drawing than the controls. The conclusion made was that though children with autism and Asperger syndrome could generate possible novel changes, they were less creative than the controls.

Craig and Baron-Cohen (1999) distinguish between two types of creativity: the first entails the production of *novel but real-world* events (reality-based creativity); the second, the production of *novel but purely imaginative* events (imaginative creativity).

However, bearing in mind that autistic people's cognitive processes are qualitatively different relative to the non-autistic population, their creativity and imagination would be qualitatively (and contextually) different. They would probably find it more difficult to imagine 'a flying elephant', but they could design whole new systems in the imagination (as Temple Grandin, who has created equipment for cattle plants, has done) that satisfy the definition of the first type of creativity (reality-based creativity). The examples of the second type (imaginative creativity) can be found in the artistic and literary works of autistic individuals. Their work speaks volumes.

Eric Jiani Phipps, an adult with ASD, is a talented artist whose works are fascinating and intriguing. Since he was a child, Eric has always liked inventing his own imaginary worlds and then expressing these worlds through models, maps or drawings. Through his art that has developed enormously, Eric feels he is moving closer to finding his place in the real world. Figures 4.6 and 4.7 can give the reader the idea of 'non-impaired imaginative creativity' of people with ASD.

Figure 4.6 'Megalopolis', by Eric Jiani Phipps

Figure 4.7 'Sermon at the Edge of the World', by Eric Jiani Phipps

How could we question the ability of the reality-based and imaginative creativity of such people as Tito?

> [At the time of writing Tito was 12 years old] …I tried to grow myself mentally, so big, that I could reach the door of the room by merely stretching my hands. I could bang the door mentally… I imagine. And I imagine a great deal. From concrete to abstract as abstract gives rise to the concrete… (Mukhopadhyay 2000, p.27)

More and more autistic individuals have had their books published – a real testament to their creativity and imagination. They display their unique styles of writing and very individual use of figures of speech. So far there has not been any research study that specifically investigates any variations in expression between male and female autistic authors, though there are some subjective observations of differences of behavioural and communicative features between boys and girls with ASD (see, for example, Attwood 1998). It would be interesting to investigate gender differences in writing styles of autistic individuals.

Another fascinating phenomenon is autistic poetry. A huge proportion of people with ASD writes poetry. It is this genre that seems to give them the freedom of expression; the genre where they can put aside all the literary conventions and use the language that seems to correlate to different perception and thinking.

What they say

Visual thinking has enabled me to build entire systems in my imagination. (Grandin, 1996a, p.19)

...I, and several others I know, have extremely vivid imaginative powers and enormous creativity... Imagination has helped me write poetry and prose filled with graphic images. It enables me to hear words and music I write 'inside' my head before they are typed, printed, written, spoken, sung or played, and given 'lives' of their own. (Kochmeister 1995, p.5)

There has often been the stereotype that people with autism lack imagination... I have seen wonderful art by people with autism, seen displays of humour, non-verbal, typed and spoken, however surreal, self-directed and 'autistic' in nature. I have seen amazing surreal and creative uses of objects used in experiences of 'art', 'music', 'construction' and kinaesthetic play in spite of labelling such as 'inappropriate use of objects' by non-autistic psychologists seeking to assess levels of 'abnormality' and 'disability'. I have also worked with children and adults, non-verbal and verbal, who have displayed interaction either with their reflection as another person or playing or dialoguing with someone 'invisible'. This doesn't mean they actually see or hear them. (Williams 2003a, p.209)

Regarding the so-called lack of imagination, consider this. I have read Wendy Lawson's poetry, a lady with Asperger's Syndrome who was diagnosed in August 1994 at the age of 42. She has written much better poetry than I could ever compose. After being diagnosed she has written her own biography, has her own website and is an accomplished speaker. Before her diagnosis she achieved academic qualifications. This was after spending 25 years on wrongly prescribed anti-psychotics for her 'Schizophrenia'. Sounds familiar. These are remarkable achievements by anybody's standards. Is someone capable of these things lacking in imagination? (Phillips 2002).

IQ and autism – 'autistic intelligence'

Big world people [non-autistics] can be considered idiots in the autistic world, too, just as it can be the other way round. (O'Neill 1999, p.55)

Measuring non-autistic people by this [autistic] type of
development would often find them failing miserably and
appearing to be thoroughly 'subnormal' by 'autistic' standards.
(Williams 1996, p.235)

What is intelligence?

There is no single definition of intelligence that has been universally accepted
and we have to deal with a wide class of vague descriptions such as 'the ability
to carry on abstract thinking', 'an innate, general cognitive ability' (Burt
1955), 'the aggregate or global capacity of the individual to act purposefully,
to think rationally, and to deal effectively with the environment' (Wechsler
1958). So very often intelligence is (unsatisfactorily) defined as that quantity
that the intelligence tests measure.

What do we measure with IQ tests?

About 70 to 75 per cent of autistic people are considered to be intellectually
disabled, although there are discrepancies in performance between verbal and
non-verbal intelligence.

If we assume that autistic people live in a different perceptual world from
non-autistics, and develop different cognitive mechanisms and styles, then
what do we really measure with the standard IQ tests that do not take into
account all these differences? It is as if we tested the IQ of a blind person by
asking him to name the colours of the objects in front of him. Even using his
hands (tactile recognition) he would not be able to pass the test successfully.
Does it mean that he would be diagnosed as intellectually disabled?

As autistic individuals have different information-processing strategies
and styles, they might struggle with tasks presented in a conventional,
non-autistic way (for example, a child working in 'mono' may be presented
with multisensory information). The IQ tests are designed to determine
whether a person is developing within normal range or is 'slow' or 'stuck' in
his or her development. However, as autistic people follow a different path in
their development, they are not just 'less developed versions' of non-autistic
people, but rather people who have developed, sometimes substantially, along
a very different track from non-autistic people, while acquiring a whole range
of adaptations, compensations and strategies on the way.

Their abilities, while 'invisible', may be so unusual that no existing test can measure them. For instance, how could you measure (and appreciate) the abilities described by Donna Williams:

> I could tell from the change in the pattern of a footstep or the slightest change in the sound of the vehicle pulling up outside the feel of the occurrences about to happen. I could tell in the shifting pattern of movements, from strong to erratic, to flowing, to extreme, the range of possibilities that would follow. I could tell from the sound with which a glass was put down, in response to the sound of another glass being put down, the basic feel or 'edges' of the interaction that would take place. I could tell from the incongruence between what was being portrayed and what I could sense, whether chaos was impending or fear and reactiveness was in the air... I wasn't 'psychic' in the common media sense of the word. It was merely that my system was quicker, less mechanical, less plodding than the system of interpretation. (Williams 1998, p.46)

What we really measure with IQ tests of autistic people is how well a person can function (or even communicate his functioning) in a different perceptual/ cognitive/linguistic/social world using any perceptual/cognitive/language systems available to him (but unidentified by the test). These tests do not identify 'autistic intelligence'. This is unfortunate, because if we have knowledge of the 'inner abilities' and mechanisms they have acquired, we can better teach autistic persons to function in the non-autistic world and, consequently, they could score a higher IQ.

Sharisa Kochmeister has both cerebral palsy and autism and does not speak. At the age of four Sharisa was said to have IQ of 24; at the age of 12 her IQ was assessed as being 10. After two years of facilitated communication (FC) she achieved an IQ score of 142 and was able to attend classes in regular high school. She now types independently:

> I disagree with much of what professionals think they know about autism and people with autism. Most of us are not retarded, we do both have and comprehend feelings, we are capable of both imagination and abstract thinking, and we do experience pain, pleasure, sadness and joy. While it may seem that we don't understand things, this is not true. The real difficulties occur in speed and style of processing, digesting, and responding to what has been presented. This is largely due to an over abundance of internal communication rather than a lack of it. It is exceedingly difficult to communicate with others when one's time is so

taken up with attempts to make sense of a world one finds so confusing. This is the true curse of autism – great ability to absorb coupled with poor ability to process and react. (Kochmeister 1995, p.11)

Another example of the 'uselessness' of standard IQ tests for measuring intelligence of autistic individuals:

> When I was assessed in 1994, my overall IQ was said to be 83. The assessor noted that I '…operate at the lower end of average ability…' In the year 2000 I began my PhD programme. This will be my fifth tertiary qualification, four of which I completed within eight years! I doubt that I have an intellectual quadrant graded at 83, when 100 is considered to be average. What this does show, however, is that having autism influences the way I learn and experience life. Therefore, it will impact upon my apparent IQ functioning because IQ tests are written for neuro-typical individuals and are usually administered and scored by neuro-typical means! (Lawson 2001, pp.67–8)

Stephen Wiltshire, one of the most gifted savants, who has a immense ability in visual recognition and drawing from memory, did very poorly in general intelligence tests, scoring a verbal IQ of 52.

Asperger himself recognized 'autistic intelligence' as a sort of intelligence that is unconventional, unorthodox, strangely 'pure' and original, akin to the intelligence of true creativity, scarcely touched by tradition and culture. Very often, autistic people's intelligence is underestimated and unnoticed.

In addition to inadequate tests, the matter is complicated (and aggravated) by 'unprofessional' professionals: those who are inexperienced and lacking knowledge about autism but who are in the position to evaluate autistic individuals' abilities and deficits. I remember being present at the evaluation of IQ of an autistic boy with behavioural problems by a clinical psychologist. The boy, whose native language was different from English, but who attended an English school and had no problem with receptive language, was offered tasks to measure his non-verbal intelligence. The performance was poor because the boy's attention was anywhere but at the task (was he bored?). The mother could not believe her eyes, as he was able to do similar tasks at a very early age. The psychologist refused to listen to her opinion and declined her offer to test the boy in English. ('What's the point if his expressive language is not very good?') The verdict was: the boy's IQ was about 40. Some additional information: the boy is very good at mathematics and languages. He can read and write. At school he actively participates in all the activities with minimal support. So what was this evaluation about?

Obviously, some autistic individuals may be intellectually disabled, just as some non-autistic people are. However, the poor results of the IQ tests may be accounted for by different reasons. Due to certain perceptual and cognitive differences, the autistic person either may not understand what is expected from her or may be unable to access her 'mental database' at the moment of testing. Besides, very often, smart autistic individuals are bored or even offended by the questions of the examiner and may give incorrect answers on purpose or refuse to cooperate altogether (as happened with the autistic boy described above).

A brilliant explanation of what might influence the score of the standard (non-autistic) tests in autism is given by Temple Grandin, whose intelligence cannot be questioned:

> Five years ago I took a series of tests to determine my abilities and handicaps. On the Hiskey Nebraska Spatial Relations test, I got an average score because it was a timed speed test. I am not a fast thinker; it takes time for visual images to form...

> As a child I got scores of 120 and 137 on the Wechsler. I had superior scores in Memory for Sentences, Picture Vocabulary, and Antonyms-Synonyms on the Woodcock-Johnson. On Memory for Numbers I beat the test by repeating the numbers out loud. I have an extremely poor long-term memory for things such as phone numbers unless I can convert them to visual images. For example, the number 65 is retirement age, and I imagine somebody in Sun City, Arizona. If I am unable to take notes I cannot remember what people tell me unless I translate the verbal information to visual pictures...

> I got a second-grade score on the Woodcock-Johnson Blending subtest where I had to identify slowly sounded-out words. The Visual Auditory Learning subtest was another disaster. I had to memorize the meaning of arbitrary symbols, such as a triangle means 'horse', and read a sentence composed of symbols. I could only learn the ones where I was able to make a picture for each symbol. For example, I imagined the triangle as a flag carried by a horse and rider.

> Foreign languages were almost impossible. Concept Formation was another test with fourth-grade results. The name of this test really irks me, because I am good at forming concepts in the real world. My ability to visualize broad unifying concepts from hundreds of journal articles

has enabled me to outguess the 'experts' on many livestock subjects. The test involved picking out a concept such as 'large, yellow' and then finding it in another set of cards. The problem was, I could not hold the concept in my mind while I looked at the cards. If I had been allowed to write the concept down, I would have done much better. (Grandin undated)

Temple Grandin's visual–spatial ability is so phenomenal that it cannot be measured by any existing standard spatial test.

It is worth mentioning what autistic people themselves think about IQ tests.

What they think

…It is a myth that severely autistic people are all retarded, mentally. Actually, some people with severe Autism are brilliant. Also, a single individual can show both low-functioning and high-functioning in different areas… Frequently, autistic people's intelligence is underestimated. Many professionals still claim that the majority of autistics score within the mentally retarded range on IQ tests. This doesn't mean the majority of them are mentally retarded, however. There's a lot more to overall intelligence than an IQ test can show… (O'Neill 1999, pp.15, 55)

Many [autistic] children are labeled low-functioning and have low IQ scores. Some may be retarded, but others may receive a low-functioning label because their sensory processing problems make communication difficult. (Grandin 2002, p.7)

Too high a value in society is placed on IQ levels. I used to think they were valid but now, the more I study them, the more sceptical I am growing about their value. For me IQ tests just prove one's abilities at IQ tests. I think that they are inappropriate for many people with Autistic Spectrum Conditions, and particularly people with ADHD or Kanner's Autism to take, because they can't often concentrate long enough to do the tests.

IQ tests often concentrate on language in parts, so someone with classical Autism will not do well there, and will obtain ridiculously low scores which in some cases don't reflect their actual ability. IQ tests don't measure savant ability, such as my calendar calculating. They don't measure musical ability, which many Autistic people have. They don't measure drawing ability, which Steven Wiltshire had…

At secondary school on Tuesday 10th November 1987 I had an IQ test. I didn't know what it was at the time and wasn't bothered. I learned years later that I had scored 99. However, I had an IQ test in 2000 and scored 121. Then I had one a while later scored 114. To what extent can reliance be placed on them? (Phillips 2002)

In a court, one is innocent until proven guilty. So it should be for people with 'autism'. When people with 'autism' are spoken to or shown things as though they were intellectually retarded until they demonstrate that they are not, this is like judging them guilty until they prove themselves innocent.

One man with 'autism' who I know of was taught the ABC and given soft play in place of regular classes until he was in his teens, when he began communicating. He then let people know how he was not only sick of soft play but had learned the ABC back when he was three years old…

I am not suggesting that people with 'autism' should be assumed to be intellectual geniuses. I *am* suggesting that people with 'autism', regardless of level of functioning, should not be *assumed* to have intellectual retardation. I am suggesting that they be spoken to and shown these things in language that is concrete, concise and to the point and in language that is slow and clear with a minimum of unnecessary, excessive or distracting information. (Williams 1996, pp.115–16)

Donna Williams (1996) distinguishes between functional and intellectual retardation. The first one is to do with how a person *functions* in the world based on the capacity to act on the information in the context it happens. The second is about capacity to accumulate knowledge. A person can have no or little intellectual retardation because of his unimpaired capacity to accumulate information and still have difficulties to access or act on this knowledge caused by information-processing problems.

Autistic savants

The phenomenon of autistic savants provides strong evidence that there can be many different forms of intelligence, that may be independent of each other. The studies by Beate Hermelin and her colleagues in the early 1980s showed that visual savants, for instance, were far better than normal people at extracting the essential features from a design, and that their memory was not photographic and eidetic, but, rather, categorical and analytical, allowing them to select certain features and use them to build their own images

(Hermelin 2001). These studies give some evidence that there might be different forms of intelligence, each with its own characteristic features and styles.

Areas of skills traditionally attributed to savants are:

- musical ability (usually perfect pitch)

- artistic ability (usually drawing, painting or sculpting)

- pseudo-verbal ability: an exceptional ability to remember, spell and pronounce words with a very limited capacity to *understand* words

- mathematical abilities (including lightning calculating, or the ability to compute prime numbers)

- calendar calculating

- mechanical skills (taking apart and putting together complex mechanical and electrical equipment)

- geographical ability: reading maps, remembering directions, locating places

- coordination, a remarkable ability to balance things

- spatial skills: the ability to estimate the size or distance of objects with great accuracy

- language ability (rare): polyglot savant

- outstanding knowledge in specific fields (such as statistics, history, navigation).

These extraordinary abilities (capabilities) are often seen as a sign of dysfunction rather than an 'islet of intact ability' (Frith 1989). However, if we recognize the different cognitive mechanisms involved, we could assume that these abilities become dysfunctional in the environment that operates using different forms of processing and expressing information.

Besides, while recognizing different types of abilities in 'diagnosed' autistic savants we often ignore (or do not notice) the abilities that are not so spectacular in individuals with low-functioning autism. These abilities may include:

- extrasensory perception

- sensory (unusual discrimination abilities in smell, touch, vision, etc.)

- perfect appreciation of passing time – without knowledge of or access to a clock.

There are two necessary characteristics of the savant syndrome:

1. A remarkable ability to memorize or to repeat an operation endlessly.

2. A means of given expression to this ability.

'Unrecognized savants' may lack the second characteristic while possessing the first. Some autistic savants are found undiagnosed among the general population or misdiagnosed among people with intellectual disabilities. Because their skills are not spectacular, they are often not identified. Thus, autistic children with high intellectual ability may be placed in special education classes where all the attention is focused on remediation of their deficits while ignoring their exceptional abilities ('invisible' to their teachers).

What they say

I have often wondered if Asperger people are able to appreciate colour, taste, sound and texture to a higher degree than non-Asperger people? Perhaps there is a way such talents or heightened senses can be harnessed? Of course Asperger people are already benefiting from these gifts because they know the joys of such treasures, but their joy can easily be turned into frustration and anger or sadness and fear by the words of others who do not understand. (Lawson 1998, p.7)

The important thing is that people with these skills aren't sold short and that the non-autistic world would realise that 'savant skills' are not limited to the places where stereotyped impressions expect them to be. In my view, they can and do extend beyond art, music, mathematics and 'calendar memories'. In my experience, they can extend into mimicry, speed-reading, automatic writing, the acquisition of foreign languages and, in some cases, to the intermittent presence of so-called 'clairvoyance'. Taking into account these wider areas in which 'savant skills' may be found, a larger percentage of so-called 'savants' may be present among the 'autistic' population than is presently realised. (Williams 1996, pp.254–5)

Dr Howard Gardner, professor of education at Harvard University, used the performance of autistic savants as evidence that there can be many different forms of intelligence, all potentially independent of each other. He developed the theory of multiple intelligences and described it in his book *Frames of Mind: The Theory of Multiple Intelligences* (1983). Gardner suggests that the traditional notion of intelligence, based on IQ testing, is far too limited and does not reflect the unconventional abilities of a person. Dr Gardner proposed at least eight different types of intelligence, all of which must be taken into account in order to get an idea about a person's abilities and potential:

- visual/spatial intelligence – ability to perceive visually
- verbal/linguistic intelligence – ability to use words and language
- logical/mathematical intelligence – ability to use reason, logic and numbers
- bodily/kinaesthetic intelligence – ability to control body movements and handle objects skilfully
- musical/rhythmic intelligence – ability to produce and appreciate music
- interpersonal intelligence – ability to relate and understand others
- intrapersonal intelligence – ability to self-reflect and be aware of one's inner state of being
- naturalistic intelligence – ability to recognize and classify the naturalistic environment.

Some types of intelligence singled out by Dr Gardner are close to the 'cognitive languages' distinguished in this book.

Different ways to process information are reflected in different learning styles, i.e. the ways we acquire knowledge. Learning style is often not a matter of preference, but it is the way a person compensates for his or her weaknesses and adapts to the environment. Some learning styles will work better than others. Most people learn via several modalities (visual, auditory, verbal). Others (for example, autistic individuals) use different strategies. If a person works in 'mono', learning only through one channel, it is difficult (if not impossible) for him to focus on more than one thing at a time. Or, if there is delayed processing, there is a difficulty in generalizing information.

What they say

Being autistic does not mean being unable to learn. But it does mean there are differences in *how* learning happens. Input-output equipment may work in non-standard ways. Connections between different sensory modes or different items of stored data may be atypical; processing may be more narrowly or more broadly focussed than is considered normal. But what I think is even more basic, and more frequently overlooked, is that autism involves differences in what is known *without* learning. Simple, basic skills such as recognizing people and things presuppose even simpler, more basic skills such as knowing how to attach meaning to visual stimuli. Understanding speech requires knowing how to process sounds – which requires recognizing sounds as things that can be processed, and recognizing processing as a way to extract order from chaos. Producing speech (or producing any other kind of motor behavior) requires keeping track of all body parts involved, and co-ordinating all their movements. Producing any behavior in response to any perception requires monitoring and co-ordinating all the inputs and outputs at once, and doing it fast enough to keep up with changing inputs that may call for changing outputs. Do you have to remember to plug your eyes in order to make sense of what you're seeing? Do you have to find your legs before you can walk? Autistic children may be born not knowing how to eat. Are these normally skills that must be acquired through *learning*? (Sinclair 1992, p.295)

Chapter 5

Autistic Culture?

I needed an orientation manual for extraterrestrials. Being autistic does not mean being inhuman. But it does mean being alien. It means that what is normal for other people is not normal for me, and what is normal for me is not normal for other people. In some ways I am terribly ill-equipped to survive in this world, like an extraterrestrial stranded without an orientation manual. (Sinclair 1992, p.302)

Recently the term 'autistic culture' has appeared as a reference to the autistic way of perceiving, understanding and reacting to the world, although very often autistic people are described as being 'acultural' (Baron-Cohen 1993; Jordan and Powell 1995) or 'dyscultural' (Richer 2001). Some autistic individuals do feel that there is something so different about an autistic way of perceiving and thinking that it is justifiable to define it as a different culture. They believe that they are outside non-autistic culture and distinguish, for example, between 'the world' and 'my world' (Williams 1999c) or 'big worlders' and 'autistics' (O'Neill 1999). However, if a person does not belong to the culture into which she is born, it does not necessarily mean that she is acultural or dyscultural. Below we will consider a controversial issue concerning the possibility of describing an autistic population as belonging to a different culture.

One of the definitions of 'culture' is a particular form or type of intellectual development comprising patterns of learnt behaviour, shared knowledge and beliefs that are integrated in accordance with some learnt dominant value systems. With this in mind, the analysis of any behaviour must be undertaken in the context of culture as value systems and norms may be completely different from one culture to another.

Any culture emerges from a shared sensory-perceptual experience which, in turn, leads to shared knowledge about the world, patterns of behaviours, traditions, beliefs, etc. Although we all live in the same physical world our experiences are not necessarily the same (see Chapters 3 and 4). As a result, we might move in different cultural worlds; different perceptual, social, linguistic, etc. worlds. If autistic experiences are different from non-autistic ones (and they are!), the autistic world will differ from the non-autistic.

While autism is not a culture in the strict anthropological sense of the word, it *functions* as a culture, as it affects the ways people behave, understand and communicate with the world.

To be able to move between different cultures we have to become 'multicultural'. Mesibov and Shea (1996) stress that the role of any person working or living with autistic individuals should be 'that of cross-cultural interpreter – someone who understands both cultures and is able to translate the expectations and procedures of the non-autistic environment' (1996, p.1) to the person with autism. In order to successfully teach students with autism, we must understand their culture, and the strengths and deficits that are associated with it.

To belong to a certain culture we have to share patterns of behaviours, beliefs, traditions, etc., based on a similar knowledge of the world around us. Although there are no two individuals who perceive the world similarly, and each individual develops her own image of the world around her, these individual 'worlds' share enough common features for us to understand each other and 'belong' to one and the same culture.

Schutz (1962) introduces the concept of a personal and shared stock of knowledge about the world which every individual develops, and distinguishes into two parts one's knowledge about the world:

- the 'common world', constructed through social interaction with people of the same culture and characterized by a shared common experience of things, events, situations, feelings, beliefs, etc.

- the 'private world', constructed through an individual's private experience of certain events which differs for each person.

As people share the 'common world' knowledge, communication between them is possible even when much that is being talked about is not mentioned as each expects that the adequate sense of the matter is known to the other (Garfinkel 1967).

Figure 5.1 Shared knowledge makes communication possible, by Ian Wilson

If there is no shared knowledge about the world, communication is either impossible or, at the very least, there are misunderstandings. In this case both parties must express everything explicitly, as nothing can be taken for granted. Figures 5.1 and 5.2 illustrate these two types of communication.

Figure 5.2 Communication is difficult if there is no shared knowledge, by Ian Wilson

Where does this shared knowledge come from? The obvious answer is that our understanding of the world is shaped by the culture into which we were born through social interaction. However, before this 'shaping' takes place, we have to receive the information ('raw material') about everything around us through our senses and get it processed, categorized and stored in the brain. The way we do this depends on the way our senses work, the cognitive structures and mechanisms we develop, and the cognitive strategies and styles we acquire. As these structures are similar in non-autistic people, the 'construct' of the world and the experience of it is also similar, common to all, shared.

To understand other 'cultures', say, autistic culture and autistic people's knowledge of the world, we have to understand the ways they experience and construct it, their perceptual and cognitive styles and mechanisms. It will help us 'discover' the knowledge and experiences they have and the language they use to communicate and to formulate their thoughts and ideas.

For example, we would discuss the picture of the 'Mona Lisa' differently with a blind person, a child and a French person who has just started learning English. In each of these cases we adjust our language and mode of transmitting the same information in accordance with the peculiarities (lack of vision, limited knowledge about the subject, limited vocabulary) of each of our communicative partners. It makes the communication possible and, we hope, successful.

Strange as it seems, we do not bother to do the same when communicating with autistic people. We know they have difficulties (differences?) in certain areas, but do we always adjust our communication system and style to theirs?

Very often our assumptions – for example, that they are aware of some things and are ignorant of others – are based on our own understanding, feelings and experiences. And if a person does not respond in the way in which we assume he has to respond (if he had a shared understanding and a shared system of communication), we conclude that he is either incapable (severely intellectually disabled) or stubborn and naughty. Let us make a different assumption – people with autism are quite capable of understanding, relating and communicating with us, but we have neither shared systems and tools nor shared experiences with them. Our aim must be to learn about their experiences in order to get shared concepts and to create shared systems and tools, making communication possible. The more shared information and experiences we have, the easier communication will be.

Here we have to consider the role of language in cultural development and in the construction of a 'cultural-linguistic world'. As language is a convention, it is a model of a culture and of its adjustment to the world (Hill

1958). Edward Sapir, an outstanding linguist, hypothesized that our view of the world is shaped by the language we learned as a child. To Sapir, the 'real world' is to a large extent unconsciously built upon the language habits of the group speaking this language. The worlds in which different cultures live are distinct worlds, rather than the same world with different labels attached, as no languages are sufficiently similar to be considered as representing the same social reality (Sapir 1929).

This thesis was further developed by Benjamin Lee Whorf, who studied the language of the Hopi Indians and showed how their view of the world was closely related to the grammatical categories of their language. Whorf (1956) introduced a principle of relativity that holds that 'all observers are not led by the same physical evidence to the same picture of the universe, unless their linguistic backgrounds are similar, or can in some way be calibrated' (p.214). Whorf concluded:

> We cut nature up, organize it into concepts, and ascribe significances as we do, largely because we are parties to an agreement to organize it in this way – an agreement that holds throughout our speech community and is codified in the patterns of our language. (Whorf 1956, pp.213–14)

Although this hypothesis has been criticized, there are certain developments that seem to confirm the core idea of it. Take, for example, the consequences of the expansion of the English language in former colonies. The Kenyan novelist and playwright, Nguigi wa Thiong'o, having witnessed the changes brought by the English language to his native culture, concludes:

> Language is a carrier of a people's culture. Culture is a carrier of a people's values. Values are a carrier of a people's outlook or conscious-ness and sense of identity. So by destroying or underdeveloping people's languages, the colonizing nations were deliberately killing or underdeveloping the cultures, values and consciousness of the people. And by imposing their languages, they were also imposing the culture, values and consciousness carried by them. (wa Thiong'o 1984, p.xiv)

Raymond Williams, in his book *Culture and Society* (1983), argues that some important social and historical processes occur *within* language. Williams analyses changes in meanings of old words and the appearance of new ones (neologisms) in their connection to the changes in the cultural development of people speaking the language, and views linguistic changes as barometers of changes in society and culture.

Although the Sapir-Whorf hypothesis (that our ways of looking at the world are formed by the categories of the language we speak) is not considered proved and much more emphasis is made on the 'universal grammar' of all languages (Chomsky's 'transformational grammar' (1957)), the idea of social-cultural differences caused by differences in languages is worth considering, especially if we deal with verbal *versus* non-verbal languages.

Although all verbal languages do have common underlying structures ('universal grammar'), each language arranges different categories in a different way. This idea was emphasized by Hjelmslev (1961):

> Each language lays down its own boundaries within the amorphous 'thought-mass' and stresses different factors in it in different arrangements, puts the centers of gravity in different places and gives them different emphases. It is like one and the same handful of sand that is formed in different patterns. (p.52)

The meaning of any word is closely related to the experiences of the members of this particular culture to the object/event the word refers to. We learn to structure experience and thought as they are structured by a certain social group (Brown 1958), and languages differ in the way they reflect cultural attitudes and experiences. For instance, in the languages of Eskimos there are more than 20 words to designate ice, depending on its strength, ways of formation (coastal, sea), etc.

Berlin and Kay (1969) studied colour terms in different languages. They found that although languages did differ in how they subdivided the light spectrum, the effects on colour perception seemed minimal. However, it is possible to hypothesize that the 'nameless colours' can be ignored as 'unimportant'. It has been found that although the boundaries of colour categories are established by physiology of the colour receptors, these boundaries show some plasticity and can be moved depending on subcategorization and naming alone (Bornstein 1987). Here we deal with 'acquired distinctiveness' and 'acquired similarity' of cues: two stimuli would look more alike if they had the same name and more different if they had different names (Gibson 1969; Lawrence 1950). As Miller put it, 'many of the differences we perceive among things and events would not be noticed if society had not forced us to learn that they have different names' (Miller 1951, p.199). Even more complicated are differences in grammatical categories.

The child acquires these 'cultural-linguistic categories' as she shares the experiences of the people around her and thus enters the culture into which she is born.

Although there are language universals common to all verbal languages, these universals are reflected in each language differently. Therefore we may speak about the linguistic world of each culture.

It is interesting to note that users of different sign languages demonstrate differences in their shared beliefs, attitudes and customs, thus revealing distinct cultural groups that are not simply signed versions of the spoken cultures within which they live (Hall 1989; Padden and Humphries 1988; Rutherford 1988).

This is even more true concerning 'non-verbal languages'. The 'sensory concepts' acquired by a child 'speaking' one (or several) of these languages do not represent 'shared knowledge'. However, the child uses these 'categories' and relations between them to understand the world. Here we may apply the Sapir-Whorf hypothesis – different languages conceptualize the world in different ways.

In order to speak a foreign language fluently and effectively, a person must learn to use the categories of the language in the same way as the native speaker and not just learn the vocabulary and grammatical rules.

There are two types of contact between members of different cultures: one results in the process of acculturation, i.e. the adaptation or adoption of a different culture (often a more 'superior' nation subsumes an 'inferior' nation), a second one brings a cultural exchange between 'equal partners' that enriches both sides.

In our situation, non-autistics try to 'acculturate' autistic people, i.e. make them take over more and more non-autistic ways until they lose all their own and become (or, at least, appear to become) non-autistic. However, this process is unlikely to be successful. Moreover, it is often very painful for the 'minority' (the autistic population). What we can do, instead, is to undertake cultural anthropology (the comparative study of our two cultures) in order to establish a cultural exchange that is beneficial for both parties.

In order to understand 'autistic culture', non-autistic people have to take into account possible perceptual and cognitive styles and the 'inner language(s)' of autistic people. It will enable us to learn the language we may share and make communication between the two cultures effective. Having become 'bilingual', those who live and/or work with autistic individuals will be able to help them acquire a second language, i.e. a non-autistic system of functioning. One should remember, however, that no matter how fluent autistic people may become in this language, it will be always a foreign language to them (even if they are able to master it and 'forget' their 'native tongue') and we must respect their cultural difference.

What they say

Because autistics think so differently from non-autistics, there is a natural separation between them. That doesn't actually have to be a bad thing. It's rather like a cultural difference between people of different nations. Some people who grew up in Europe and are very immersed in a European way of life, may be startled, confused, overwhelmed by moving to Vietnam – especially if the individual doesn't speak Vietnamese. An acclimatization process occurs, however, so in time, the European takes on the Vietnamese way of life. That does not happen with an autistic, except occasionally superficially. An autistic person can learn to mimic others, but never truly grows to understand why they do what they do. (O'Neill 1999, p.80)

You try to relate as parent to child, using your own understanding of normal children, your own feelings about parenthood, your own experiences and intuitions about relationships. And the child doesn't respond in any way you can recognize as being part of that system. That does not mean the child is incapable of relating *at all*. It only means you're assuming a shared system, a shared understanding of signals and meanings, that the child in fact does not share. It's as if you tried to have an intimate conversation with someone who has no comprehension of your language. Of course the person won't understand what you're talking about, won't respond in the way you expect, and may well find the whole interaction confusing and unpleasant. (Sinclair 1993, p.2)

Cultural exchange involves the sharing or swapping of different forms of the language and ways of interpretation all of which have arisen from essentially the same sensory, perceptual and cognitive mechanisms. Yet, hard as one might try, it may be much easier for a human being with interpretation [i.e. non-autistic] to have a cultural exchange with an octopus with interpretation than it may be for a person with interpretation to comprehend someone who functions without it, primarily on the level of sensing [i.e. autistic]. (Williams 1998, p.107)

Chapter 6

What Language Are They Speaking?

I turned to see Kath crying.

'I never thought he had any language,' she said. 'Now I see he does. I just don't know how to speak it… We think it is we who have to teach autistic people…now I see it is us who have so much to learn from them.' (Williams 1999b, p.170)

I tried to grasp the Millers' efforts. They tried equally hard to come to grips with mine… They were coming from a foreign place and speaking a foreign language just like I was. I began to see that given how totally different our underlying systems were, it was a miracle that we bothered at all. (Williams 1999c, pp.97–8)

We assume that language is necessarily verbal (i.e. comprising of words). That is why we say that children are verbal if they can talk (no matter that their verbal output is just a combination of echolalic phrases) and that they are non-verbal if they cannot produce verbal output. Donna Williams brilliantly illustrates this misleading conclusion with a story about a 'talking' parrot:

> People buy a parrot and they think that they teach it to speak. In spite of teaching, the parrot learns (maybe he is bored out of his mind or learns he gets rewarded for performing). The people are impressed because they now have a 'clever' parrot. Their parrot can 'do things'. An expert comes along and says the parrot only appears to speak. But the parrot did have language. Beyond cheap tricks, the parrot has always had language. It had and always will have its own. (Williams 1999c, p.20)

As the original experience of the world of autistic children is sensory-based, their original internal language (as a tool of formulation and expressing thoughts) consists of sensory-perceptual (multidimensional) images. This 'language' becomes central to their intellectual and emotional development.

Thanks to this internal (very real) language autistic children can experience thought as reality. It means that when they think about something, they relive it visually, auditorily and emotionally. O'Neill (1999) compares it with 'watching a movie: a mind-movie' – the pictures of thoughts in this movie 'transport you and create emotions as you view scenes'. It is not uncommon to see an autistic child giggling to himself. One of the reasons might be that the child is reliving some funny moment, using recorded, stored sensory images. What is very difficult for the parents to comprehend (and accept) is that a child might laugh or giggle non-stop when someone is crying. It might be one of the defensive strategies used by the child – when he is sad he tries to lessen it by 'feeling the cheerful emotions of a happy mind-movie' (O'Neill 1999, p.38) or he might be just confused and even frightened by all the emotions around him. In these cases, giggling does not mean that the child is happy about the situation.

Autistic children, like non-autistic ones, learn through interactions with the world, but this interaction is qualitatively different. They learn their language(s) through interaction with objects and people on the sensory level. That is why their 'words' have nothing to do with the conventional names for things and events that we use to describe the function of these things and events. Their 'words' are literal, they store sensations produced by objects through interaction, and they 'name' them accordingly. One sense (sometimes several) becomes dominant for storing memories, developing 'language', and constructing thoughts.

Contrary to a recent stereotype, not all autistic people think in pictures. In fact, those with severe visual perceptual problems have great difficulty easily retrieving mental pictures in response to words (Williams 2003b). Instead, they may use auditory, kinaesthetic or tactile images, for example:

> I learned sound pattern and the feel of words in my mouth and sound pattern in my ears. I learned the emotional tone of phrases in advertise-ments…but without any gestural signing to link experiences to the blah-blah NO IMAGES HAPPENED and the interpretation was lost. Unlike Temple, I do NOT think in pictures. I imagine primarily in feel, movement, kinaesthetic and via the acoustics made by the object when struck. I 'visualise' like a blind person. (Williams 2003b, pp.1–2)

Despite all the differences, the one thing in common for all these languages is that they are non-verbal and 'sensory-based'. Perceptually-based rather than meaning-based development leads inevitably to a lack of understanding of socially accepted categorizations (Powell 2000). Here we may talk about visual, auditory, tactile, kinaesthetic, olfactory and gustatory languages.

- *Visual language*: Children use visual images.

- *Tactile language*: Children 'speaking' tactile language recognize things by touching them, feeling textures and surfaces with their hands, their bare feet or their cheeks, or putting them in their mouth. Through touch they get the information about the size and form of things, but not about their function or purpose. They store the information for later reference and may find similar objects (for instance, a plastic cup and a glass cup) to be completely different 'words' in their vocabulary because they 'feel' different.

- *Kinaesthetic language*: Children learn about things through the physical movements of their body. Each thing or event is identified by certain pattern of body movements. They know places and distances by the amount and pattern of the movement of the body. They may bite objects and even people if they store the information by the way it feels when bitten.

- *Auditory language*: Children remember objects and events by 'sound pictures'. If the object is 'silent', they may tap it, recognizing it by the sound it produces. Unsurprisingly, spoken words are often perceived as mere sounds. It is difficult to sense or feel a ball, for example, in the auditory frame *ball*. While such children do not recognize something if given its verbal (conventional) name, they may identify it by the sound it produces while bouncing, the smell or the feel on the hand.

- *Smell language*: Objects and people are identified by smell. Olfactory memories ('words') neurally, are almost indelible as they may be remembered even in the case of an amnesia (Sacks 1995).

- *Taste language*: Children lick objects and people to feel the taste they give on the tongue.

Each child may use one or several 'languages' to make sense about the world. Given the perceptual problems they experience (fragmentation, hyper- or hyposensitivities, etc.), one or several systems may become inconsistent and/or meaningless, and they have to use the remaining ones to check the information with which they are flooded.

Each child has unique sensory-perceptual profile and has acquired (voluntary or involuntary) compensations and strategies to recognize things and make sense of the world. One and the same child may use different systems at different times depending on many factors that can influence the 'perceptual quality', such as stress, fatigue and 'environmental sensory pollution' (bright light, noise).

At the early stages of our work with a child, we should not dictate what mode of communication the child must use. We have to find the mode that is most natural to her, i.e. most close to her inner system, and on the basis of this communication system (shared with the child) we may introduce the conventional communicative rules and means and teach conventional concepts. In other words, we have to find out what language each child 'speaks' and introduce verbal language on the basis of her 'native tongue'.

> *Igor, a six-year-old autistic boy, puts every thing he is given into his mouth. His teacher shouts a loud 'No' and relocates the thing (a toy car) beyond his reach. At this moment any teaching stops (at least for the boy). No matter how many times the teacher would repeat 'This is a car. Say, this is a car. Look, it's a car,' Igor is unable to connect the sensation/feeling (or lack of any sensation/feeling) in his mouth with the noise produced by his teacher.*
>
> *Ann smells everybody and everything. 'It's rude to smell people. Don't do that again,' says her support worker. But how on earth will she recognize people and things?*

The usefulness of verbal language for an autistic child will depend on the degree to which he shares meaning of the verbal words with people from whom he learns the language. 'It is in the language and through the language in particular that the success and failure of the constitution of the common and own worlds are most impressively revealed' (Bosch 1970, p.61).

We can teach children with autism to speak (use) a verbal language and even think in it, first only 'outside of their world' (as if they are tourists who come to the country to practise the language of this country). Some of them (with early intervention) may even forget their own language and use only a 'foreign' one (like a small child who was brought to a foreign country and acquired the language of this country) (Williams 1996).

To start, we have to identify their language and speak to them through *their* words. To teach them to verbalize their thoughts, we have to 'hear' their thoughts, i.e. interpret them from whatever language they use, and 'wrap them up' into words. This way they are more likely to connect words with meanings (experiences). It is necessary to avoid long introductions as context through words is likely to confuse them and definitely does not help comprehension:

> The linking of words with sensory experience means that if I hear the word 'shoe', I link this with the sound it makes being thwacked on the floor. If I hear the words 'patent leather', I link this with cold shiny smoothness. If I hear the word 'silk', I link this with its feather-like flow, its sheen and the whisper of a 'whitt' sound that happens when I run my hand over its stretched surface quickly. If I hear 'picture', I re-experience running my fingers around its frame, the cold of its glass and the sound it makes being tapped. If I hear the word 'printer', I re-experience the sound pattern of my own printer printing out. If I hear the word 'biscuit', I re-experience the crunch and the feeling of it as I ate it… I have built word searching skills through sensory triggers and as a result been more quickly able to make personal meaning out of the sound patterns that are words. (Williams 1996, p.156)

Even if we become 'bilingual' and can understand their language(s), still there may be translation problems, as there are no direct 'word-for-word' translations in the qualitatively different systems we use.

As our conventional linguistic representation of the world is so different from that of 'autistic words', it is often a hard job to understand autistic symbols that seem totally unrelated (from our point of view) to the things and notions they represent. Park and Youderian (1974) reported the use of visual symbols by a 12-year-old autistic girl Jessy Park. Jessy used symbols of doors and clouds to represent such abstract concepts as 'good' and 'bad'. For example, 'pretty good' in Jessy's interpretation was seen as two doors and two clouds; 'very bad' – zero doors and four clouds.

Verbal autistic children often do not use language in the same way we do. In order to get any meaning of what they hear they have to connect verbal symbols with their mental symbols:

> For a long time there were many words that didn't connect so I used whichever ones I could find in their places. These were often phrases I'd heard or jingles or bits of songs and that doesn't make for saying what

you really intended even though it can be sculpted to sound all right. By touching, smelling, crumpling, feeling, jingling and tasting things, I came to be able to better recall what I *intended* to say. The word 'paper' was recalled often by its sound (when crumpled) and texture and visual impression and use so, for example, I would ask for the 'flat, square, white, cr-cr-cr, writing thing' instead of asking for 'paper'. By having contact with the object and commanding myself to name it (which is not the same as trying to recall its name), I could sometimes tap the thing and the word would come out. (Williams 1996, p.156)

If they see our sincere desire to understand them they do cooperate and try to express themselves more clearly. Paradoxically, they often try to teach us how teach them. It is not their fault that we often do not see very subtle clues they give us.

> *Alex kissed his mother's forehead. 'Potato,' he said, smiling happily. Mother saw he wanted her to sit with him and 'talk'. She had learned to recognize these subtle signs of Alex's 'social mood'. 'Potato?' she asked. 'What do you mean? Are you hungry?' He kissed her again. 'Potato,' and another smile. He definitely looked happy. 'Oh, I understand. Mummy's forehead feels like potato to you. And you like potatoes. You say you love your mummy, don't you? I love you too, sweetheart.' This was yet another lesson the boy gave to his mother. They both equally struggled to learn a 'foreign language'. Crazy? Not them.*

What they say

Because of the specific skills associated with having a fairly-high verbal IQ, I can put words together in a way which can usually be pretty well understood, and would not be identified as 'sounding autistic'. But this, to me, is as though I were very fluent in a foreign language. My 'native language' doesn't seem to have any words…thus, if I had to use only it, I too would be nonverbal. It is only the use of adaptation which permits me to use words as I do. (Spicer 1998, p.4)

I linked meaning with words when I was about nine when I got a picture sentence dictionary and linked the tiny (and tiny = cohesive) images with the physical experience of the words they stood for – and then translated these images into kinaesthetic experience related to the picture (i.e: prodding motion for cushion, tapping motion for the sound of cup, swirling motion for the inside of bowl, patting motion for a cat, the movement associated with the acoustics produced by running fingers through a comb for the image of comb, etc.) and then back to the written in order to understand the spoken in order to translate the heard...long track and big consequences for processing delay. (Williams 2003b)

For me, successful 'social' contact depended on someone else interpreting my own signals. Some of my attempts at communication were fairly conventional, as when I put my arms up towards a person with my hands stretched up because I desperately needed to be picked up or lifted over an obstacle. However Jay [her mother] noted that if I turned my hands outward when I put my arms up to her, I was asking for a boost for a somersault, rather than some help in climbing up. If she interpreted wrongly, things could get very noisy. (Blackman 2001, p.11)

Indeed, IF things are BAD ENOUGH, you will eventually decide that further attempts at communication (NC [autistic] style) WILL only bring on more trouble, so you STOP trying to communicate...

You will even punish parts of yourself that won't cooperate, with YOURSELF, trying to be what THEY want you to be. You won't understand why they never seem to understand, what you try to tell them, even after you have tried, as HARD as you DARE. You are very likely to be prevented from developing what YOU CAN DO WELL, because their system failed to realize the true content of your attempts to communicate. (Morris 1999)

Indeed, how does one explain the color red, to a person who has never perceived it? NOW imagine the problem of attempting to explain to another person, a whole set of senses (sights, sounds, smells, etc.) that are perceived differently, or possibly never have been perceived, particularly when that person doesn't speak your native language. Simplifying that, just describe the light display (with full meaning) that NT [neurologically typical] people witness in mid to late December each year in the northern hemisphere, to a person who has been blind since birth, and speaks only Swahili, while you must use the pure native Navajo language. (Morris 1999)

In Chapter 1 we identified the elements necessary for communication to take place. Now we may return to these elements keeping in mind the issues we have discussed. They are:

- A receiver, i.e. someone who receives information. A person who relies on monoprocessing, may be unaware of the presence/absence whom they are supposed to address, as all their energy is directed towards performing a learned phrase/sentence.

- Something to communicate about, i.e. an awareness of one's needs, ideas, etc. Autistic people have needs but sometimes they may not be aware of them (in the case of sensory agnosia, for instance).

- Communicative intent, i.e. a desire/necessity to affect the receiver's behaviour, emotions, ideas, etc. Very often, in order to prevent challenging behaviours (tantrums), the needs of children with autism are anticipated and they have no opportunity to develop communicative intent. Alternatively, their desire to communicate may be ignored altogether (say, in institutionalized settings). Research has shown, however, that very often autistic children do not lack communicative intent, but rather show a limited ability to use verbal or non-verbal communication for different purposes, and often use unconventional means of communication (their own means of communication: their language that we do not share).

- A medium of transmission, i.e. a means of communication *shared* by both participants. As we discussed above, someone with autism might use a different language to communicate and is likely to have difficulty in using any conventional system for communication in all but the most basic ways.

However, it is important to remember that:

> [Non-autistics] can be ignorant of the autistic's struggles to communicate. In this case, more care must be taken to learn how to interpret autistic languages… Communication in Autism is not a 'failure'. It is not non-existent. It's simply different, in some way eccentric in an interesting way, and in some cases dormant. (O'Neill 1999, p.47)

PART 2

*Language Characteristics,
Learning Styles
and Development in Autism*

Chapter 7

Language Learning Styles

> As an adult my method for learning a foreign language may be
> similar to how a more severely impaired autistic child learns to
> understand language. I cannot pick words out of a conversation in
> a foreign language until I have seen them written first. (Grandin
> 1996b)

Although all normally developing children acquire language at approximately
the same time and following similar patterns of development, it has been
established that there is a wide variety in language-learning strategies. Several
strategies of language acquisition have been identified: 'referential – expressive' (Nelson 1973), 'intonation – word' (Dore 1974), 'nominal – pronominal' (Bloom, Hood and Lightbown 1974) and 'analytical – gestalt' (Peters
1983; Prizant 1982) strategies.

Referential children tend to acquire a high proportion of object names (for
example, ball, dog, spoon) and also seem more concerned with solitary play
with objects. *Expressive* children acquire words and phrases that carry out
particular social interactions (for example, mummy, daddy, yes, no, please,
stop it, go away) and spend more time in social interaction than solitary play
with objects.

Dore (1974) distinguishes between 'message-oriented' and 'code-oriented' children. *Message-oriented* children acquire a rich repertoire of
intonation patterns that are used to carry out a variety of social functions.
Code-oriented children use words primarily to identify and describe objects and
events in the environment. The code-oriented children (corresponding to
Nelson's referential children) acquire a vocabulary more rapidly than
message-oriented children and tend to use more nouns than pronouns in their
first sentences.

Gestalt *vs* analytic style

Prizant (1983a) distinguishes two types of language acquisition and use, characterized by differences in the mode of learning basic units, growth of vocabulary, generalization and ways of development. A comparison between analytic and gestalt modes in language acquisition (Prizant 1983a) is summarized in Table 7.1.

Table 7.1 A comparison between analytic and gestalt modes in language acquisition and use

Characteristics	Analytic mode	Gestalt mode
Basic units	Single words	Words, multiword utterances, phrases, sentences
Early development	From single words to two- and three-word utterances, to express semantic and relational meanings	Multiword utterances function as single units
Growth	Acquisition of grammatical functions	Analysis and 'breaking gestalt units' (unanalysed chunks) into constituent components and movement to analytic mode
Flexibility	Language is flexible from early stages	Language is relatively inflexible in early stages
Generalization	Language use is generalized to classes of objects, events	Language remains specific to situational contexts and particular objects

(Adapted from Prizant 1983a)

Prizant (1982) suggests that autistic children use a gestalt strategy in language acquisition, i.e. they imitate unanalysed chunks of speech (this is called *echolalia*) and only at later stages of development do they learn how to break down these units into meaningful segments. This can account for the pattern of language acquisition manifested by many autistic children: from echolalia with no or little evidence of comprehension or communicative intent, through mitigated echolalia used for a variety of communicative functions, to spontaneous speech. A gestalt strategy is also reflected in other peculiarities of the use of language by autistic children, such as, for instance, the insistence on certain verbal routines (Prizant and Wetherby 1989). In a gestalt mode, language is relatively inflexible in the early stages with limited generative use

(Prizant 1983a). Despite seemingly complex grammatical structures, gestalt 'words' are very limited – they 'mean' specific situational 'notions'. For example, 'It is getting dark' (= 'we are not going for a walk' regardless of the time of the day) cannot be easily modified to show changes in the situation, as it is 'one word'.

While some normally developing children do manifest a gestalt style in language learning, for autistic children it seems to be a dominant style.

It is typical for an autistic child to insist on a specific, ritualistic set of questions and answers. If her 'communicative partner' varies, even in the smallest detail (the intonation, word order, word replacement), the child may respond with a tantrum. A slightest change in the 'dialogue' confuses the child. If she does not recognize the 'gestalt word' (the whole dialogue), she does not understand it.

Blackburn (1999) explains that treating a verbal stimulus analytically involves breaking it into (and thus, having to analyse and relate) more discrete units; thus it is not surprising that a gestalt mechanism is preferred. It becomes easier if the message is written down, as non-transient signals like writing simply allow more time for the child to analyse the pieces individually, since they don't disappear and thus do not have to be either processed simultaneously or stored in working memory.

The use of a particular strategy (or strategies) is closely related to the cognitive styles the child uses, as language serves as a tool for cognitive operations. Although non-autistic children may use different strategies to acquire the language, the outcome – development of speech and language as a tool for communication – is the same. In autism, the picture is more complicated.

To enhance the communication of autistic children, we must take into account how they learn to communicate and which communicative tools they use. The identification of language-learning strategies used by an individual child is vital for the appropriate intervention approaches for this particular child.

The differences in learning strategies can be caused by the differences of many factors involved in the process, such as genetically inherited features, cerebral hemispheric organization, the relative timing of the emergence of cognitive structures (Bates 1979), the relative timing of acquiring the language and of the onset of sensory processing problems, and the learning environment.

Cerebral hemispheric organization

The fact that the human brain is unsymmetrical is well known. Each hemisphere has its own way of perceiving and interpreting information: the left one, verbally, and the right one, non-verbally. In normal development the dominance of the left hemisphere is established when language develops, and from this point it determines the intellectual processes of abstract thinking and logical reasoning. This hemispheric lateralization manifests the full intersensory integration and integration of sensory processing with language thinking. If in early development this integration does not occur, it results in various disabilities and impairments.

In the general population between 90 and 95 per cent of people have a dominant left hemisphere and use *left-brain logic* (*convergent* thinking); the remaining 5 to 10 per cent use a different thinking style (*divergent* thinking). The dominance of the right hemisphere in the 5 to 10 per cent of the general population does not lead to any disability, however, as the functions of the left hemisphere are not impaired. However, they have a different pattern of lateralization: their right hemisphere or both hemispheres play a critical role in language (Banich 1997).

Besides, males and females seem to have somewhat different patterns of lateralization, with males being more right-hemisphere dominant than females (Baron-Cohen 1998). This leads Baron-Cohen (1998) to the conclusion that autism may be the extreme version of 'male brain'.

It was hypothesized (Dawson *et al.* 1986) that in early development autistic children may tend to rely on the cognitive strategies associated with the right hemisphere. Dawson and colleagues suggested that a shift from right- to left-hemisphere processing of speech might occur in later development. This may account for the shift from gestalt to analytic style of language acquisition (Prizant 1983b).

The indirect evidence of the right-hemisphere dominance in the autistic population comes from the studies of autistic savants. Their superabilities seem to be connected with the right hemisphere of the brain. Hendrickson (1996) suggests that in the autistic brain, the right cerebral hemisphere favours the development of the five senses at the expense of the mediation of the left cerebral hemisphere. The degree of the right-brain dominance in autism varies greatly. According to Hendrickson (1996), in the case of autistic savants, one or more of the right brain's senses becomes a kind of substitute language and becomes central to the intellectual and emotional development of the autistic person.

The research has shown that auditory experience is unnecessary for the normal development of left-hemisphere language specialization, and lateral specialization for language is generally similar for deaf native speakers and non-deaf native speakers of oral language (Virostek and Cutting 1979). The pattern of sign language deficits in the deaf population after left-hemisphere damage is similar to those seen with spoken language. This provides further evidence that the left hemisphere is specialized (in most cases) for language (Benson and Zaidel 1985).

However, the right hemisphere does seem to contribute to language processing (Code 1987) as the neurological structure necessary for language exists in the right hemisphere as well as the left (Jaynes 1976). In a child, a major lesion of Wernicke's area on the left hemisphere, or of the underlying thalamus which connects it to the brain stem, produces transfer of the whole speech mechanism to the right hemisphere. A very few ambidextrous people actually do have speech on both hemispheres. Thus the usually speechless right hemisphere can under certain conditions become a language hemisphere, just like the left (Jaynes 1976).

Young children with right-hemisphere lesions display delay in word comprehension and the use of symbolic and communicative gestures. These problems are not found in adults with lesions in their right hemisphere. Stiles and Thal have suggested that there may be a link between the word comprehension problems of children and the right hemisphere, because to understand the meaning of a new word, children have to integrate information from many different sources, including auditory input, visual information, tactile information, memories of the immediately preceding context, emotions – in short, a range of experiences that define the initial meaning of a word and refine that meaning over time (Stiles and Thal, as cited in Elman *et al.* 1997, pp.309–10).

Another phenomenon that may cause problems in language acquisition is establishing hemispheric dominance. Doman (1987) suggests that as language functions in the dominant hemisphere, a failure to establish dominant or controlling organs on the same side of the body can often lead to problems with language-related activities including speaking, reading and writing. To be completely efficient a child should be right-handed, right-footed, right-eared and right-eyed; or left-handed, left-footed, etc. Dominance is usually established by the age of six years. After that age a child has become fixed in her method of accomplishing acts such as writing with the left hand, kicking with the right foot.

Mixed dominance means that information processing does not occur in a correct fashion. For example, a child may take visual information through his right eye and put it in his left hemisphere, or take it in through his left hand and store it in his right hemisphere. Also, if the child neglects to take in information from one side and place it in one hemisphere, he is not establishing firm pathways into his brain whereby he can efficiently process that information. These children take in the information but are not able to locate it when they attempt to retrieve it (Doman 1987).

Research (James and Barry 1983) has provided some evidence of a significant developmental delay in the establishment of cerebral lateralization in autistic children. An autistic child with left–right hemisphere integration problems is often unaware of the information her brain has processed subconsciously (sometimes the amount of the information and knowledge she subconsciously possesses is much more than non-autistic people have). So when she surprises other people with her knowledge of something, she is equally surprised herself. The disadvantage of this, however, is that she cannot consciously get access to this information when she needs it, if it is not triggered from the outside. When she is triggered she can function appropriately on 'autopilot'. Without any external triggers, she is confused and unable to perform the activity she has done many times before (Williams 1996).

Left–right hemisphere integration problems affect a child's ability to connect his thoughts to words as well. So he often speaks 'stored language' when triggered without meaning what he is saying, as verbal utterances are not necessarily connected to his thoughts, feelings, wants or needs.

Children with these problems often acquire compensatory strategies to cope with different situations. Thus, they may copy or 'echo' other people's actions or words, or they may look for any trigger to respond appropriately. If the trigger is not found, they use their 'stored language' (for instance, questions they are usually asked in similar situations) to trigger other people to respond, giving *them* triggers to react.

> *The family is having a meal. Alex addresses his mother: 'Do you want more potato?' His mother has accepted the routine and perfectly understands that her son wants more potato but 'forgot' how to ask, so she gives him a trigger he has asked for: 'Do you want more potato?' The boy happily admits, 'Yes, please'.*

What they say

Some cases of 'dyslexia' and learning disabilities have been considered to be due to a problem with the integrated use of left and right brain hemispheres. The same problem may also be at the basis of certain feedback difficulties for some people with 'autism'. Examples of this might include:

- problems in maintaining a simultaneous awareness of internal 'self' and external 'other' (rather than switching between awareness of only one or the other).

- problems getting expression and understanding to work smoothly together (such as simultaneously monitoring one's speaking and also processing what one thinks about what someone else has just said).

- problems with the interruption of subconscious automatic thinking, behaviour or expression into the place where conscious, intended and voluntary thought, behaviour or expression would normally be used (affecting conscious and voluntary access and control over thought, action or expression). (Williams 1996, p.68)

Dr Merzenich (the University of California, San Francisco) believes that such disorders as dyslexia, other language-related disabilities and autism are not simply inherited illnesses but inherited brain weaknesses which become disorders when the ever-changing brain 'gets stuck in the wrong gear', and that it might be possible to reverse them by retraining the brain (Merzenich *et al.* 1996). There have been developed different programmes aimed at 'reshaping' the brain; for instance, special exercises to improve the ability of the two hemispheres to work together, different techniques to establish a dominant hemisphere and 'patterning'. However, research on the effectiveness of these programmes is needed.

Another interesting approach to explaining language acquisition connects language learning with motor development. As early as the first day of life, the baby moves in precise and sustained segments of movement that are synchronous with the articulated structure of adult speech. In contrast, microanalysis of pathological behaviour (for example, that of subjects with aphasic, autistic and schizophrenic conditions) reveals marked self-asynchronies. Delayed auditory feedback also markedly disturbs this self-synchrony (Condon and Sander 1974). The research identifies a complex interaction system in which the organization of the baby's motor behaviour is synchronized with the organized verbal behaviour of adults in his environment. If the infant, from the beginning, moves in precise, shared rhythm with the organization of the speech structure of his culture, then he participates developmentally through complex sociobiological entrainment processes, in millions of repetitions of linguistic forms, long before he later uses them in speaking and communicating. By the time he begins to speak, he may have already laid down within himself the form and structure of the language system of his culture (Condon and Sander 1974).

Neural imaging has revealed that 'language areas' in the brain are connected to their 'sensorimotor roots'. For instance, activation in Broca's area is observed when subjects plan, convert non-speech mouth movements or perform complex sequences with the hand and fingers. In fact, Broca's area is active when the subject merely observes such movements by another human being, or reacts to static objects (for example, tools) that are associated with specific movements (Bates and Dick 2000; Rizzolatti and Arbib 1998).

What they say

I still have many problems with rhythm. I can clap out a rhythm by myself, but I am unable to synchronize my rhythm with somebody else's rhythm. At a concert I am unable to clap in time with the music with the rest of the people. A lack of rhythm during autistic piano playing is noted by Park and Youderian (1974). Rhythm problems may be related to some autistic speech problems. Normal babies move in synchronization with adult speech (Condon and Sander 1974). Autistics fail to do this. Condon (1985) also found that autistics and, to a lesser extent, dyslexics and stutters have a defective orienting response. One ear hears a sound sooner that the other. The asynchrony between ears is sometimes over one second. This may help explain certain speech problems. People still accuse me of interrupting. Due to a faulty rhythm sense, it is difficult to determine when I should break into a conversation. Following the rhythmic ebb and rise of a conversation is difficult. (Grandin undated)

Timing of acquiring language

The neuron plasticity of the brain has long been recognized by the scientists: the brain has an ability to adapt as it develops. However, there seem to be critical periods of sensitivity to environmental input – so-called 'windows of opportunities' – when the brain is able to rearrange functions of different regions. The critical period for language acquisition/learning is considered to be the biologically determined period in which the brain has plasticity for acquisition of any language. As time goes on, the plasticity of the brain decreases, the 'windows of opportunity' are shut, because the brain is working on the use-it-or-lose-it principle (Purves 1994). That is why brain injuries affect people differently depending on their age. If brain damage occurs in language areas that are not developed before the age of two, the brain can reorganize extensively, creating language areas in different regions. For instance, in some cases where babies suffered injury of the left hemisphere, language deficits were not apparent, because the right hemisphere contained the language centres which took the 'job' of the damaged parts. Similarly, the eventual proficiency in sign language by deaf people is greater the younger one is when exposed to that language (Bjorklund 1997). By four to six years of age, there is less language plasticity; after the age six or seven, the window of opportunity for forming language connections is largely gone and language loss can be permanent (Ratey 2001). The brain behaves as if it has become set in its ways and basic skills not acquired by that time usually remain deficient for life (Lenneberg 1967). That is why late development of language areas can account for language impairments.

It is interesting to note that second languages learned after this critical period are stored in different systems from those of the native language, while people who are bilingual from birth have the same areas for their native and second languages (Ratey 2001). It is widely believed that the earlier the person starts learning a second language, the more successful she will be. However, it is also known that acquisition of different aspects of language (such as pronunciation and grammar) is different: adults can learn the grammar of a new language more easily and rapidly than children but they will always speak with a foreign accent. Seliger (1978) suggests that there may be multiple critical or sensitive periods for different aspects of language acquisition. For instance, the period during which a native accent is easily acquired appears to end earlier than the period for the acquisition of a native grammar. There is a tendency by mature speakers learning a second language to interpret sounds in a foreign language in terms of sounds found in their native tongue. It may be a cause of permanent foreign accent (Flege 1981).

The sooner the intervention begins for children with language problems, the better the opportunity they get for achieving language functioning.

Timing of the onset of sensory processing problems

The timing of the advent of sensory processing problems may play a crucial part in the child's verbal development.

Temple Grandin hypothesizes:

> The exact timing of the sensory problems may determine whether a child has Kanner's syndrome or is a nonverbal, low-functioning autistic. I hypothesize that oversensitivity to touch and auditory scrambling prior to age two may cause the rigidity of thinking and lack of emotional development found in Kanner-type autism. These children partially recover the ability to understand speech between the ages of two and a half and three. [Those] who develop normally up to two years of age, may be more emotionally normal because emotional centers in the brain have had an opportunity to develop before the onset of sensory processing problems. It may be that a simple difference in timing determines which type of autism develops. (Grandin 1996a, p.50)

Tanguay and Edwards (1982) hypothesize that distortion of auditory input during a critical phase of early development may be one of the causes of impairments in verbal language and thinking. Those children who do not get enough undistorted speech through their dysfunctional auditory system may be unable to discriminate among speech sounds and fail to develop language, and gradually lose any contact with the world around them (Grandin 1996a).

Another reason for language delay and/or impairments can be hypersensitivity to sensory stimuli, when, for example, too-acute hearing (quite common in autism) makes certain sounds and noises intolerable for a child and leads to frequent shutdowns of the auditory system. This results in self-imposed sensory deprivation that, in turn, may cause secondary impairments (Bogdashina 2003; Grandin 1996b):

> Auditory and tactile input often overwhelmed me. Loud noise hurt my ears. When noise and sensory stimulation became too intense, I was able to shut off my hearing and retreat into my own world. (Grandin 2002)

> When a baby is unable to keep up with the rate of incoming information, its threshold for involvement or attention is not great before aversion, diversion or retaliation responses step in, or plain and simple systems shutdowns: nobody's home. (Williams 2003b, p.50)

With severe sensory processing problems, it is no wonder that verbal language is no more than noise and has nothing to do with either interaction or interpretation of the environment.

What they say

By the time of birth, the interruption in development of the neocerebellum has already occurred and no amount of wishing is going to change that. Then, aggravating factors such as toxins and complex organic compounds act to further lower the individual's maximum level of functioning. In time, the autistic brain does develop at a much steeper rate than what is otherwise expected, even to the point of almost catching up with its non-autistic counterpart (Hashimoto *et al.* 1995, cited in Hawthorne 2002). Thus, as the autistic individual gets older, coordination among the various areas of the brain improves, allowing for better attention shifting. However, the deficiency of Purkinje cells continues throughout life, apparently, leaving the individual vulnerable to repeated flooding of information picked up by the various senses. The frustration continues. (Hawthorne 2002)

In pulling away, I may not have received stimulation that was required for normal development. Possibly there are secondary central nervous system abnormalities that happen as a result of the autistic child's avoidance of input. The initial sensory processing abnormalities that the child is born with cause the initial avoidance. Autopsy studies indicate that cerebellar abnormalities occur before birth (Bauman 1991; Bauman and Kemper 1994). However, the limbic system which also has abnormalities is not mature until the child is two years old. The possibility of secondary damage to the central nervous system may explain why young children in early intervention education programs have a better prognosis than children who do not receive special treatment. (Grandin 1996b)

This wasn't just to do with how I understood verbal language, but also how I understood both visual language and the visual impression of objects and people. When I heard people speaking, I assumed they were mostly just making noise patterns... The speech of others was like a mosaic of tumbled sound, some patterned, some not, some with rhythm, some not, some with strange and interesting sound combinations... People's facial expressions seemed idiosyncratic contortions. As faces, they were so very hard to recognize because they never remained constant... Objects were known mostly by their placement, movement, acoustics or texture. Visually, it depended on which angle you came at them. They seemed ever changing and visual recognition was always so delayed that other means of ascertaining the use or familiarity of something was much more immediate. (Williams 2003a, pp.62, 63)

Learning environment

The learning environment and approaches to the child affect her ability to learn the language. If children with major sensory processing problems (for example, hypersensitivities to auditory, tactile and visual stimuli) are placed in the highly stimulated environment (for instance, bright wall decorations, a lot of noise and movement around them) with a highly intrusive speech development programme, they are unlikely to perceive speech accurately, and could even suffer from painful stimuli. While children who are hyposensitive most of the time, on the contrary, need as much sensory stimulation as possible. (See Chapter 12 for more on environment and interaction styles.)

Chapter 8

Speech and Language Development in Non-autistic and Autistic Children

> Yet without being taught, we'd still make sound patterns; given
> just two of us, we'd probably still form some type of
> communication system that vaguely resembled language even if it
> wasn't a pre-existing one. (Williams 1998, p.73)

At about the same age all normally developing children, no matter what culture they are born into, manifest similar patterns of speech and language acquisition.

Pre-verbal/pre-linguistic development

Long before the children learn to use language as a means of communication they develop non-verbal communicative behaviours that underlie all later language acquisition and its reflection in speech. This pre-verbal period of communication development can be described as movement from pre-intentional to intentional communication and from pre-symbolic to symbolic language development. The pre-verbal communicative behaviours are roughly similar in non-autistic children and are easily understood and interpreted by their carers. However, autistic children seem to fail to develop these conventional non-verbal communicative skills and, even if they use sounds and words, their 'communicative load' is different.

Babies know quite a lot about language before they start saying their first words. They are born with the ability to discriminate sounds from any language (Eimas, Miller and Jusczyk 1987; Streeter 1976; Trehub 1976) but being exposed to one particular language babies gradually (after approximately nine months) lose this ability and can only discriminate the sounds of the language spoken around them. For example, Japanese people cannot hear the distinction between English 'r' and 'l', whereas English children do not hear any difference between some Japanese sounds. Babies seem to be preparing for the sounds of their native language even before they are born. Newborns prefer the voice of their mother over that of strangers (DeCasper and Fifer 1980) and can distinguish their own language from a foreign one (Mehler *et al.* 1988).

Even crying is sometimes considered as a language (Lester and Zeskind 1978) that represents an adaptive communication system facilitating an infant's chances of survival. Lester and Zeskind (1978) note that crying is more than just a reflex and is better understood as a motor response to distress followed by sound. The cry seems to carry information that affects the infant–caregiver relationship because adults react differently to the cries of high-risk and low-risk babies. The cry of high-risk babies not only differs acoustically but also is perceived differently – as a signal of the need for special attention (Lester and Zeskind 1978).

Though crying cannot be formally defined as a language, it serves as a tool normal babies use to communicate with their mothers. Already at this stage mother and child 'speak the same language'. Research has shown that mothers of normal babies could 'interpret' the cries communicating different needs. In contrast, mothers of autistic children sometimes found it difficult to understand 'the message', as the cries of their babies are often idiosyncratic (Ricks and Wing 1975). It means that already at this early stage of communicative development 'the foreign language' of an autistic baby is not understood by the mother and results in the failure of 'intentional communication', which normally begins at about nine months. The vocalizations of older non-verbal autistic children remain idiosyncratic. In some very interesting research (Ricks 1979) the expressiveness of the vocalizations of non-verbal autistic children (between three and five years old), non-verbal intellectually disabled children and eight-month-old normal children was compared. All the children were presented with stimuli designed to elicit different emotional states (surprise, pleasure, frustration, need). All the children's vocalizations were recorded and then presented to the children's parents to 'interpret'. The results showed that all the parents could match the vocalizations of the intellectually disabled and normal children with the correct emotional state, though the parents of intellectually disabled and normal children failed to identify their own offspring. In contrast, the parents of autistic children could not only match their child's vocalizations with the emotions expressed but also recognize their child; however, they couldn't interpret the vocalizations of other autistic children. These results were interpreted as the vocalizations of autistic children being expressive but idiosyncratic: they were meaningful only for their parents and not for other people.

Could we consider these results as that autistic children 'speak a different language' understood only by their parents who, after years of living together, have learned (subconsciously, intuitively) the 'language' their children 'speak'?

> *We were talking in the kitchen of a one-room flat in Kiev. All of a sudden Tanya, the mother of a six-year-old non-verbal autistic boy, rushed out of the kitchen into the room where her son was watching TV. 'He is in trouble', she said. And she was right: the boy was stuck between the TV set and the wall with a screwdriver in his hand. How could she know this? Andrew's 'vocabulary' was not large: he was able to produce very few sounds and his 'favourite' was 'ah-ah'. As he was 'ah-ah'ing' most of the time, his 'word' seems to be polysemantic and could mean anything. How did his mother know all the meanings he applied to it?*

The pre-verbal communication of normally developing children is often described as serving two functions: *protodeclarative* (establishing joint attention on something, usually accompanied by a pointing gesture) and *protoimperative* (getting something the child wants from the adult (Bates *et al.* 1979). Some pre-verbal autistic children seem to be able to use proto-imperatives but not protodeclaratives (Curcio 1978). Unlike normal or intellectually disabled children, autistic children, while communicating with adults, fail to establish such protodeclaratives as eye contact and joint attention by pointing.

Speech development begins with the precursors of language from birth. They include the baby's perception and production of sounds, gazes and vocal exchanges with the carer. Already the one-month-old baby is believed to 'tune into' the speech he hears and to begin to discriminate distinctive features (Bloom and Lahey 1978).

At about the age of three months babies use intonations similar to those used by people around them. They engage in eye-to-eye contact with their carers and accompany this 'eye talk' with vocalizations that indicate that some communicative aspect is present. Autistic babies are reported to lack or have very limited non-verbal and vocal interchanges with their carers.

Phonological development

At the age of about four months the baby starts babbling and producing different speech sounds. It is difficult to establish the purpose of babbling and its connection to word structure. It has been suggested that babbling reflects the biological maturation of the central nervous system (Oller 1980; Stark 1986) as it does not seem to depend on external reinforcement – deaf children babble at the same age as hearing children. At about ten months the baby seems to discover that sound is connected to meaning and babbling becomes more consistent; the baby produces certain sounds and intonational patterns to refer to different objects and events. These patterns are called 'vocables' (DeVilliers and DeVilliers 1978) and the process is often referred to as 'jargon babbling'. At the end of this period babies start producing 'protowords' – invented or derived forms used in specific situations (Menn 1976). It is interesting to note that 'gestural babbling' has been reported by the researchers studying the development of deaf children (Petitto *et al.* 2000). The discovery of babbling in another modality confirms the hypothesis that babbling represents a distinct and critical stage in the language acquisition (Petitto *et al.* 2001).

The recent research conducted by Professor Ann Petitto and colleagues shows that by interpreting the baby mouth motion during babbling it might be possible to diagnose language/communication problems/disorders already at this stage of a child's development (as early as 5 to 12 months) and start early treatment. It depends upon which side of the mouth babies open more widely. As language is linked to the left hemisphere and smiles to the right hemisphere's emotional centres, researchers (Holowka and Petitto 2002) claim that if the babies open the right side of the mouth wider than the left side ('right-mouth asymmetry') it means that the language centre in the brain is active, if the babies' mouths open more on the left side during babbling, then the left hemisphere is not developing properly and there might be problems with language acquisition.

The end of the babbling period is marked by the appearance of the first words at the age of about 12 months. At the same age a deaf child in a sign environment begins to produce single signs (Siple 1978).

These first single words ('holophrases') are used as sentences ('holographic speech'). They are characterized by the consistent usage of the words, spontaneity of usage and evidence of understanding (Dale 1976). It is difficult to identify the part of speech of these first words as they often have multiple meanings. For instance, 'ball' may mean not only a ball itself, but also 'Give me the ball', 'That's a ball', etc.

During this period children master the pronunciation of the words they are using. Although their phonological development can be delayed (Tager-Flusberg 1981), autistic children are reported to have no serious problems with articulation of the sounds (Bartolucci *et al.* 1976) (however, in my practice, the number of autistic children with articulation problems has been considerable).

This period of single words lasts approximately until the age of 18 months. It is characterized not only by an increase in the vocabulary the baby can understand and use, but also by the way the infant uses the words. Phonological development does not stop with the appearance of phrases and sentences, but continues until the child masters phonological rules.

The order of the emergence of speech sounds, the errors made, the whole pattern of phonological development in autism – although they might be delayed and proceed at a slower rate, they do not seem to differ from those of non-autistic children.

Phonological development also includes the acquisition of appropriate prosodic features: stress, intonation, pitch, volume, etc. Already during the first year, normally developing children acquire the prosodic patterns of their native language. By the end of the second year children can use prosody to perform different pragmatic functions and communicate social and affective information (Furrow 1984). By puberty children have mastered the whole prosodic system of their language (Myers and Myers 1983). In contrast, autistic children manifest clear deficits in prosody that persist through adulthood and do not depend on the level of verbal functioning (Kanner 1971; Ornitz and Ritvo 1976). Simmons and Baltaxe (1975), studying adolescent autistics with linguistic impairments, suggested that autistic children may lack the ability to perceive the features that may be crucial for decoding and encoding linguistic signals. Although some autistic people can imitate speech accurately, including the intonation patterns, pitch and rhythm, it seems unlikely that they can comprehend the pragmatic and social-emotional meanings of the prosodic features they imitate or perceive.

Grammatical development

When a child is about 18 months old, she starts to formulate two-word sentences. Bloom and Lahey (1978) describe two stages of language patterning development (between the ages of 18 and 24 months):

- sentences in a *linear syntactic relationship*, when the relational meaning of two words is determined by the meaning of one word, for example, 'more milk'

- *hierarchical syntactic structures*, when words with a semantic relation between them are combined, such as subject and predicate (noun and verb); the meanings of the words are not determined by the meaning of one word as in a linear syntactic relationship.

The one-word sentences (holophrases) develop into phrases and short sentences. Children begin to use different words to name the same things that they previously referred to with single words.

At the age of about two years simple two-word sentences appear with definite syntactic structure. These first structures are called *telegraphic speech* and they consist mainly of nouns and verbs.

Dale (1976) believes that it is with the appearance of two-word utterances that language truly begins, because now children are able to express an infinite number of ideas with a limited system of words and rules of their combination.

By the age of four years children start using auxiliary verbs and adding inflections: first the plural of nouns, then the tense and person of verbs, and then possessives. During this period they often overregulate inflections, for instance, 'Daddy comed home' (Dale 1976). This shows the way they learn language – by learning patterns and then fitting all the words to these patterns. They seem to possess the knowledge of deep structures and acquire the skills to form surface structures of the sentences (Chomsky's transformational grammar).

Bates and Goodman (1997) hypothesize that syntax abilities parallel very tightly vocabulary size over a wide variety of ages, and the degree of grammatical competence children acquire is strictly linked to the lexical stage at which they are. Children with vocabularies under 300 words have very restricted grammatical abilities: some combinations, a few functional words, but little evidence for productive control over morphology or syntax (Bates and Goodman 1997). From this perspective, Tager-Flusberg (1989) concludes that autistic children with no considerable delay of vocabulary acquisition develop grammatical competence with ease, while autistic children with a very limited vocabulary remain at a very simple level of grammar development. However, it has been reported that autistic children in their grammatical development often rely on echolalia, which suggests that they do not analyse what they hear or say: they exhibit the gestalt mode of grammar acquisition (Schuler and Prizant 1985).

Semantic development

Semantic development is much slower than phonological and grammatical development.

Kess (1976) distinguishes two main characteristics of semantic development:

- vocabulary constantly increases

- the relationship between words is constantly reorganized (for instance, at the initial stage of semantic development a child calls all animals 'a dog'; later he distinguishes between different words to refer to different animals).

DeVilliers and DeVilliers (1978) give an account of children's acquisition of language from the words for objects (nouns) and action (verbs) to the relationships among objects and their positions in space and time. The authors note that the initial use of verbs reflects changes in objects (broke, open) or personal actions (run, kick). Relational words (big, little, more) appear quite early; however, their correct usage depends on the child's cognitive knowledge about spatial relations.

The DeVilliers state that the most difficult relational words for children to master are *deictic* words: words that identify objects not by naming them but by relating them to the speaker: *this, that, here, there;* or by relating them by time: *now, later, yesterday, today, tomorrow.* To master these words children have to understand the speaker's perspective and its dependence on the context: if a speaker is on one side of the street and you are on the other, *this* side of the street for the speaker is *that* side for you (DeVilliers and DeVilliers 1978).

In spite of extensive research, semantic development is the least understood aspect of language development. When a child speaks a word, it tells us little about the meaning of that word to the child, and about the relationships among the words in a child's vocabulary and how they are combined into sentence meanings (Dale 1976).

The relationship of thought to language becomes most obvious as the vocabulary develops and the conceptual system changes. Children start relating words by meanings and grammar instead of by sounds; associations and meanings become richer and more expressive as language and thought constantly supplement each other (Travers 1982). Autistic children seem to stay at the stage of 'labelling' longer, and some of them stop at this stage.

During school years children master more complex concepts and develop a good grasp in the use of different semantic categories of words, e.g., analogies, similes, metaphors, etc.

Despite the research findings suggesting that autism involves a fundamental deficit in acquiring basic conceptual knowledge (see, for example, Fay and Schuler 1980), some professionals argue that autistic children have no difficulty in acquiring conceptual categories or meanings (Tager-Flusberg 1989). Tager-Flusberg (1989) thinks that the difficulty in conceptualization may be true for children with low-functioning autism and not for verbal children with high-functioning autism. However, we may argue that although individuals with high-functioning autism do achieve the ability to organize conceptual knowledge for categories of concrete objects, they apply different cognitive strategies. For instance, unlike most people who think from general to specific, autistic individuals often move from specific images to generalization and concepts.

For normally developing children variations in rates of language acquisition are minimal. Table 8.1 presents the main stages in speech development that children follow, whatever their native language is.

There seem to be several 'scenarios' for the language acquisition of autistic children. Some autistic children start developing language at the usual age or a bit later, but at around the ages of two years and a half and three lose it. This language loss may be temporary or permanent. Some children start talking again in a few months or a year, but their language development after the interruption differs from that of normal acquisition. One of the possible explanations of this phenomenon has been put forward by Temple Grandin:

> The first kind of child may appear deaf at age two, but by age three he or she can understand speech ... The second kind of child appears to develop normally until one and a half or two and then loses speech. As the syndrome progresses, the ability to understand speech deteriorates and autistic symptoms worsen. A child that has been affectionate withdraws into autism as his sensory system becomes more and more scrambled. (Grandin 1996a, p.55)

Table 8.1 Some normal developmental milestones of communication / language development

Age	Pre-verbal and non-verbal communication	Phonological development	Number of words	Semantic development	Grammatical development
From birth to 5–6 weeks	Cries, coos				
3–6 months	Has 'special' cry for hunger, or when uncomfortable or annoyed, understood by carer; 'eye talk' accompanied by vocalizations; smiles, laughs	Uses intonations similar to those by the carers; babbles			
6–9 months	Uses voice to attract attention; attempts to imitate gestures	Produces 'vocables' or 'jargon babbling'; starts producing 'protowords'			
9–12 months	Makes sounds during speech-action games, songs, rhymes with an adult; 'protodeclarative' and 'protoimperative' communication	First words	3 or 4	First words ('holographic speech')	One-word sentences ('holophrases')

Continued on next page

Table 8.1 continued

Age	Pre-verbal and non-verbal communication	Phonological development	Number of words	Semantic development	Grammatical development
18 months	Understands non-verbal communicative cues (gestures, facial expressions, intonation, directed eye gaze)		3–50	Some words for objects	Phrases
2 years	Follows simple commands	Continues to master the use of prosody for pragmatic functions	c. 250	Action words	Two-word sentences with definite syntactic structure
4 years	Joins in games; shares toys; takes turn with other children	Continues developing control over tone patterns, pitch, etc.	c. 1500	Relational and positional words	Auxiliary verbs, inflections; asks wh-questions
6 years			2000+		Complex sentences

There is a suggestion (Siegel 1996) that the early language acquisition is a fundamentally cognitively different type of process than later language acquisition, as it may have to do with internal changes in connections in the brain. Uta Frith formulated an interesting theory on two ways of learning language. The first one (used by autistic children) relies simply on making associations between sights and sounds and learning these associations in a rote fashion. The second way (non-autistic children) is by tracking the speaker's intention and making associations only when the spoken word maps onto the world in the speaker's eyes and in the listener's ears. Children who cannot track the speaker's intention give up and lose their associations, probably because they are not useful (Frith 2003).

What they say

I loved the sound of my own voice but there was no such thing as my first words or, if so, not until I was about nine. At two and a half I didn't respond to language. At this same time I was heard to be chattering to myself in the voices of my grandparents, regurgitating a two-hour long conversation between them in the voices used. I remember being three, four, five and still not responding to people with please, thank you, yes or no… Yet I sang all the time and I had, by the age of five, a huge repertoire of television advertisements and jingles. By the age of seven this had expanded to copied sentences that fitted certain patterns…

By the age of nine I began to use my own words, 'foosh' for cat, 'degoitz' for Exposure Anxiety, 'whoodely' for the sound of air moving inside glass goblets as I ran my hand about inside them. I had names for fruit and food I liked and stated these out loud upon seeing them like I was addressing a friend. At school, though, functional verbal communication was near impossible with my teachers and, because my use of language wasn't well understood, I was treated mostly as uncooperative and a behaviour problem until I was about eleven. Those who spent much time with me found the language I had either underused or overused, self-directed and without apparent meaning or purpose, and annoying and disruptive. (Williams 2003a, p.191)

I first started intentionally trying to squeeze meaning out of language when I was about ten. At this time I knew that words were theoretically meaningful based on previous experience, but as I heard them again, their meaning was as elusive as ever. The clarity was fine and I would play about with their shapes and the spaces between syllables and words but it just didn't go anywhere. Later, the category the word belonged to would be triggered so I'd come up with all its opposites or its possible similes or all the words it rhymed with or that had a similar shape but the word or sentence that had triggered these responses basically remained gobbledeegook until the moment passes and it was all unimportant (then it sometimes sunk in, by which time I generally didn't care, nor attended to its comprehension. (Williams 1996, p.92)

Now I think that the use of speech and of other sensory activities that are normally lumped together as 'communication' are themselves a kind of sensory exploration. One's sense of oneself as a person is augmented and developed in that process. The spoken environment is a peculiarly human invention, and like all other environments is learned by experience, both as a receiver and as a speaker. But for me all was distorted and unpredictable. It was only as an adult aunt that I learned that the babbling of a baby and adolescent gossip are both an essential part of learning and exploration. I did make sounds of course. All my life I cooed and chanted vaguely and hummed happily, and so drawn a sense of awareness from my own voice. (Blackman 2001, p.11)

There is a large group of children labeled autistic who start to develop normally and then regress and lose their speech before age two. These early regressives sometimes have a better prognosis than late regressives. Those who never learn to talk usually have severe neurological impairments that show up on routines tests. They are also more likely to have epilepsy than Kanner or Asperger children. Individuals who are low-functioning often have very poor ability to understand spoken words. Kanner, Asperger and PDD children and adults usually have a much better ability to understand speech.

Children in all of the diagnostic categories benefit from placement in a good educational program. Prognosis is improved if intensive education is started before age three. I finally learn to speak at three and a half, after a year of intensive speech therapy. Children who regress at 18 to 24 months of age respond to intensive educational programs when speech loss first occurs, but as they become older they may require calmer, quieter teaching methods to prevent sensory overload. If an educational program is successful, many autistic symptoms become less severe. (Grandin 1996b)

Chapter 9

Impairments of Social Communication in Autism and Language Peculiarities Specific to Autism

> Because I didn't use speech to communicate until I was twelve, there was considerable doubt about whether I would be ever able to learn to function independently. No one guessed how much I understood, because I couldn't say what I knew. And no one guessed the critical thing I *didn't* know, the one missing connection that so much else depended on: I didn't communicate by talking, not because I was incapable of learning to use language, but because I simply didn't know that that was what talking was for. Learning *how* to talk follows *why* to talk – and until I learned that words have meanings, there was no reason to go to the trouble of learning to pronounce them as sounds. (Sinclair 1992, p.296)

Impairments of communication are seen as one of the essential diagnostic features of autism. Moreover, it is delay or atypical path of language acquisition that is most 'visible' for the parents and the first sign for them that something is wrong with their child.

The pre-verbal communication of children with autism

People with autism manifest problems both in verbal and non-verbal communication. These problems occur very early when youngsters seem to have great difficulty acquiring joint attention behaviours (pointing in order to ask for objects, showing and giving objects to others to share interests, etc.). Autistic babies have problems with the development of pre-verbal communication. We can easily interpret a normally developing baby's communicative intent via tone of voice and bodily gestures, because we share her perceptual world. Understanding is possible, whereas with an autistic infant the situation is different.

The verbal communication of children with autism

It is estimated that about one third (Bryson 1996) to one half (Lord and Paul 1997) of people with autism never develop any functional speech: they are functionally mute. Those who do develop speech exhibit problems in prosody, semantics, syntax and pragmatics. All autistic people are on a continuum of communicative and verbal language skills: ranging from those who never develop any verbal language to those who are very fluent in their language use but lack 'communicative feel' in their attempts to interact with other people.

The diagnostic characteristics of qualitative impairments in communication used in ICD-10 (WHO 1992) and DSM-IV (APA 1994) based on the Triad of Impairments, are as follows:

1. Delay in, or total lack of, the development of spoken language, not accompanied by attempt to compensate through alternative modes of communication, due to lack of appreciation of the social uses of communication.

2. Lack of understanding that language is a tool for communication.

3. Lack of reciprocity in conversational interchange; for example, the inability to initiate or maintain a conversation with others. May be able to ask for their own needs but have a great difficulty in talking about/understanding emotions, feelings, thoughts and beliefs of their own and other people.

4. Idiosyncratic language (echolalia, literal use of language, neologisms, etc).

5. Lack of use and understanding of gesture, miming, facial expression, vocal intonation, etc. as tools of conveying information.

6. Impairment in make-believe or social imitative play.

7. Inadequate emotional reaction to verbal and non-verbal approaches by others.

Research has shown, however, that it is often not the lack of communicative intent (the desire to communicate) but rather a limited ability to use verbal or non-verbal communication for different purposes, and often the use of unconventional means of communication (their own means of communication and their language we do not share).

The communication/language problems in autism vary significantly from one individual to the other. Some may be unable to speak, whereas others may have extensive vocabularies and may be very articulate about the topics of special interests while quite helpless in social conversations.

Lack of expressive verbal language – 'autistic muteness'

> If you think a lot and have things you need but no speech it means you have to be smarter and more alert than anyone else. But they assume you don't know anything. One thing I know for sure is that talking is not intelligence. It is a way of communicating it but that's all. (DePaolo 1995, p.9)

It is estimated that 40 to 50 per cent of autistic people never develop a verbal language and are functionally mute. Some mute individuals do produce intelligible utterances, at least once, and then become mute again for many years or even for life.

> *Mother was packing bags – her husband, his brother and her autistic non-verbal son (Alex, three and a half years of age) were going to the country to visit their relatives. Alex was in bed but not asleep. He seemed oblivious to all the 'fuss' in the room, flicking his favourite toy in front of his eyes. In the middle of Mother's 'I've put Alex's pyjamas in...' the three adults heard a very clearly articulated question from the NON-verbal boy: 'Will Mummy go with us?' Surely they could not been hallucinating! Not three of them! 'Alex, sweetheart, what did you say? Please, honey, say it again!' Alex was lying in bed, flicking his toy in front of his eyes, seemingly oblivious to the fuss around him. Was he talking or wasn't he?*
>
> *Alex did not say another word for four more years, when he was seven...*

The causes of 'autistic muteness' may be different for each person and often multifaceted. They may include motor problems, anxiety or stress.

Two possible explanations are:

1. They can understand speech but cannot talk (motor problems, anxiety).

2. They do not understand speech (sensory processing problems).

Motor problems

Motor problems may be one of the causes of 'autistic muteness':

> One day, when I happened to utter the word 'car' by mere chance, I tried and started practising it over and over again. Overjoyed, mother took the sound as my beginning to speak… She picked up my toy car and said 'car' to me. I said 'car' too after her… She picked up a ball and asked me what it was. 'Car,' I said again knowing very well that it was a ball. It was 'car' and only 'car' which my tongue had practised to tell. So when she asked again whether I was hungry, I remember replying again with 'car'… I recall those moments when I tried to tell something other than the word 'car', and to my great disappointment, I found my voice saying just the very word 'car'. (Mukhopadhyay 2000, p.12)

Stress and anxiety

> I had 'forgotten' the natural sequence of connections needed to make consistently comprehensible language. Articulation was happening without vocal connection. My lungs and diaphragm were responding to [my] intention to speak but either my jaw, lips, and tongue weren't on speaking terms or my voice box walked out on the job. (Williams 1999a, p.90)

Jasmine Lee O'Neill (1999; 2000), an autistic woman, gives us several possible explanations for autistic muteness and distinguishes several types of this phenomenon. She considers autistic muteness as an emotional and cognitive issue. She describes selective mutism (when a child chooses to whom to talk and in which situations) and elective mutism (when a child does not talk at all, for whatever reason for this may be).

> *Helen, an 11-year-old girl with autism, goes to mainstream school and does very well at all the subjects. But no one at school has ever heard*

her speak. She used to sit quietly in the classroom rocking her body and seems oblivious to everything and everybody around her. However, her written work is always neat and correct.

Her mother says she talks to her family at home, always whispering, but if there is nobody else present. If the family's friends come to visit, she turns into 'a silent statue', never uttering a word. Helen can speak loudly but only if she is alone in her room. Her mother listens to these one-way conversations from behind the door with tears in her eyes: 'Why does she talk to the empty room about whatever's happened at school, and never ever talk to us like this? She can talk, can't she? Why can't she talk all the time?'

Helen's ability to speak seems to be affected by the stress of strangers being present and any unfamiliar environment.

We take the ability to speak for granted and often erroneously assume that a child who is mute either is being deliberately rude or indifferent to others. Autistic children do not plan whether to talk or not to talk. They do not speak because they either are unable to speak or do not understand 'what it is all about', and not because they do not want to communicate with us. In many cases, they are too overwhelmed to speak. It is our task to decrease the stress by making the environment more 'communication-friendly' and adjusting our interactive style to theirs.

Although we do have to try to teach autistic children a verbal language (a shared means of communication), talking should never be forced on them. To find a shared way to communicate with the non-verbal child is of paramount importance. As the child has inner language (which is strikingly different from that used around him) he is often struggling to express himself from the 'inside-out', using the tools available to him (we call these attempts to communicate 'erratic or challenging behaviour'). We, on the other hand, could teach the child a form of communication we could understand (this is discussed further in Part 3).

When the child does start to talk, her speech is characterized with specific 'autistic' features as if the child was speaking a foreign language. Autistic children seem to acquire language intellectually as an adult would have to learn, say, Russian or Japanese.

Before we start discussing peculiarities of verbal behaviour exhibited by autistic children, I'd like to remind you about a very important point which is briefly summarized by O'Neill (2000): '[Verbal] Language has a different usage for an autistic person than it has for a non-autistic person'.

The major specific peculiarities of 'autistic language' which have been identified by the researchers are the following.

1. Echolalia

2. Pronoun reversal

3. Extreme literalness

4. Metaphorical language

5. Neologisms

6. Affirmation by repetition

7. Repetitive questioning

8. Demanding the same verbal scenario

9. Autistic discourse style

10. Poor control of prosody.

Echolalia

Echolalia is the parrot-like repetition of another person's spoken words. There are usually distinguished two types of echolalia: *immediate echolalia*, or repetition of words and phrases just heard, and *delayed echolalia*, or repetitions of words and phrases heard in the past. Some researchers (Roberts 1989) identify one more type of echolalia, *mitigated echolalia*, which is speech that consists of learnt phrases of various sizes which are manipulated so that they result in new utterances.

Immediate and delayed echolalia can be observed in normal language acquisition as a language-learning strategy. An echolalic utterance is usually equivalent to a single unit (word) for a situation or event. However, in normal development it is a short phase and is accompanied by many modifications that children make in the learnt patterns of words and sentences. Eventually children learn to break down the echolalic chunks into smaller meaningful units as part of the transition to a rule-governed language system (Prizant and Rydell 1993). In autism echolalia is not just a stage of language acquisition, it lasts much longer, sometimes well into adulthood, or even remains the only verbal means of expression a person possesses. Thus, we may talk about echolalia as one of the symptoms of autism.

In the past it was believed that echolalia was an abnormal, self-stimulatory and obsessive behaviour, devoid of any communicative function, and that it should be eliminated and replaced by more appropriate 'communicative' behaviours (for example, Lovaas 1977). The main techniques used were based on behavioural modification methods. However, the results were unsatisfactory. At present, however, echolalia is considered as the child's attempt to communicate and should be 'shaped' into communicative verbal utterances. But why do children do it? What are the functions of echolalia? Is there any communicative purpose in it?

Many autistic individuals testify that echolalia may be both communicative and non-communicative. Much research has been aimed at analysing echolalia in autism. Several explanations of echolalia functions (both non-communicative and communicative) have been suggested.

The presence of echolalia indicates that a child is able to attend to speech alone and screen out other environmental sounds and noises, even if for a short time. But it does not necessarily mean that the child understands the meaning and purpose of speech.

Frith (1989) thinks that echolalia manifests detachment between more peripheral processing systems and a central system concerned with meaning: that echolalia shows that a child selectively attends to speech and is able to produce heard utterances, bypassing the interpretation of what has been said into meaning. They let messages come in and go out without any understanding of the meaning these messages convey. For instance, a child was given a biscuit and told: 'Say thank you, Paul.' Child: 'Say thank you Paul.'

Uta Frith (1989) accounts for this phenomenon as weak central coherence: an autistic child attends only to small bits of information, he cannot comprehend the context and does not understand the deeper intentional aspects of communication because he lacks central coherence drive. As we have discussed earlier, it is better explained as the gestalt perception of speech blocks, where the meaning of the whole block is understood only by the child producing echolalia which has nothing in common with our intended meaning.

Prizant (1983a) suggests that echolalia is one of the features of the gestalt mode of language acquisition when a child uses whole chunks of verbal utterances as single units. There have been attempts to single out functional categories of echolalia. Prizant and Duchan (1981) proposed seven functional categories of immediate echolalia and 14 categories of delayed echolalia. They found that echolalia may or may not have communicative intent.

According to Prizant and Duchan (1981) functional categories of immediate echolalia are:

- communicative: turn-taking, declarative, yes answer, request

- non-communicative: nonfocused, rehearsal, self-regulatory.

Functional categories of delayed echolalia (Prizant 1983a) are:

- communicative: turn-taking, verbal completion, providing information, labelling, protest, request, calling, affirmation, directive

- non-communicative: nonfocused, situation association, self-directive, rehearsal, labelling.

Mitigation seems to be comparatively rare in autistic children but nevertheless important. Mitigated echolalia may be seen as a positive linguistic sign that a child moves from gestalt to analytical mode of language acquisition.

There seems to exist another type of echolalia – *sophisticated echolalia* – that may be present in adults with high-functioning autism and/or individuals with Asperger syndrome (see Chapter 10).

Let us consider communicative and non-communicative echolalia.

Non-communicative functions

Echolalia as stereotyped behaviour described as 'self-stimulatory' and 'obsessive' devoid of any communicative function. 'Non-communicative echolalia' (usually delayed echolalia) is often considered as form of babbling when the child may simply enjoy the sounds of words (Attwood 1998).

> *Alex, eight years old, happily repeats 'timokha' when he is excited. His mother can see that he is relaxed and happy. But where did he take this 'word' from? What does it mean? On some occasions, when he is anxious about something and looks as if he were deaf, he starts producing grunting sounds to himself. Is it because he wants to bring sound to his 'silent' world? Interestingly, when his mother (who is at her wits' end and cannot tolerate these any longer) starts imitating him, he vigorously denies her right to do this – 'Stop it'.*

> *Vicky, an 11-year-old autistic girl, when frustrated, repeats 'Again, again, again', rocking her body.*

A lot of autistic people will produce sounds, words or phrases to themselves, just in order to get some auditory and/or tactile pleasure. In this case, these sounds, words or phrases have no meaning at all. They are not linguistic units, they are 'auditory/tactile toys' ('sensory-linguistic toys') to play with. They have neither linguistic meaning nor communicative function. We find many examples of young autistic children using 'adult' words. The words are usually long and morphologically complicated. They seem to be chosen for their unusual sound structure or the feeling they produce on the tongue. Kanner (1943) reported that Donald, an eight-year-old child he described in his paper, liked to say the word 'chrysanthemum'.

This 'sensory' use of words is meaningful for autistic children. Instead of trying to stop them producing 'silly sounds', you could share the meaning (and it is one step forward to learn their 'language') and gradually (if it really irritates you) you could give them some sort of substitute (something else that brings the same sensation/stimulation) or just accept it as their eccentricity. One should think very carefully whether it must be eliminated.

What they say about non-communicative echolalia

…the sounds of certain words can roll about deliciously and provide auditory stimulation… Repeating sound patterns is comforting. It also simply feels nice. Other people do things that simply feel very good. Why shouldn't an autistic do that as well? (O'Neill 1999, p.25)

Autistics often use the speech they have in ways other than communication with another individual. They talk to themselves more than to others. They also often enjoy repeating specific phrases and words. They pick up certain words or tunes that they favour. The ring of these in their minds feels nice as a form of self-stimulation. So, there definitely is a purpose for them doing this. It is not meaningless. It probably is meaningless to non-autistics. But that doesn't mean to say that it be eliminated. Other basically non-communicative uses of speech in Autism include choosing a word, phrase, or tune, and repeating it to yourself when you feel stressed. It is a way of calming yourself…senses play an enormous part in this. Imagine that you simply love the sound of the words 'purple fur'. Don't consider what the words' actual definitions are. Only pretend you feel vocal intonation. Pretend it makes you shiver in glee, as well as feeling relaxed. This is a lot like using mantras in meditation. Whenever you become upset, you turn to your own little mantra to help you focus inside yourself, and comfort yourself. You can use your special private words to just feel good, too. Repeated in sequence, it makes calmness settle over you, 'Purple fur, purple fur, purple fur'. Also words can sound funny and make you giggle. (O'Neill 1999, p.48)

Communicative functions

Immediate echolalia is seldom completely non-communicative (Jordan and Powell 1995). It can be seen as carrying a communicative intent and inter-preted as 'I don't understand'. It increases when children are confused and cannot work out what is going on around them.

For an autistic child echolalia may be the only means of communication at his disposal and it can be used to start developing dialogue (Prizant and Wetherby 1985). Any approach based on this interpretation of echolalia should build on the level of communication manifested in the echolalic response (Jordan and Powell 1995).

Echolalia can be a means to 'win time' (in the case of delayed processing) or to 'get the meaning' from what has been said as some people understand speech better if they repeat the message. Repeating things other people say helps to clarify the meaning in an autistic person's mind as it aids the cognitive process: an autistic child will repeat a question someone asks her to be able to hear the words in her own voice – to take an external stimulus inward, accept it and prepare a reply (O'Neill 1999). For example, Donna Williams (1999c) states that she could comprehend only about 5 to 10 per cent of what was said to her unless she repeated it to herself. Immediate echolalia in this case is a strategy to 'translate' verbal words into meaningful inner language (whether visual, kinaesthetic or olfactory, etc.) Thus, while repeating the sentence, either loudly or silently (silent echolalia), they elicit pictures, tactile, olfactory images (whatever their 'inner' language is) in their mind. It is a kind of 'reverse thinking' (Williams 1999c). Using this strategy, they gradually can develop skills to speak meaningfully without any noticeable delay. However, acquiring these 'immediate translation' skills sometimes takes years and a lot of practice.

Echolalia can be interpreted as a request; for instance, when a child wants a biscuit he says: 'Do you want a biscuit?'

Autistic children appear to learn the language (even without any understanding that language is a tool for communication) through the rote learning of echolalic patterns. Their first speech may be meaningless repetitions of television jingles, songs, nursery rhymes, etc. Sometimes 99 per cent of their verbal repertoire is a stored-up collection of literal dictionary definitions and stock phrases (Williams 1999c).

What they say about communicative echolalia

As an echolalic child, I did not understand the use of words because I was in too great a state of stress and fearful reaction to hear anything other than patterned sound... The development of my speech was fuelled largely by the repetition of a story-book record and jingles on the television. When I later repeated phrases, it was simply because I sensed that some sort of response with sounds was required. Mirroring...was my way of saying: 'Look, I can relate. I can make that noise too.' If echolalic children often do better, it is because, in their own way, they are trying desperately to reach out and show they can relate, if only as mirrors. (Williams 1999b, p.181)

Research has shown that echolalia increases when there is too much information to be processed and the child cannot cope with it (gestalt perception): the easiest option for him is to use the language that is already 'there', in his short-term memory, and repeat the utterance. When the processing demands or pressure to speak are less, then echolalia decreases and gives way to more spontaneous speech (Jordan and Powell 1995).

What we can do to help

One of the strategies to help 'shape' echolalia into meaningful speech is to back it with a substitute close to the child's inner language – pictures, tactile images, movements, etc. – emphasizing the key words. It will allow the child to break the gestalt-word down into meaningful 'syllables' that eventually will be learned as words. Other things to consider when working with echolalic children:

- if echolalia is used to 'win' time or clarify the meaning to be able to hear the message in her own voice, give the child more time to process and respond

- if it is used as a request, teach the child to make changes in sentence structure (i.e. moving to mitigated echolalia)

- if echolalia is the only means the child uses to communicate, introduce other means of communication

- as echolalia increases in stressful or confusing situations, create a 'stress-free' environment.

Pronoun reversal

All children come through a stage when they experience difficulty in using pronouns, especially *I/me* and *you*. In normal development, however, children soon overcome it once they have established a sense of self and have practised the use of the appropriate forms in pretend play with social roles ('mothers and daughters', etc.). For children with autism the confusion over the correct use of the pronouns is very profound and even autistic adults sometimes use their proper names to refer to themselves or to others.

Several explanations of the phenomenon have been suggested. One, that pronoun reversal is the reflection of lack of differentiation between the self and others, has been proved wrong, as research has shown that autistic children can use proper names with correct reference (Jordan 1989).

The difficulty seems to be rooted in the *deictic* nature of pronouns: that they are used to refer to roles in conversational situations and not to 'label' people 'for ever'. The same problem arises with other deictic words – such as *this, that; here, there; yesterday, today, tomorrow* – which label objects, people, situations for a certain time and then 'jump' onto other objects, people and situations. For an autistic child it is difficult to grasp why 'today' will become 'yesterday' tomorrow, or why the toy is 'here' for him but 'there' for Mummy, etc.

As we have seen, autistic children have difficulty in understanding that one and the same thing (or person) can have several 'names' attached to them.

What they say

Too many people make a ridiculous big hoo-ha about these things [pronouns], because they want to eradicate this 'symptom of autism' or for the sake of 'manners' or impressiveness. Pronouns are 'relative' to who is being referred to, where you are and where they are in space and who you are telling all this to. That's a lot of connections and far more than ever have to be made to correctly access, use and interpret most other words. Pronouns are, in my experience, the hardest words to connect with experienceable meaning because they are always changing, because they are so relative. In my experience, they require far more connections, monitoring and feedback than in the learning of so many other words. Too often so much energy is put in teaching pronouns and the person being drilled experiences so little consistent success in using them that it can really strongly detract from any interest in learning all the words that *can* be easily connected with. I got through most of my life using general terms like 'a person' and 'one', calling people by name or by gender with terms like 'the woman' or 'the man' or by age with terms like 'the boy'. It didn't make a great deal of difference to my ability to be comprehended whether I referred to these people's relationship to me in space or not. These things might have their time and place but there are a lot of more important things to learn which come easier and can build a sense of achievement before building too great a sense of failure. (Williams 1996, pp.160–1)

Extreme literalness

> I take what is said by others very literally. My brain is incapable of understanding grey, subtle areas in language. (O'Neill 2000)

Autistic children have great difficulty in understanding the pragmatics of language; in other words, they use and interpret language literally and focus on what the words mean and not what the speaker's intention is. For example, an autistic child knocked over your favourite vase and to your 'Thank you very much' replies 'You are welcome'. Sarcasm, irony and humour are often beyond their understanding (though they do have their own sense of humour). For them, semantics is important, and they cannot see why you use words that mean one thing to express something else.

> *Alex was very twitchy during his snack in the kitchen. He was 'kicking the air' and giggling. Accidentally he touched a caretaker who was making a cup of tea. The caretaker (unfamiliar with autism) was irritated ('Couldn't this boy see other people around him?') and snapped: 'You kick me again and…' He was not able to finish his*

threat because Alex followed his instruction 'to the letter' – he kicked him.

> *Josh is 'playing with words': 'Mash, cash, lash, crash, slash...'*
> *His mother (encouraging him to rhyme the words): 'So, what rhymes with 'mash', Josh?' Josh: 'No, it doesn't.'*

Children with autism fail to understand conventional or polite modes of expression. For instance, if told, 'Would you stop talking please and get on with your work?', they might say 'No'. It is neither rudeness nor disobedience on their behalf. They interpret the question literally and answer it honestly.

Another example, 'Take the register to the office', is very ambiguous: the child is not told explicitly to take it to the office and leave it there. She may bring it back and be very confused when the person who gave her this instruction becomes cross ('Didn't I tell you to take it to the office?').

Because of their literal interpretation, autistic children may experience difficulties in understanding idioms and metaphorical expressions. This may lead to misunderstanding (and mistreatment):

> Teachers find it impossible to understand that an intelligent and apparently verbally fluent child who, told to 'pull their socks up!' bent down and pulled their socks up, as David A. did, was not trying to make fun of them, and reactions could be violent: 'When I was seven I had a teacher who used to give instructions in such a way that *if* I followed them literally I would be wrong. Then she would slap my hands with a ruler. I didn't understand that until I was about twelve' (Jim). (Sainsbury 2000, p.92)

Some autistic children seem to have difficulty accepting synonyms. They cannot grasp that two or more different words can refer to the same thing, or that one and the same word can have different meanings in different contexts. It is hard for them to understand that words that have the same pronunciation may have different spellings, or that words that are spelled differently can sound the same.

— *It is too noisy here.*

— *No, it is one noisy here.*

It is typical for autistic children to have difficulty with homographs; for instance, they pronounce 'tear' wrongly in 'there was a big tear in her dress' (Happé 1997). Happé notes that autistic individuals make relatively little use of preceding sentence context in pronouncing the homographs, and this may be an indication of an autistic impairment in extracting meaning in context.

The literal understanding of verbal language is observable in the autistic way of language acquisition. One verbal word has only one 'inner image' (whether visual, kinaesthetic, olfactory, etc.), something the child can refer to in his mental 'vocabulary'. We may explain this phenomenon by examining the origin of 'autistic words' and the way they form concepts (see Chapters 3 and 4).

From an autistic point of view, language is 'heavily polluted' with unnecessary ('untranslatable') 'bits and pieces'.

> *An autistic boy who, at the age of 13, became interested in the meaning of words asked whomever he was talking to questions like 'What does "isn't she"/"we don't"/"yes, it will", etc. mean?' It was nearly impossible to keep a conversation going with him. However, he was very sincere in his attempts to really understand the meaning of the words that seemed useless to him.*

> — *Alex, Mummy is at home, isn't she?*

> — *What does 'isn't she' mean? Does it mean 'inside'?*

What they say

By around eight years old, I had become a very proficient comprehender as well as word caller… Words were beginning to mean far more to me than actions were. I remember following directions, literally and to the letter. As was her habit, Mom insisted I be able to see the roof of my house from wherever I was. This was her way of insuring I never wandered off too far. One afternoon, I remember making my way to my elementary school playground, never fearing that four blocks was too far away. After all, I told my mother when I returned home and found her terribly upset, I had been able to see the roof of my home. So what if I had had to climb to the roof of my school to do so. That's how I understood language. Words had yet to develop into metaphors or similes or analogies or main ideas. It was all about details and pedantic rules and one-way semantics. I never considered a statement had more than one meaning. I always assumed the meaning I inferred was the intent of the speaker… My parents…found themselves weighing their every directive to be certain I would not find a way to weave their words with mine... Typically, my teachers took it upon themselves to analyze this pedantic behaviour of mine and...their fondest memories of me included adjectives like obstinate, disobedient and everyone's favorite, mentally retarded. Because my parents were learning how to talk to me, it never occurred to them that I was not following other people's directions. (Willey 1999, pp.18–19)

When they learn one word they just don't know that it can have variables... Being able to read greatly helps the autistic with mastering language... It is highly difficult to explain to an autistic person often that the word 'die' is not the same as the word 'dye'. They hear that both have an identical sound, so they are influenced by the first. (O'Neill 1999, p.51)

Consider the following example. When a child with ASD is engaged in behaviour that a parent wants to curtail, the parent might say 'You can't do that!' Unfortunately the child *is doing it* and due to the child's literal translation, will most likely not understand the instruction as intended by the parent. The child may even consider the parent to be stupid! But when a parent says 'Stop, come away from...and move over to me please', then the child with ASD understands what is expected of them and is more likely to comply. If a parent does not understand the literality of their child with ASD, then they will interpret their child's lack of compliance as wilful disobedience. Stress and anxiety for all will only increase. Another example of this is the following: By shouting 'We don't have yelling in the house' and the boys are yelling, the youth with ASD, who takes words literally, might assume you are lying or are stupid, because probably all three of you are yelling in the house! Understanding literality as an active component of ASD will enable parents to respond more confidently towards their child with ASD, who in return will feel safer and less likely to demonstrate self-injurious or destructive behaviour. (Lawson 2001, pp.85–6)

Metaphorical language

The term *metaphorical language* was coined by Kanner. To autistic people certain words may have some private meanings different from their common definitions. These definitions make sense only if you know their origin. Kanner (1943) provides a good example of autistic metaphors while describing one of his patients, a seven-year-old autistic boy. The boy's seemingly meaningless announcement, 'Annette and Cecile make purple', got its explanation when the original situation was revealed. The boy had five bottles of paint which he named after the Dionne quintuplets – Annette was blue and Cecile was red. To successfully interpret the meaning of such metaphorical expressions, one has to know the origin of these 'words' that is not always possible.

What they say

...for years I have used the spontaneous word, 'Bertie!' to say how I feel. Although 'Bertie' the word is flourishing, Bertie the long-haired dachshund dog has been dead for about fifteen years... 'Bertie', underpins several emotions, and the other person has to understand exactly what his link with the present is to be able to respond meaningfully.

'Bertie!' I will snarl at Jay [mother] when I think she has been neglectful or unsympathetic towards anyone (not just me). She struggled unsuccessfully with Bertie's summer eczema for years before she had him put to sleep. I am simply having a memory-jerk into the mood that I personally was in when I saw him being led out of the door for the last time. 'Bertie' is also my generic word for canine. That is the second use of the word. 'D-o-g' is an exotic import which has only recently come easy to my lips, though I had been taught it for many years... When I stand without distress, and gaze over a large walkway flooded with people and completely dogless, one would think that this should be a 'Bertie'-free zone, but the furry long dog is still floating around somewhere in my speech processing. 'Bertie'. My tone is interested, conversational even. Across the furthest corner I have spied a slightly built, dark-haired man with horn-rimmed glasses. What I am saying is, 'Oh, is that Dad? No, it can't be, but he is very similar to how Dad looked when I was small.' This was true of course of how Dad was when Bertie, his little mate Alex and...luscious litters of sausage-shaped puppies competed with Dad's feet... This sensory trigger that releases the speech relates to the emotion I was experiencing at the time I first processed the sound. (Blackman 2001, pp.44–5)

Neologisms

Verbal autistic children are known for their ability to create new words which are understood only by them (though parents are often able to 'get' the meaning). Each child may have his own personal vocabulary. For instance, an autistic boy calls lipstick 'paintlipster'.

Affirmation by repetition

The absence of the 'yes' concept and its corollary, affirmation by repetition, was noted by Kanner (1943) in his observations of people with autism. 'Yes' is often a difficult word for autistic children to use and understand. (You cannot sensorily define 'yes'.) Instead, the child who wants to respond in the affirmative will repeat the question he was just asked.

For example, for Donald the word 'yes' meant for a long time that he wanted his father to carry him on his shoulders. The origin of this meaning was: once his father, trying to teach Donald to say 'yes' and 'no', asked him whether he wanted to be carried on his shoulders. The boy showed his agreement by echoing the question. His father, however, insisted on the 'proper' answer: 'If you want me to, say "yes", if you don't want it, say "no".' Donald said 'Yes' and stored the meaning of the word 'yes' as 'I want my father to carry me on his shoulders' (as a whole situation, not as a concept of agreement).

Repetitive questioning

Autistic children often ask the same questions again and again and again. Although they know the answer they want to hear it again and again. The problem is that the answer must always be the same, and if their 'communication partner' does not know the 'right' answer (including the same word order, intonation, etc.), a tantrum may follow.

A child repeats the same questions not for the sake of getting information, but to maintain a predictable reaction, i.e. be reassured everything is going fine. The safest way to handle the situation (if you are unaware which answer is in the child's 'script') is to 'kick the question back' to him – 'You tell me why/what/when…'

Another successful strategy is to write the answer down (if the child can read) and show it to him. The effectiveness of using the written word may come in part from the novelty of the procedure and in part to the change from the auditory to the visual, as the written word may be a mode more accessible to the autistic individual for transmitting information (Schuler cited in Sullivan 1980)

What they say

Another big reason for doing what I do is to get a reaction from people that I am ready for, such as asking a question to hear a certain word or phrase in the answer or to re-enact a scenario involving others that I have experienced many times before. This quite often may also be entertaining or it may be to delay or dodge a less pleasant or less predictable issue. (Blackburn 2000, p.5)

Demanding the same verbal scenario

Autistic children often demand that the other person initiate conversation by saying exactly the same words they have used in similar situations. They demand, 'Say _____'. Some children do not mind 'replaying the whole verbal scenario' themselves. Others always insist on their 'fellow-actors' saying their 'lines'.

Autistic discourse style

The speech of children with autism may be overly formal, pedantic in both vocabulary and grammar.

They may assume either that their communication partner does not share their knowledge or that everybody knows what they do. In the first case the child may give a very detailed description of what he is talking about, making his 'monologue' sound very pedantic (and boring). If he is interrupted, he goes back and starts from the very beginning. Those who assume knowledge in their listeners equivalent to their own may produce ambiguous utterances where no joint reference or shared knowledge has been established. For instance, they may say things like 'He did it' with no indication of who 'he' or what 'it' is (Jordan and Powell 1995).

Poor control of prosody

Many autistic individuals speak with peculiar prosodic features, such as a monotonous flat voice and idiosyncratic intonation, rhythm and stress. They fail to use or understand intonation as communication and are often unable to 'interpret' the speaker's intentions/attitudes that are expressed by the intonation patterns (that often contradict to the literal meaning of the utterance).

What they say

There was another problem: the way I spoke. I would often fluctuate between accents and pitch and the manner in which I described things. Sometimes my accent seemed quite 'polished' and refined. Sometimes I spoke as though I was born and bred in the gutter. Sometimes my pitch was normal, at other times it was deep like I was doing [an] Elvis impersonation. When I was excited, however, it sounded like Mickey Mouse after being run over by a steam-roller – high-pitched and flat. (Williams 1999b, p.76)

Chapter 10

Fluent Speakers – So What's the Problem?

Never mind what I say, Robert! I am always saying what I shouldn't say. In fact, I usually say what I really think. A great mistake nowadays. It makes one so liable to be misunderstood. (Oscar Wilde, *An Ideal Husband*, Act II)

Some individuals with autistic spectrum disorders (ASD) (especially those with high-functioning autism and Asperger syndrome) possess well-developed spoken language, with good vocabulary and perfect grammar. However, they still have difficulties with pragmatics (using language for communication) and non-verbal communication.

A good verbal arsenal does not seem to make it any easier for autistic people to interpret non-verbal cues in order to find out the intentions of the speaker. They find it hard to 'read' the meaning of gestures, facial expressions and 'eye-talk', and have to learn theoretically the art of conversation, with all the rules of how to initiate the conversation, take turns in the process, be polite (and even lie!).

What they say

It's hard for me to tell when someone is lying. It took me a very long time, and a lot of painful experience, just to learn what lying is. And in the social area, as with everything else, I have trouble keeping track of everything that's happening at one time. I have to learn things other people never think about. I have to use cognitive strategies to make up for some basic instincts that I don't have. In the social area, as with everything else, there are a lot of things that I don't understand unless someone explains them to me. (Sinclair 1992, p.302)

Another important element of social interaction is eye contact. As for many people on the autism spectrum, eye contact was difficult for me and can still be. People with autism have great difficulty in processing the huge quantities of nonverbal data coming from the eyes and the face. Attempting to do so takes away cognitive energy from processing conversation. For situations that require perceived eye contact, I say 'fake it, but don't break it.' Others probably are unable to differentiate whether I am looking between their eyes, at the bridge of their nose or in their eyes. (Shore 2003, p.89)

It has been noticed that autistic people find it hard to perceive the mental states of others. This capacity is called Theory of Mind (ToM) and a hypothesis was put forward: autistic people lack ToM (Baron-Cohen, Leslie and Frith 1985; Frith 1989). According to this hypothesis, the social and communication impairment in autism results in a kind of blindness to socially meaningful stimulation – *mind-blindness* (Baron-Cohen *et al.* 1995). However, given the differences in sensory perceptual experiences and cognitive representations, non-autistic individuals may be said to lack Theory of Autistic Mind.

What they say

Theory of mind plays a very strong presence in my life. However, every person has a different kind of theory of mind. I have my own theory of mind, which is different from people who do not have autism. Communication is a two-way street, and it takes two people to have a conversation. It also takes two people to mess up a conversation. Not all of this problem is caused by people with autism. People without autism have a lot to learn about the art of conversation with people who do not converse in the same way, whether it is verbal, non-verbal, or sign language. We can think of the idea of theory of mind as an assumed 'people without autism' theory...

Theory of mind has its validity and makes good points of what is noticeable, but it needs to be fleshed out by people with autism and our thinking, experiences, and way of life. The way that people with autism think is just as valid as the thoughts of people who do not have autism. These are two valid opinions. (Bovee undated)

I keep reading that autistic people lack empathy and are unable to take other's perspective. I think it might be more fair to say that autistic people lack certain expressive and receptive communication skills, possibly including some basic instincts that make communication a natural process for most people, and that this, combined with any cognitive or perceptual differences, means that autistic people do not *share* others' perceptions... When I am interacting with someone, that person's perspective is as foreign to me as mine is to the other person. But while I am aware of this difference and can make deliberate efforts to figure out how someone else is experiencing a situation, I generally find that other people do not notice the difference in perspectives and simply *assume* that they understand my experience. When people make assumptions about my perspective without taking the trouble to find out such things as how I receive and process information or what my motives and priorities are, those assumptions are almost certain to be wrong... If I know that I do not understand people and I devote all this energy and effort to figuring them out, do I have more or less empathy than people who not only do not understand me, but who do not even notice that they do not understand me? (Sinclair 1989)

In the past few years, I have begun realise that my outlook on life is vastly different to that of most other people. I had always assumed everyone operated as I did, and felt about things as I do. Intellectually, I realised that people are individual and different, but it has only just occurred to me *how* extensive is that difference. (Lawson 1998, p.116)

As people began to explain how other people experienced my behaviour, I came to learn that all behaviour had two definitions: theirs and mine. These 'helpful' people were trying to help me to 'overcome my ignorance' yet they never tried to understand the way I saw the world. (Williams 1999b, p.76)

Let us consider some other common problems experienced by 'fluent speakers'.

Receptive language

People with autism may have problems with comprehension because of processing problems. As the problems they experience are often 'invisible', the interlocutor assumes that communication is successful:

'Yes', my mouth was saying automatically in response to the external blah-blah as the battle raged inside of me. I had no idea what I'd said yes to and was too distracted to even worry whether the yes would bring me bad consequences... 'Is it okay?' 'Yes,' I replied automatically as usual, having only half understood the words. Unless someone gave me an explicit choice – 'Do you want this *or not*' – I usually felt compelled to go along, not understanding that in fact I had a choice. (Williams 1999a, pp.45, 28)

They often cannot keep up with the rate of 'verbal flow'. When they are trying to find the right words to say, others are already talking about different things. They need time find the right words and say them.

Expressive language

The 'fluency' of the speech of people with autism seems to depend on what they are talking about. If the conversation concerns the subject of their special interest their speech may be fluent, complex and sophisticated. If they are not interested in the subject of the conversation, they may struggle to utter the simplest words.

They may be literally 'lost for words', for example:

At the prompt of 'what is it you want?', my first answer was 'I don't know' (though I did know but couldn't connect and access). My mind ran amok with stored evasive responses. I had wanted to say 'a pottery wheel'. The stored picture that jumped into my head came, first, from a category of 'things we couldn't have'. Instead of saying 'pottery wheel', I blurted 'cat'. When that response was checked, I again wished to say 'pottery wheel' but the stored picture that jumped into my head...came from a category of 'things we already had in our house' and I said 'ironing board'. There was no way that I wanted an ironing board nor a cat... I had been preparing a pottery shed for the past weeks and was thinking of a pottery wheel but was totally unable to organise fulfilling or even expressing the want without being prompted or triggered to do so. (Williams 1996, p.232)

What they say

I have a more subtle, but often far more annoying type of communication deficit – I may get out exactly the word I want, only to be horribly misunderstood. I used to think my mother was an 'idiot' because I would ask her questions or say things to her, and get a reply that made no contextual sense; I might ask a question about one subject, and get an answer about another, totally unrelated subject. When I started to get out in the world a little more, however, I found this sort of thing to be extremely common problem with the majority of the people I met. Since I am the common factor, the logical explanation is that I am not expressing myself well (i.e. in a way other people can understand). I often cannot figure out why they don't understand what I've said. I suppose that most people may meet someone they cannot get through to, but for me it's a constant (and frustrating) problem. (Blackburn 1999, pp.4–5)

Speaking for me is still often difficult and occasionally impossible, although this has become easier over the years. I sometimes know in my head what the words are but they do not always come out. Sometimes they do come out [but] they are incorrect, a fact that I am only sometimes aware of and which is often pointed out by other people. (Jolliffe, Lakesdown and Robinson 1992)

Literalness

No matter how 'verbal' autistic individuals are they tend to interpret everything literally. Eventually they may learn the meaning of idioms and common metaphorical phrases. However, they still experience difficulty in understanding 'empty' words, irony and humour. They may get in trouble because of trying to do 'the right thing', i.e. what there are told, following the instruction to the letter:

> Once, my mother told me that if a teacher said such-and-such to me, I should tell her to go and jump in a lake. Unfortunately I took this completely literally and proceeded to tell the teacher to go and jump in a lake and couldn't work out why she got upset, since I'd been being good and doing what I was told to do. I had been told by everyone that I should tell the truth and that lying was bad, so I couldn't understand why people got upset when I told them they were stupid. Literal understanding of instructions was typically interpreted as sarcasm or 'trying to be clever'. (Sainsbury 1999b, pp.91–2)

> I remember, when I was about seven, how I got a slap in the face after walking into someone's house and announcing, 'It's very dirty in here' and following it up by enthusiastically informing the host that he 'only had one arm'. This was fairly typical of me, and I came to earn myself a

reputation as rude, hurtful and outspoken. Later this same quality sometimes came to earn me respect as someone who was 'never afraid to say
what she thinks'. (Williams 1999b, p.50)

If we think about the words and conventional phrases that we use from the
autistic perspective, the logic of the following arguments is unbeatable: if you
feel terrible why say 'I'm fine'? If you are not interested in how I feel why ask
'How are you?'

Language as 'stress reliever'

In stressful situations autistic people may talk to themselves in order to
'unwind':

> After every social encounter...I go through a period of what seems to
> be a kind of 'letting off steam'. I wait until I'm alone, and then, when I
> am able to relax my shell of control, I twitch and vocalize. My hands
> jump around, flying this way and that, or gesturing elaborately about
> nothing. Meanwhile, my voice speaks nonsense. I say 'my voice speaks',
> because the words are unvoluntary. My conscious, deliberate mind is
> not involved. I don't know what I will say until I hear myself say it.
> Occasionally, I discover that I'm not as alone as I thought I was. The
> apparently deserted street is inhabited by a man crouching down to
> inspect the tire of his car, and I wonder for the rest of the day what he
> thought when this literally jerky middle-aged woman walking by all
> alone suddenly barked out, 'I don't love you'. Or 'elaborate retirement
> options'. Or 'thirteen purple penguins'. Or whatever phrase that
> non-voluntary portion of my brain happens to be using for decompres-
> sion that day. Sometimes it's nothing more exciting than 'no, no, no, no,
> no, no, no' repeated until I can stop. (Meyerding undated)

It is necessary to note that there is increasing evidence that some children and
adults with ASD develop signs of Tourette syndrome (motor, vocal and
behavioural ones) (Attwood 1998). It is the uncontrollable utterances which
are used as a stress reliever that is one of the examples showing a link (or even
overlap) between ASD and Tourette syndrome. Like autistic people with
involuntary vocal manifestations, Tourette syndrome sufferers cannot control
their own speech sometimes and exhibit vocal utterances unconnected to the
situation.

Sophisticated echolalia

To 'disguise' their difficulties in understanding social and communicative conventions people with high-functioning autism and Asperger syndrome may employ echolalia. However, it is a 'sophisticated' echolalia that is not easily detected by 'outsiders'. In this case, it is a survival strategy in a social world they do not quite comprehend:

> I guess I had been one of the luckier ones. I had been both echolalic and echopractic, able to mimic sound or movement without any thought whatsoever about what was heard or seen. Like someone sleep-walking and sleep-talking, I imitated the sounds and movements of others – an involuntary compulsive impressionist. This meant that I could go forward as a patchwork façade condemned to live life as a 'the world' caricature. Others called 'autistic' who were neither of these things sometimes paid the price of being incapable of any sound or action at all. They, at least, probably maintained a sense of self. Ironically these people, and not those like me, were the ones who were labeled 'low functioning'. (Williams 1999c, p.9)

> [When all else failed] I used to rely on a 'fitting in' trick that is nothing more than a sophisticated form of echolalia. Like a professional mimic I could catch someone else's personality as easily as other people catch a cold. I did this by surveying the group of people I was with, then consciously identifying the person I was most taken in by. I would watch them intently, carefully marking their traits, until almost as easily as if I had turned on a light, I would turn their personality on in me. I can change my mannerisms and my voice and my thoughts until I am confident they match the person I wanted to echo. Of course, I knew what I was doing, and of course, I was sometimes embarrassed by it, but it worked to keep me connected and sometimes that was all that concerned me. It was simply more efficient for me to use the kinds of behaviours other people used, than it was for me to try and create some of my own... It is simply easier to echo, more comfortable and typically more successful superficially to pretend to be someone I am not. (Willey 1999, p.57)

> Over the years, I usually tried to contain my excitement and joy over life's happenings and watched to see what makes other people happy or sad. If they laughed or were unmoved, then this was my signal that it was all right for me do likewise. This process was hard work and although it helped me to be more observant of others, it robbed me of spontaneity and enjoyment of the richness of my own experience. (Lawson 1998, p.116)

What they say

...often my strengths mask my very real disabilities... I feel that in many ways my ability quite often proves to be my biggest disability. (Blackburn 2000, p.7)

the fact that communication *is* the problem means that I can't communicate *what* the problem *is!* Since I *can* talk, many people have trouble seeing me as having a communication problem, *per se.* (Blackburn 1999)

Because of the specific skills associated with having a fairly-high verbal IQ, I can put words together in a way which can usually be pretty well understood, and would not be identified as 'sounding autistic'. But this, to me, is as though I were very fluent in a foreign language. My 'native language' doesn't seem to have any words...thus, if I had to use only it, I too would be nonverbal. It is only the use of adaptation which permits me to use words as I do. It is not my fault that my makeup happens to include the technical ability to use words in certain ways, in imitation of what I see other people doing. Some autistic folks multiply large numbers; I construct large sentences... Examining the structure and flow of the words I write might lead one to make assumptions about me based on these observations. Such assumptions would likely not be correct. What appears to be seamless integration is actually the skillful use of 'interface layer', a veneer... It serves to mask, mute, and 'adapt away' my differentness for the convenience of those around me. (Spicer 1998, p.13).

Autistic people don't really understand how somebody could have bad intentions, yet still act friendly on the outside. That paradox is confusing for a person who needs to see things literally as they are, and not befogged with deceit. A person like this simply can't grasp how another person can be acting nice only to play tricks or to really harm the disabled individual. An autistic person can learn that things like that do happen, yet can never actually understand why they happen...autistics do need to be guarded from people with bad intentions. They are naïve socially. Their innocence and literalness prevent them from being able to distinguish between foe or friend in many cases... Autistic people generally don't know the things others know naturally. They can't be taken for granted, and they can't be expected to know something just because others know it. (O'Neill 1999, pp.86–7)

Guidance for communicating and interacting with autistic people (Modified from Blackburn 1999 and Dekker undated)

Autistic people have unique ways of communicating and interacting that are rooted in their unique ways of thinking and experiencing the world. While there is much variation between autistic individuals, the following guidelines are a few good things to consider when communicating with autistic people:

- *Distance*: Many autistic people are hypertactile and may be afraid that people who get too close might touch them, or they may simply feel uncomfortable with the nearness of people (especially strangers). Some autistic people may enjoy physical contact in some situations and not mind closeness as much. However, unless you know this is true, it is a good idea to be 'better safe than sorry'.

- *Olfactory issues*: It is better not to wear perfume if you know you are going to be around autistic people.

- *Rate of approach*: It is not a good idea to approach an autistic person too quickly, or from behind.

- *Different rhythm of interaction*: In contrast to non-autistic people who tend to experience silence as uncomfortable and to attempt to fill it with small talk, autistic people prefer to say what they have to say, then stop talking and wait for the other to respond.

- *Less non-verbal communication*: Autistic people communicate mostly with words, not with body language and facial expressions.

- *Be careful with emotions*: It is best not to be too emotional when speaking to an autistic person. Autistic people find it difficult to interpret this extra information. Besides, they may find emotional outbursts too loud, unpredictable and overwhelming. (However, contrary to popular belief, many autistic people do have an acute sense for the emotional state another person is in. They can 'pick up emotional waves' even if the person tries to hide them.)

- *Directness (just facts)*: When dealing with autistic people speak matter-of-factly and to the point. Giving a lot of empty words or over-explaining may overwhelm many autistic people with too much information to be processed, causing confusion. It is best simply give all the relevant details in short simple sentences, without unnecessary decorative words.

- *Literal interpretation*: Autistic people rarely 'read between the lines'. They take words literally, usually use words directly and say what they mean, without wrapping up their message into idioms or tone of voice, etc.

- *Listen, accept, respect*: Everyone deserves respect. Autistic people should not be used or patronized (that is often the case). It is good to take other people's differences into account but not to treat someone as helpless or incompetent because of it. People should listen to each other, accept each other's needs and problems, and respect them even if they do not understand them.

PART 3
Key Strategies to Enhance Communication in Autism

The main goal in any communication approach is to teach a child spontaneous communication. No one treatment method has been found to teach communication in all autistic individuals. Any approach used should improve useful communication. For some, verbal communication is a realistic goal. For others, it may be communication by gestures or symbol systems.

In order to 'find' the right method to communicate with each particular person, we have to start with the assessment of this person's strengths and use them as a basis for intervention.

Chapter 11

Communication/Language Assessment Strategies – Communication Profile

It is very important to plan what we are going to achieve and how we are going to achieve it. This starts with assessing the autistic person's strengths and weaknesses. Then we can work out our priorities and strategies. You have to discuss and agree with other people involved how you are going to do it. It is important that everybody knows what the others are doing, so that the autistic person experiences consistency and continuity of approach.

The ultimate goal of the assessment is to determine the needs of the autistic person and develop communication systems suitable for this particular person (see Table 11.1). The unique communication/language profile of each person should be assessed and used to develop that person's communication potential.

Sensory components

Sensory perceptual assessment is vital in any communication profile in order:

- to adjust the environment to the needs of the individual and protect the person from painful stimuli and/or reduce the confusion caused by possible distortions

- to identify the optimum rate of incoming information the person can cope with

- to identify the preferred communication channel used by the person

- to identify the interaction style to be used with the person.

Table 11.1 Components of the assessment of communication in autism

Components	Objectives
1. Sensory	To adjust the environment to the needs of the individual in order to protect him from painful stimuli and/or reduce the confusion caused by distortion.
	To identify the 'right' language to be used with this particular individual.
	To identify the communicative style.
Expressive ability	
2. Atypical communication behaviours	To determine what strategies the person currently uses to 'get his message across'.
	To identify communicative functions the person expresses.
3. Muteness	To determine whether there are motor problems.
	To determine whether there is (no) understanding of verbal language.
	To find out whether the person has auditory processing disorder.
4. Ability to use non-verbal communication strategies	To find out whether the person can use and understand conventional non-verbal communication (gestures, facial expressions, etc.).
	To identify the person's strategies, means and functions of non-verbal communication.
5. Atypical use of verbal language	To determine the functions and meaning of 'verbal messages' used by the individual.
	To distinguish between non-communicative and communicative echolalia.
	To identify communicative functions of echolalia.
6. Functional use of verbal language	To determine to what extent the person can use verbal language to express different communicative functions.
7. Communicative functions expressed	To identify communicative functions the person can express at present and the means of communication used to express these functions.
Comprehensive ability	
8. Ability to understand verbal and non-verbal communication/ language	To adjust the language (both verbal and non-verbal) used with the individual.

One of the possible sensory profiles is the Sensory Perceptual Checklist – Revised (SPC-R) (Bogdashina 2003). It is designed to collect information about an individual's behaviours as they are related to sensory-perceptual functioning. Seven sensory modalities (visual, auditory, tactile, olfactory, gustatory, proprioceptive, vestibular) are assessed across 20 sensory-perceptual phenomena. Special graphs – Rainbows – identify strengths and weaknesses within each modality. Information obtained from this or any other similar tool may be useful in identifying problem 'sensory domains' (visual/auditory/ tactile, etc.), specific problems in each particular area (for instance, fragmentation, distortion, hyper-/hyposensitivities, delay of processing) and the strategies the person has acquired to cope with them. These 'problem domains' will be addressed from two perspectives – from outside (adjusting the environment) and inside (desensitization). For example:

> *John was screened for possible sensory problems. His SPC-R revealed his hypersensitivity to bright lights and bright colours. It was decided to switch off fluorescent lights if there was enough natural lighting. John was encouraged to try wearing sunglasses (and he did!). He chose the colour of the glasses himself (grey) and the changes in his behaviour were seen almost immediately – fewer stimms, better concentration on the task and less anxiety.*

An analysis of sensory processing difficulties may assist in understanding puzzling behaviours which have proven difficult to change. Intervention chosen to accommodate to individual difficulties is likely to result in improved adaptive strategies.

Strengths and interests in certain domains may serve as powerful reinforcers and can be used as objects/activities to release stress and anxiety for the individual.

The SPC-R provides information about the preferred sensory modality to get information in and the inner language of the individual. This preferred sensory modality is likely to be the preferred communication channel. This information helps choose the 'language' to be spoken to a person (visual, tactile, kinaesthetic) and to 'translate' the environment into the chosen mode. For instance, a visual environment would not work with a tactile-speaking child who experiences severe visual distortions. The environment should be structured in a way that enables communication with each particular person with the methods of instruction being matched to the person's learning style.

The identified preferred modality will be used for introducing verbal concepts at the initial stages of the programme.

With development you may decide to change the preferred channel; for instance, from a kinaesthetic to a verbal one or from visual to auditory.

The SPC-R also helps identify the interaction style to be used with the individual and the rate of giving the information the individual is able to cope with.

Atypical communication behaviours

It is important to identify and analyse communicative functions of so-called aberrant, bizarre and socially unacceptable behaviours. Due to the pervasive impairments in social cognition, especially in imitation and joint referencing, the communication attempts of autistic children are often idiosyncratic (Mundy, Sigman and Ungerer 1989). Challenging behaviours such as aggression, self-injuring and tantrums are often used to seek attention, escape from a difficult task or a confusing situation, protest against changes of routine or regulate interactions in a predictable manner. These behaviours *are* meaningful and often serve as (unconventional) means of communication used by the child who cannot 'get his message across' in any other conventional way.

Let us not forget that our ways may look equally idiosyncratic to them (for instance, hugging hurts; why ask 'How are you?' if you are not interested?).

Muteness

There is increased evidence that in some autistic individuals lack of speech (muteness) may be related to issues other than social-cognitive abilities (Prizant 1996). Prizant argues that motor speech impairments can be a significant factor inhibiting the speech development in some autistic children:

- Some people are able to acquire the ability to communicate via alternative communication devices and/or sign language (for example, Blackman 2001; Mukhopadhyay 2000) although they cannot produce meaningful utterances.

- Some people exhibit oral motor problems such as difficulty in coordinating movement of lips, tongue, voice box, jaw, etc. These features are consistent with the symptoms of developmental apraxia of speech. The symptoms are:

- o   use of primarily vowel-like vocalizations

- o   limited consonant repertoire (as consonants require greater motor-planning ability)

- o   intelligibility decreasing with the length of utterance (single word and single syllable production may be more clear than extended utterances or multisyllabic words)

- o   differences in automatic *versus* volitional speech (echolalia may be more clearly articulated compared to spontaneous speech attempts) (Prizant 1996).

If an autistic person has an understanding of language and an ability to communicate via alternative means but no or unclear speech, assessment of the oral and speech motor systems is necessary. Clinical observation and evaluation should include the following areas (Crary 1993):

- *Non-speech motor functions:* posture and gait, gross and fine motor coordination, oral movement coordination, mouth posture, swallowing, chewing, oral structure, volitional *vs* spontaneous movement.

- *Speech motor functions:* strain during speech attempts, groping of mouth, deviation in prosody (rate, volume, intonation, etc.), fluency of speech, hyper/hyponasality, etc.

- *Articulation and phonological performance:* amount of verbal output, sound repertoire, intelligibility and type of errors.

- *Language performance:* comprehension and expression, type of utterances, semantic and syntactic ability, effect of increased length of input.

- *Other:* ability to sustain and shift attention, reaction to speech, distractibility (Crary 1993).

However, it can be difficult to evaluate the oral-motor and speech-motor problems in autistic children due to their communication problems, hypersensitive oral mechanism, hyposensitive proprioceptive system, etc.

If possible, an audiometric assessment should be conducted: impairments in auditory processing and hearing acuity need be ruled out before formal intervention procedures begin. Depending on the person's level of communication and awareness, audiological testing may be used to verify that hearing is within normal limits. If the person is unable to participate in audiological testing, auditory evoked-response (AER) studies can be used. AER studies detect significant deviations in auditory processing.

Ability to use non-verbal communication strategies

It is necessary to find out whether the person can understand and use conventional non-verbal communication (gestures, body language, facial expressions, eye contact) and to identify the person's strategies, means and the functions of the non-verbal 'arsenal' at her disposal, such as, for example:

- primitive contact gestures

- referential gestures (pointing, showing)

- mimes.

Atypical use of verbal language

It is necessary to analyse the following:

- The individual vocabulary that the person uses; for example, 'dog' = 'I want to go for a walk'.

- Non-communicative echolalia: Is it used as a 'sensory toy'? If so, either give the person a substitution (something bringing the same sensation/stimulation) or just accept it as her eccentricity (see Chapter 9).

- Communicative echolalia (any speech/vocalization is assessed as communicative if there is intent or desire to convey a message to someone else):

  o Is it used because the person does not understand what he is asked? If so, decrease confusion, overstimulation, anxiety and stress. Use the person's language to 'translate' what has been said. Create a stress-free environment.

  o Is it used to win time (in the case of delayed processing) and/or clarify the meaning to be able to hear the message in her own voice? If so, give the person more time to process and respond.

    o Is it used as a request? Teach the person to make changes in sentence structure (i.e. moving to mitigated echolalia).

Functional use of verbal language

In order to get an accurate picture of the person's use of words symbolically and referentially it is necessary to assess his ability to use and understand symbols in both verbal and non-verbal communication.

- Do the words have referential meaning? Or do they refer only to specific objects, situations or events, and only those objects or events?

- Does the person use the words he knows to initiate an interaction or just respond to it?

Communicative functions expressed

Does the person exhibit communicative intent, i.e. does he anticipate an outcome?

> *N. puts his shoe on the table in front of his carer to communicate that he wants to go for a walk. When the carer says, 'No, we can't go now', N. repeats his request 'louder' — he puts both his shoes on the table.*

It is not uncommon for autistic children to lack communicative intent. They may be unaware that they can use communication to get something or ask somebody to do something for them.

It is necessary to identify the communicative functions the person can express at present and the means of communication used to express these functions (see Table 11.2).

Communicative functions include:

- instrumental (request, objection, discomfort, frustration, boredom)

- social (greeting, calling, joint attention, request information, etc.)

- expressive (comment, emotions, mental states).

Table 11.2 Communicative functions and the means to express them

Communicative functions	Means of communication					
	Behavioural	Gestural	Vocal	Verbal	Signs/ mimes	Objects/ pictures
Instrumental: request, objection						
Social: greeting, calling, request information, joint attention, sharing interests						
Expressive: comment, emotions, mental states						

The means used to express these functions and their sophistication:

- behavioural (often idiosyncratic, unconventional; for example, aggression, self-injury, tantrums, withdrawal)
- gestural (contact gestures, when a child manipulates an adult's hand; pointing; showing; mimes etc.)
- vocal (sounds to express pleasure or distress)
- verbal (echolalia, spontaneous speech)
- sign language
- using objects
- using pictures
- using written language
- combinations of the above.

Wetherby (1986) points out possible discrepancies in the sophistication of the communicative means a person may use for different communicative functions. For instance, a child may use a spontaneous speech for instrumental purposes, echolalic speech or primitive contact gestures for social interaction, etc.

While considering the strategies and abilities to communicate the child uses, the focus should be on current competence and ability, rather than simply listing absent behaviours that need to be developed and/or prioritizing so-called 'deficits' for eradication (Prizant 1983b).

In general, autistic children find it very difficult to initiate communication. Research findings (Stone and Caro-Martinez 1990) show that, on average, autistic children initiate communication three or four times per hour in unstructured situations, whereas normally developing two-year-old toddlers communicate spontaneously about 200 times per hour (Wetherby *et al.* 1988).

Autistic children who are still at the early stages of communication development are able to express a limited range of communicative functions. Their communication is focused on expressing their needs. Although in this case their communication is often spontaneous, their understanding of communication is one-sided, i.e. they transmit the message without taking into account the receiver's response or even the receiver being present or absent. Their one-sidedness in communication is reflected in their inability to repair the communication breakdowns. Thus, to determine the child's communicative competence we have to identify the strategies the child uses to repair the conversation (for example, the child repeats the same word or gesture, or modifies it).

If the child tries to modify a message the adult does not understand, it means that the child understands at least some meaning and significance of interaction and moves from one-sidedness to the reciprocity of communication. To show the child that communication is a two-sided process, it is very important to teach him strategies to initiate, repair and sustain the conversation, and turn-taking.

Ability to understand verbal and non-verbal communication/language

An assessment of the autistic child's comprehension of verbal language is important so that you can adjust the language you use with the individual to her level of understanding. It is not uncommon to overestimate the person's understanding of language, as they often read non-verbal cues and seem to understand more than they actually do. For instance, the carer takes a towel and says to the child, 'Bath time'. The child may read the towel-message without understanding what has been said.

It is important to find out whether these non-verbal cues are necessary for the child to comprehend the message. If he understands the linguistic aspects of the message, it is important to determine whether he is able to comprehend single words within the message, multi-words guided by semantic relations (i.e., understanding based on knowledge about word classes and relations), grammatical constructions (i.e., syntactic and morphological rules) or connected discourse (Wetherby and Prizant 1992).

The language used with the individual during natural interactions should be adjusted to the level of his understanding. Using language that is beyond the individual's comprehension is likely to be confusing and frustrating and may lead to tantrums, aggression or withdrawal.

Assessment strategies

Traditional formal language assessment instruments are usually unsatisfactory for assessing autistic children. The assessment strategies that have proven successful are:

- observation of the child in familiar and unfamiliar settings, interacting with familiar and unfamiliar others in order to assess a child's language in different environments

- interviews with significant others

- a checklist of possible communicative behaviours, communicative means used and communicative functions expressed spontaneously in natural environments.

The assessment findings provide the basis for an intervention programme.

Chapter 12

Communication Environment and Interaction Styles

Communication environment – creating the 'umbrella'

The term *communication environment* (Potter and Whittaker 2001) refers to factors in the child's everyday environment which might affect her ability to communicate; for instance, general noise level, how the classroom is organized, the interaction styles adults use to talk to the child, etc.

As each child has his own ways to perceive and interpret information it is important to take into account his sensory-perceptual profile. One child may experience pain from the sounds we cannot hear, another may see a 60-cycle flicker of a fluorescent lamp that causes her perceptual distortions and even pain, etc. If we want a child to develop communication skills, we must create an environment where she feels safe and motivated.

Imagine the situation. Your arm is broken and the pain is intolerable. The sound of a siren comes into your ears and makes it almost impossible to hear anything. To make things worse, everything is jumping around you – colours, things, people – disappearing and re-appearing again and, on top of that, someone (with very good intentions, of course) insists 'Hello. How are you? Say "Good morning" and I'll give you a crisp', while pulling faces. How would you feel? Brrr. Would you be motivated to communicate or would you try to find a quiet place and 'heal your wounds'?

Now project your imagined experiences into the 'autistic situation', described by Donna Williams:

> Entering the infant room, I saw a girl about four years old curled up in the dark interior of a crate. Her eyes were sharply crossed, her fists clenched into balls. The staff had been advised that in the safety of her

self-controlled isolation, she might begin to explore her surroundings. Hung inside the crate were various mobiles and objects... The two supervising staff were excited by the novelty of their ideas and the equipment for the little girl. Like overenthusiastic relatives on the first meeting with a newborn child, they were half in the tiny crate with her. I stood there feeling ill as they bombarded her personal space with their bodies, their breath, their smells, their laughter, their movement, their noise. Almost mechanically, they shook rattles and jiggled things in front of the girl as if they were a pair of overzealous witch doctors hoping to break the evil spell of autism. Their interpretation of the advice seemed to be overdose her on experiences... I got the feeling that if they could have used a crowbar to pry open her soul and pour 'the world' in they would have done so and would never have noticed that their patient had died on the operation table. The little girl screamed and rocked, her arms up against her ears to keep their noise out and her eyes crossed to block out the bombardment of visual noise. I watched these people and wished they knew what sensory hell was. I was watching a torture where the victim had no ability to fight back in any comprehensible language... She had no words to put to what was happening, to analyze or adjust to it as they did... It was medieval. These people had been told to use something that might work but no one had told them why or how... They were surgeons operating with garden tools and no anesthetic. (Williams 1999c, pp.25–6)

Autistic children are often bombarded with sensory (often painful) stimuli. They are vulnerable to distractions from the environment and have difficulty filtering out background stimuli. The first thing to do is to find out which of the stimuli disturb the child and create a 'sensory umbrella' in order to protect him from the 'sensory rain'. The problem is, each child has his own sensory experiences and what is safe for one child is harmful for another (Bogdashina 2003). It means each child will need an individual umbrella which he can open up any time he needs it.

The TEACCH programme (Mesibov 1992) stresses the importance of making the physical environment predictable and unthreatening. It is achieved by:

- providing a physical layout with visually clear boundaries for different areas

- using natural lighting if fluorescent light flickering is distracting/painful for the individual

- reducing all unnecessary stimuli

- creating an individual timetable showing what work is to be done, when it is finished, and what happens next

- sticking to routines.

What they say

It is impossible for children to learn if they are bombarded with confusing, irritating stimuli they are unable to screen out. If clothes bother them steps need to be taken to find less irritating clothes. (Grandin 1988, p.4)

The more predictable and calm the voice, the less emotional fear is inspired. Emotional fear, however, is a two-way street. Mildly autistic children may emerge, as themselves, in an environment where they are able to relax, though not enough to 'lose themselves'… Perhaps a more severely closed-off child would learn to respond to a combination of predictability and unpredictability in a voice, though never too much unpredictability as to send a child like this irretrievably withdrawn. This is a double-edged sword. If it is too predictable, it will be tuned out, although the child will trust. If it is too unpredictable, it is hard to tune out, but the psychological barrier of distrust will be greater. (Williams 1999b, pp.180–1)

Creating opportunities for communication

Very often carers read the messages without giving a child any opportunity to transmit the message. It is crucial 'not to understand' sometimes and create as many opportunities for a child to see the power of communication (regardless of what communicative system he uses) as possible. Children should be given opportunities to express different communicative functions in specially created situations.

Several strategies to develop communication with autistic children have been proven successful:

- a proximal communication approach

- a minimal speech approach

- reduction of prompts

- a facilitative style interaction

- an indirectly confrontational approach.

A proximal communication approach

A *proximal communication approach* uses structured non-verbal interactions, involving rough-and-tumble play, imitation and creating pauses in activities. Potter and Whittaker (2001) propose the following essential elements of proximal communication:

- using tickling and rough-and-tumble play appropriate to the child's physical development
- using minimal speech
- exaggerating facial expressions and physical responses during the play
- alternating active phases with passive pauses
- responding to the child's eye gaze
- adopting the position lower that the child's gaze
- using the child's vocalizations or echolalia to develop imitation
- imitating the child's physical movements to vary interaction
- focusing on interpersonal interactions rather than introducing objects.

This approach enables children to communicate at much higher rates and for more communicative functions (Potter and Whittaker 2001).

A minimal speech approach

A *minimal speech approach* is beneficial for the children who have no or little understanding of verbal language. This strategy is used in combination with other non-verbal communication systems (objects, photos, pictures, symbols, etc.) depending on the child's 'inner language'.

The essential elements of a minimal speech approach are (Potter and Whittaker 2001):

- the consistent use of only one or two concrete words that are strictly relevant to the situation
- connecting words exactly with the situation at the time the child attends to it
- use of a clear and emphatic voice.

Reduction of prompts

Children with autism often become dependent on the *prompts* (either physical or verbal) we give them to respond to communication. As our aim is to have them respond to situations and initiate communication, we should reduce prompts as soon as possible. Research shows that an effective way to do it is to delay our response, using pauses (between five and ten seconds long) at 'critical points of activities' (Potter and Whittaker 2001).

Interaction styles

Those communicating with autistic people have to change the way they themselves communicate in order to help a person with ASD understand and communicate. The *interaction style* we use with each particular person depends on their perceptual and communication profile. For Temple Grandin, a more 'intrusive' style was beneficial as her sensory-perceptual problems were mild; whereas for somebody with severe sensory distortions, a different approach is needed:

> The teachers there knew how much to intrude into my world to snap me out of my daydreams and make me pay attention. Too much intrusion would cause tantrums, but without intervention there would be no progress. (Grandin 1996a, p.96)

A directive style vs a facilitative style

Mirenda and Donnellan (1986) distinguish between a *directive* style and a *facilitative* style of communication (see Table 12.1).

The research (Mirenda and Donnellan 1986) shows that a facilitative style of interaction with autistic children gives a higher rate of child-initiated interactions than does a directive style.

In addition to using a facilitative style while interacting with autistic children, it is important to adjust the language to their developmental level.

Table 12.1 Styles of communication

Directive style	Facilitative style
Does not allow sufficient time for initiation or language processing	Allows lags of up to 30 seconds to occur
Initiates more than half of all topics	Initiates less than one third of all topics
Uses direct questions to initiate majority of all the topics	Uses direct questions for no more than one fourth of topic continuations
Does not ask for clarification	Requests clarification when needed

(Adapted from Mirenda and Donnellan 1986)

Direct vs indirect communication

Some autistic children need intensive direct treatment that make them aware of the presence of others and does not let them 'slip' into their own world, this involves a *directly confrontational approach*. Others can often make better meaning out of what they hear or see by looking or listening peripherally (such as out of the corner of her eye or by looking at or listening to something else), a kind of *indirectly confrontational approach* (Williams 1998). For example:

> ...in my world I really wanted love to come from behind. For me this was real love. I would walk backwards towards Jay [mother] when she was watching television, and lean against her knees, waiting for a feathery kiss on the back of my head where my sensory alarms seemed to be more dozy. If she were standing up it was a more hit-and-miss procedure. I would lean slightly in her direction while looking the other way. 'Wanna be loved, but please don't hug', I might have been saying. (Blackman 2001, p.22)

> The best way I could have been able to listen to someone was for them to speak to themselves about me loud or about someone like me, which would have inspired me to show I could relate to what was being said. In doing so, indirect contact, such as looking out of a window whilst talking, would have been best. This, however, would only work once one has achieved the ability for some co-operation. In this case, this seeming indifference would actually demonstrate awareness and sensitivity to the child's problems of coping with directness. (Williams 1999b, pp.186–7)

One advantage of indirectly confrontational communication is that if something needs explaining or showing, the person explaining or showing can do so as if out loud to herself, addressing the wall or the floor, or her shoes, or the objects relating to the demonstration. The person with a problem of overload is able, similarly, to address and interact with you through speaking out loud with you 'in mind'. In this case the child will be less overloaded and more able to understand what is happening. Gradually, bridges can be built from indirectly to more directly confrontational interaction and communication (Williams 1996).

For those who cannot tolerate 'directness' yet, traditional praise and reward (applause, loud praise, etc.) may be experienced as punishment, and the person learns to avoid it at any cost, often by withdrawal and seeming loss of the skills.

The transition from indirectly confrontational to direct communication should not be rushed. We have to be 'in tune' with the child. Starting from minimal speech, to speaking aloud to ourselves or to the wall (occasionally mentioning the child's name), we can then move to speaking in the direction of the child and only then to talking face to face.

What they say

Two basic patterns of autistic symptoms can identify which children will respond well to intensive, gently intrusive teaching methods, and which will not. The first kind of child may appear deaf at age two, but by age three he or she can understand speech … The second kind of child appears to develop normally until one and a half or two and then loses speech … There are also children who are mixtures of the two kinds of autism. Children of the first kind will respond well to intensive, structured educational programs that pull them out of the autistic world, because their sensory systems provide a more or less accurate representation of things around them. There may be problems with sound or touch sensitivity, but they still have some realistic awareness of their surroundings. The second kind of child may not respond, because sensory jumbling makes the world incomprehensible. Gently intrusive teaching methods will work on some children who lose their speech before age two if teaching is started before their senses become totally scrambled. (Grandin 1996a, pp.55–6)

If loving parents can try to stand objectively away from their own emotional needs and relate to such children, always in terms of how these children perceive the world, then the children may (in being able to relate) find the trust and courage to reach out step by step at their own pace... Gain trust and encourage the child that you accept who and where they are. Through trust they may develop interest in 'the world', and at first this exploration should be on the only terms they know – their own. Only once this is firmly established should you take the safety-net away slowly piece by piece... The way out, in complete contradiction to normal interaction, is *indirect* in nature. In this way it is less all-consuming, suffocating and invasive. The child can reach out, not as a conforming role-playing robot, but as a feeling, albeit extremely shy and evasive, human being... At this point I ought to make it clear that I do not espouse soft options. One must tackle war with war and disarmament with disarmament. I am saying that the war must be thought through, sensitive and well-paced. (Williams 1999b, p.174)

Chapter 13

Selecting Communication Systems

Establishing communication and understanding between any two
people with different experiences and perspectives involves
developing a common language. An autistic person's experience
and vocabulary (verbal and non-verbal) may be so idiosyncratic
that it takes a great deal of effort on both sides to develop this
common language. Instead of attributing all difficulties in
communication to the autistic person's inability to speak your
language, why not embark on the adventure of working *with* the
autistic person to learn to understand each other's languages?
(Sinclair 1989)

If, for whatever reasons, a child does not develop a verbal language, we have to
introduce an augmentative and/or alternative language in order to arm him
with a tool to communicate and, what is equally important, a tool to assist
cognitive operations.

Fortunately, very few authors nowadays think that providing children
with alternative means of communication eliminates the need for them to
speak and will generally delay the development of language. While some
parents are reluctant to use any non-verbal system with their children as they
fear that it will hinder speech development, there is strong evidence that the
use of augmentative systems enhances the likelihood of the development or
improvement of speech (Silverman 1996).

To communicate successfully children have to have a communication tool.
We should introduce them to systems of communication as soon as possible.
The selection of a particular communication system should be based on the

child's inner language, his sensory-perceptual profile and the communicative means the child already uses to express different communicative functions.

For those who understand verbal language but have no speech, non-speech language systems (for instance, sign language or written language) may be introduced. Allen and Rapin (1993) state that autistic children who are totally mute have to be introduced to language through the visual modality. Some of these children may learn to speak when they are taught to read. For those who have no symbolic understanding of language yet, non-verbal communicative systems might be an option (the language of objects, PECS, are possibilities). (PECS is Picture Exchange Communication System and is discussed later in this chapter.) Whatever language system is selected, it should be taught as *a tool for communication* and not as meaningless noises they are asked to produce. In some schools and provisions 'communication sessions' are conducted where children are taught to respond to questions 'What is it?' or 'Show me...' without having any understanding of the process of communication. To these children they are just meaningless drills that do not help develop either social or communication skills:

> *Loren was 'taught communication' using a 'communication book'. He had to sign the reply to 'What is this?' when his teacher pointed at the picture.*

As a long-term goal is to teach a child to use and understand a verbal language, the selected communication system is not necessarily a permanent one and should serve only as a means for the child to learn another (more sophisticated) language. In fact, it is useful to select more than one system to teach. One system may be taught as a primary means of communication (for instance, speech or signs) and a different system may be developed to repair communicative breakdowns (for example, gestures, a picture system) (Wetherby and Prizant 1992).

The language system to be taught should be matched to the child's inner (internal) language in order to make it easier for her to 'translate' from external to internal 'code'. If she stores (and operates by) only 'experiences' and 'feelings of things' (in other words, her inner language is sensory-based), first we have to find out which sensory module (visual, auditory, olfactory or combination of them) she uses to get the information in and create 'words' for later reference.

The child's inner vocabulary can be visual/auditory/tactile/olfactory/gustatory images, or combinations of these. Whatever module the child uses, her inner language is concrete and literal.

Most autistic children seem to 'speak' either visual or auditory, or tactile or kinaesthetic, 'language'.

It is important to find out what language the child speaks. If we use one system (for instance, PECS) for all children in the classroom, for some it might work, for others it might not. For example, using pictures with an 'auditory' type of child won't help. It does not mean that you should 'speak several languages' but it does mean that you should know the peculiarities of each child's language in order to teach him a 'foreign' one. The aim is to teach them the language they can use to be understood everywhere and by everybody, and not only in structured settings and by very few people. (Just as, if you have a few foreign children in your class who have just arrived from, say, Japan or Lithuania, and do not know a word in English, you try to adjust your verbal behaviour to their understanding and introduce English words and structures very gradually.)

In this case, demonstrating whatever we want children to learn in real situations will be much better than verbal descriptions. If a child relies on kinaesthetic images, re-enactments, movements, mime and role play can make his interpretation of the descriptions much easier. These live demonstrations will save the child's efforts to make sense of what we want him to learn, and allow him more time and energy for doing other tasks. To conduct our lesson properly we have to remove all unnecessary information (so as not to confuse the child) and introduce new 'words' and 'phrases' very slowly (at the pace at which the child is able to cope). Gradually, more difficult concepts, such as past or future events, abstract concepts, etc. may be introduced by using external symbols (visual, auditory, olfactory – whatever the child's inner language is) to make it easier for the child to create and hold the images together.

Research has confirmed that, following the development of a system of communication, there is an increase in social awareness and a decrease in challenging behaviours.

While the child uses whichever communicative tool has been chosen, it may be useful for the adult to offer a commentary. Commenting on what the child is doing connects verbal expressions with whatever the child is experiencing. Verbal language is thus connected with the child's inner experiences.

If the right system has been chosen, there is a hope that a child will learn to code (label) her experiences and thus will be able to develop verbal cognitive structures.

Below we will discuss possible communication systems which can be used with autistic children.

Visual systems

Visual systems are very helpful for autistic visual thinkers both to understand and to express themselves. Visual communication systems can take various forms – objects, photographs, pictures, drawings. These visuals make it easier not only for autistic children to orient in the world around them but also to comprehend such concepts as time, sequence of events and abstract notions. For instance, a visual timetable is a way to show a sequence of activities in the classroom. It helps a child to see the predictability of forthcoming events and/or changes, and consequently helps the child cope with changes, reduce stress and increase independence.

Visual systems make the process of understanding and expression easier and, what is more important, help children communicate with *intention* (in contrast to just parroting words and phrases they can say which have no connection to what they want to say).

The decision of which visual system to use (objects, photos, pictures, written words or a combination of these) depends on the child's inner language and his level of understanding of a symbolic/verbal language.

Different types of pictures may be more or less meaningful for a child. One must experiment to see what works best. For example, some children find photographs easy to understand, others find them too literal, representing only the object that is on the photo and no other object. Children who react this way to photographs are more likely to be successful with drawings (Hogan 2001).

Whatever visual system is used, it is important to combine it with a written word, to develop the child's understanding of written language.

One must remember, however, that existing visual systems are limited and cannot allow the child to make complex sentences and express complex ideas, so they have to be combined with other communication means such as, for instance, written language or signing. Another limitation of visual systems is that the child must always carry them with him, and if access to them is difficult it may result in frustration.

What they say

'Compic' is a system of using picture diagram-cards to express needs, wants and interests. This makes sense but is limited when comes to complex requests and sentences so it has to be combined with other language aids… The other limitation I've seen with Compic is that non-autistic people involved in Compic communication generally don't use the same system themselves to convey what *they* mean. For some people like me, for whom the translation of blah-blah is very hard and tiring, something like Compic might have made me feel both better understood and less exhausted in keeping up as well as helped me use language with *intention* rather than just saying what I could instead of what I meant or wanted to say. It might have given me more energy to put into understanding things that I could process more easily. This would have made better sense than spending all my time mechanically plodding through the translation and retranslation of the same old words. That never built up my skills of understanding. Only cutting down on the causes and sources of information overload contributed to real development. In spite of its limitations, Compic system could be more successful with people who have trouble with fine motor skills than mime-signing. (Williams 1996, p.158)

To learn words like 'up' or 'down', the teacher should demonstrate them to the child. For example, take a toy aeroplane and say 'up' as you make airline take off from a desk. Some children will learn better if cards with the words 'up' and 'down' are attached to the toy aeroplane. The 'up' card is attached when the plane takes off. The 'down' card is attached when it lands. (Grandin 2001)

PECS

The *Picture Exchange Communication System* (PECS) was developed by Dr Andrew Bondy, a psychologist, and Lori Frost, a speech and language therapist in the Delaware Autistic Program, to help individuals with autism and other developmental disabilities acquire communicative skills (Bondy and Frost 1994). This system is based on principles of intentional communication and visual aids in the development of communication, worked out long before PECS was introduced. What PECS does is to introduce these principles as a package, to be used in a systematic and prescribed way. PECS has been proved very successful for those who either do not use (and/or understand) speech or are echolalic.

The fundamental principle of the system is to teach children communication (not just language) from the very beginning. The main techniques used to teach children to use PECS are:

- identifying reinforcers to motivate a child's communication (usually food, drinks or favourite activities)

- prompting

- shaping

- fading.

The advantages of PECS and its differences from other pictorial systems of communication are that:

- from the very beginning the interaction is intentional (children are taught to express their needs to adults who then meet those needs)

- it is the child who initiates the interaction

- communication is functional and meaningful.

As the main goal of this approach is to teach spontaneous communication, direct verbal prompts, such as 'What do you want? Show me what you want. What is it?', are avoided. From the very beginning children are taught such social and communicative skills as are needed to approach and interact with another person spontaneously.

Many traditional approaches start with teaching the child to label objects. The child responds only to prompts (either physical or verbal); for instance, the child is asked whether he wants something or is offered to sign or point to a picture. In this case the child is taught first picture discrimination, matching pictures, vocal imitations and mastering a pointing response while communication skills training has to wait. All these preparatory exercises take a lot of time and often are meaningless to the child. The child can learn to point to something he wants even if no one else is present to respond to his communicative attempt. Or the child can learn to answer questions such as 'What is this?' or respond to 'Point to…' 'Show me…' without any understanding of what it is all about.

There are several stages of introducing the PECS method, each stage building on the previous one. At the first stage a reinforcer (something the child likes) is put beyond the child's reach and a picture of it is placed in front of her. Two adults work with the child at this stage. One adult is behind the child waiting for her attempt to reach the reinforcer. Then he physically prompts the child to pick up the picture and give it to the other adult. The child immediately receives the reinforcer and a verbal comment from the adult ('Oh, you want…'). What is important is that the child is not asked what she wants and is not told to give the picture to the adult in order to receive the desired object. The child is taught to initiate interaction and this interaction is meaningful and functional for the child from the very beginning. Gradually the physical prompt is faded as the child gets the idea of the procedure.

At the second stage (often called the 'travelling' stage) the child is taught to move further to get the picture and find the communicative partner. Eventually more pictures are added, but only one is presented to the child at a time. This training takes place in different settings with different people to help the child generalize.

At the third stage the child is taught to select from two or more pictures in her communication book. The pace the child learns to make visual discriminations between symbols depends on the child's ability to match symbols. The authors (Bondy and Frost 1994) offer some useful strategies if the child experiences difficulty with discrimination of visual stimuli; for example, starting with two very different pictures (something the child likes and dislikes) or using cards of different sizes or colours to emphasize the difference between the two pictures.

As soon as the child has mastered the discrimination process, sentence structures are introduced to give her the opportunity to comment on something in addition to requesting something. During this 'building sentences' stage children are taught to make sentences on a detachable sentence strip. Such structures are introduced as 'I want' with a picture of the object they want. The child constructs a sentence and points to the pictures while the adult 'sounds' the sentence. The complexity of sentence structures grows with inclusion of attributes (colour, size, etc.), number, relative words indicating the position of objects in space, etc.

What is very important is that during these four stages it is the child who always initiates communication.

At the fifth stage the child is taught to answer the question 'What do you want?' by building the sentences she has practised at the previous stage. Only then the child is taught to label and comment on objects by answering such questions as 'What do you see?' 'What do you have?'

The research (Bondy and Frost 1994) has shown that of 66 previously non-verbal children under the age of five who were using PECS for more than one year, 44 learned to speak spontaneously and 14 developed some speech. Some children who didn't develop speech continued using PECS successfully.

As with any other approach in autism, PECS does not work for every child:

> At around the age of nine, I began to recognize pictures far more, although not line drawings because that's all they looked like – lines. I didn't interpret them and when I finally did it usually wasn't what they were trying to represent. The PECS symbol for play that involves two figures with hands throwing a ball between them was, to me, a spider… The picture for dinner looks like a face with a black eye. (Williams 2003a, p.64)

Communication via objects

Those children (both non-verbal and echolalic) who, for whatever reason, do not understand a spoken language, will benefit from being taught to communicate via objects – the closest substitute for their inner language.

For visualizers who do not understand symbols, pictures or signs, the closest to their native language would be a concrete, visible, spatial external language: a *language of objects*.

The advantage to this mode of communication is that it may cover several languages as it is not only a visual but also a tactile (when touched), kinaesthetic (when moved), auditory (when tapped) and olfactory (when smelt) mode. Children can learn the 'meaning' of objects through texture, colour, sound and smell.

However, it is important to recognize the risks of using objects for communication with an autistic individual. First, we have to remember that objects can be communicatively loaded (without our knowledge) for these children. They already speak this language. For instance, if a child is given a bag, he knows that it is time to go home. It is important to have the child understand the intentionality of communication via objects in order to prevent him from reading the messages around him (irrelevant to the situation) which we 'haven't written'. Thus, the child might get the wrong message from the 'written language of objects'. One such incident has been described by Peeters (2000): an autistic boy became very frustrated when he saw the folding chair in the corridor (and read that it meant they were going to the beach, but was taken to school instead). It took his mother some time to do a good detective job and understand the associations the boy had made and the reason for his frustration.

Thus, the language of objects can be oral (for immediate communication) and written (for reference). It is necessary to remember about the danger of written texts we have not meant to write: for these individuals they are always there. There also can be written instructions behind objects (of which we can be unaware of, but for a person they may be very 'loud'). For example:

> At home, the surroundings themselves dictated what to do. Mess told us to clean up. Papers told us to file them. Letters told us to answer them. The time told us which TV programs to watch, when to eat, bathe, dress and sleep. (Williams 1999a, p.172)

Sometimes, it may be an advantage, other times, a disadvantage for the child.

We should not assume that children with autism will understand the objects in the same way as non-autistics do. We should be aware of the different meanings objects may have for autistic children in contrast to our interpretation of them. Thus, we conceptualize the communicative value of objects according to the common stock of knowledge and experiences that we have *learnt* in our culture, whereas for them it is not the concepts but rather the sensations/experiences the objects elicit. For example, when we show someone a watch (or tap at the watch) the message is read as 'it is time to go'. If a child has no concept of time yet, for him it is the sound of tapping or the visual image of the watch or action that should be interpreted. It is our job to teach children how to 'translate' the message. If we want to speak the same language of objects, we have to teach them our meanings of objects.

Another danger of using the language of objects is the level of literalness the child has. Some children have very literal language: one thing has one word only. For instance, a child would know that a plate is a plate if it is the same plate from which she always eats. There is no such thing as 'a plate' (a concept of a plate) for her, but only 'the plate'. She cannot yet generalize objects. In this case we have to start to work with the same objects all the time, gradually introducing 'synonyms' for one and the same word (representations for objects); for example, small (toy) objects with the same communicative and semantic meaning as the real objects. If we talk about cars, we will use toy cars (not match boxes), toy spoons for spoons, etc. Once the language of objects has been successfully learnt we will introduce a more symbolic use of objects, gradually moving towards photographs, pictures, symbols.

Another thing to remember is that there are synonyms in the language of objects in autism which can be different to those in our understanding. If two things, no matter how different (for us) they are, elicit the same mental image for a child, these things will mean the same for him. For example, if two different things are made of the same material and visually or auditorily bring the same sensory image, a child might be confused which one is for what.

A note of caution should be sounded about the objects we use to represent activities (the symbolic use of objects). Peeters (2000) suggests using an 'object schedule' for classroom activities: a ball for free time, a box for work, a bag for going home, etc. There is a danger, however, of imposing a 'symbolic' meaning on a real object. If the child cannot understand that it is not an object but just a symbol for an activity (i.e., if he is still at a pre-symbolic level), then he will be very confused at learning that one can count balls, say, in his maths lesson or play with a ball at PE, because for him a ball means free time.

Peeters (2000) illustrates a child's failure to understand a task when he was given an activity to take balls from one box and put them in another one. The author describes it as a terrible mistake of the teacher since the ball had become the symbol for free time. I think instead that it was a terrible mistake to impose a 'foreign' meaning on a concrete object which was likely to bring more confusion into the child's understanding. If a child is able to comprehend the use of symbols (and this was the case – the same boy was given a card with his name or a card of certain colour to indicate that he had to consult his agenda) then it would have been more logical to introduce symbols (not concrete objects) for activities while using objects to teach children their properties and use (a ball may bounce, you can play with it, etc). Such a separation of symbols and objects also helps prevent children from reading unwritten object messages and, probably, decreases a number of tantrums that arise when a child misreads the message (folded chair for a beach, a bag for going home), as described by Peeters (2000).

Just as there are many verbal languages, so there are different 'object languages'. To share the language, we have to teach autistic children our understanding of objects. It is good to start with the 'receptive language of objects': to give them the functional meaning of objects (in contrast to sensory feelings/images) and then move to the expressive one, i.e., teach them to communicate using the 'object-words'.

To make it easier to teach children about the functional meanings of objects by reducing the informational overload, at the first stages you should communicate indirectly via objects *about* objects. Make the objects you are talking about your 'audience', with the child at the background.

The goal should be to move from concrete objects to more symbolic ones. This method of communication is more 'portable' than others, as participants may use any objects to represent other objects in whatever environment they happen to be in. Therefore, they don't have to carry around bags of 'words', as in PECS.

And another thing to remember. Not all the children lose the language of objects when they acquire a more symbolic language for communication. Some remain 'bilingual' (or sometimes 'multilingual') and can speak their native language and their second language depending on to whom they are speaking. It's wrong to consider the language of objects as a primitive mode of communication if we do not speak it. There are higher levels of this language that can communicate plenty of information for those who speak the same language. The following extract from Donna Williams's book *Somebody Somewhere* brilliantly illustrates the point:

> Night after night Olivier and I brought things for each other to experience. We were communicating, 'touching', and being moved through the medium of sharing objects. Olivier had collections of sequins and beads and spent hours and hours sewing them into intricate patterns. I left him flowers and he would talk to me through them. I did not need to explain to him that objects stood for or symbolized people. Olivier already used this system. (Williams 1999c, p.170)

What they say

In one study, aggression and outbursts were greatly reduced in very severely handicapped autistic adults by giving them an object to hold fifteen minutes before they were scheduled to have lunch or ride on a bus ... Touch was the only sense that was not confused by sensory jumbling, and holding the object let these people get mentally ready for the next event in their daily routine. (Grandin 1996a, p.150)

Most important, start with the demonstration of very simple things and single instruction, *not* multi-faceted things and complex instructions and demonstrate all things slowly and methodically without any unnecessary information (such as intonation, excessive facial expression or body language, praise or chit-chat)... It is also very important that talking via objects is free to be used as two way communication so that it is used not just for receptive language (what is going in) but for expressive language too (what is coming out)... Speaking through objects can get fluent speech going with an observable context to make it more successfully comprehensible. It can be good training to limit redundant speech and to give the person with 'autism' some idea of what knowledge is being shared by themselves and another person. It can also be good for people who have no speech or sign-language at all to express themselves in a complex way. Once speaking through objects has become a developed skill, it can gradually be used more and more symbolically so that a more flexible range of objects can be used to facilitate communication. (Williams 1996, pp.167–8)

Sign language – mime-signing – kinaesthetic 'language'

Although *sign language* was first developed as a means of communication for the deaf, it has been also used to teach people with developmental disabilities communication skills. However, it is necessary to distinguish between the natural sign languages used by the deaf community and the invented sign-based *codes* that are often used as teaching tools and that are not natural languages. Marmor and Petitto (1979) give the reasons why these sign-based codes cannot be considered as natural sign languages:

- they are artificially invented teaching devices that are not used spontaneously by any native deaf community anywhere in the world

- they are not passed down from generation to generation

- they do not delineate deaf cultural communities

- they are 'hybrids', amalgams of parts of spoken language structure and parts of sign-language structure that do not possess the full grammar of either of the two languages from which they were drawn.

With autistic and other developmentally disabled children Makaton sign language (=code) is usually used. Makaton consists of about 350 language concepts and is presented in nine developmental stages. Signs are accompanied by normal grammatical speech and natural facial expressions and body language. As autistic children are usually not good at imitation, a hand-over-hand approach to learning signs is recommended.

Sign language may be introduced either as an augmentative system to facilitate the development of speech for those who understand verbal language but have problems with expression (for instance, echolalia) or as an alternative system for communication for those whose receptive language is good but whose expressive language is absent (mutism).

The advantages of sign language for autistic children are as follows:

- Signing is both a visual and a kinaesthetic system of communication. This means it can be helpful for those who learn about the world through visual or kinaesthetic systems. A child understands the meaning of words through movements of his hands and his whole body.

- Signs can be taught through physical prompts and shaping that is beneficial for children with executive function problems (but not with tactile hypersensitivity!).

- Sign language is very 'portable' and does not need any equipment, communication books or objects.

- Sign language is a linguistic system and may stimulate acquisition of a verbal language.

The disadvantage of sign language is that it is not understood by many people.

The method of teaching autistic children sign language is the same as the one to teach any form of communication. Sign language (like spoken language) should be used slowly (to give children enough time to process it) and without any unnecessary information (to prevent overload and distraction of attention). However, it should be used simultaneously with speech to become a bridge to a spoken language.

One should remember, however, that autistic people tend to process any language literally, sign language included. That is why we need to modify the sign language for the use with autistic individuals, to avoid misunderstanding of sign words and phrases. For example, signing the squeezing of cow teats to ask for milk seems pointless to Donna Williams, as for her, with only a literal level of processing, this would be more likely to be interpreted as: 'Do you want to see a cow milked?' After all, one does not see cow teats when milk is being poured into a cup (Williams 1996).

Sign language is not successful with all autistic individuals. Research (Bonvilian and Nelson 1978) has shown that, in a study sample, although none of the nearly 70 (autistic) subjects failed to acquire at least one sign, the final outcome, in terms of each individual's linguistic performance, appeared to vary widely. Some of the children, after acquiring facility in sign language, learned to use spoken English. For those who progressed in speech as well as sign, the progress in sign language appeared crucial as a foundation for the changes in speech skills. On the other hand, a number of children never learned to use more than a handful of signs and remained mute (Bonvillian and Nelson 1978).

Sign language may be difficult for those who do not understand verbal language and are poor visualizers whose inner images are based on kinaesthesia. Signs for these children should be modified to closer match these inner images (miming).

Many autistic individuals, even without having been taught, use *mime signs* (they are not always conventional signs). Some autistic individuals (with *kinaesthetic language*) use signs as a supportive means for translating verbal words (both receptive and expressive), as they often make better sense of what has been said through the movements. Thus, when they listen or speak, they might aid their understanding and expression by using physical or mental signs in order to make better connections. For autistic children with kinaesthetic inner language, verbal language can be taught through action songs and rhymes. When used as one simple single action per word, mimes can make linear sentences.

Another advantage of using mime is that it is much more easily understood by non-autistic people, so it can be used in a wider variety of environments than conventional sign language (Williams 1996).

Kinaesthetic language helps the child to make connections between spoken words and body reactions; it is a sort of 'body mapping' (Williams 1996). If the child 'speaks kinaesthetic', label the mime with the word, so that the child can connect the experience of the movement with its verbal label. If you teach a child the word 'jump', make him jump; if you teach him the word 'run', make him run, etc. If you give the child the directions or instructions, help him to translate them into the body language; for instance, you say 'go to the left', then turn him to the left; or you say 'pick up your things and put them on the chair', then let him imitate the actions. Helping children to 'map their body' could make many tasks easier for them.

Talk to your child about what you are doing. Encourage her to imitate (to 'translate into kinaesthetic'). If the child has problems with imitation, help her to form the movement. Some autistic children were taught to draw and to write by someone holding their hands and guiding them to draw shapes, figures, letters.

Some autistic adults use these strategies to understand what they are told better. Paradoxically, we often interpret these attempts at translation as bizarre autistic behaviours and prevent them from learning (of course, with the best intentions – 'Stop fidgeting, stand still and listen to what I am telling you').

What they say about mime-signing

I personally prefer mime to using spoken language alone. It is less physically exhausting for me and I feel better connected to drawing my words through my hands than connecting to something so far removed and abstract as a collection of throat and lung exercises that are called speech. I have basically little trust of speech. I always keep checking to see whether I'm being understood. I can't actually SEE how other people can interpret the meaning of these sounds. With sign, I can see they have seen my meaning and I trust that more and can keep better track of my own expression. I also find the physical connections easier, quicker and more concise ... I know that the signing I use is more concrete than symbolic and quicker to process for meaning than more symbolic signing and that even if the signing vocabulary for the deaf is much wider than it can be with concrete mime-signing, mime-signing has an advantage over things like picture pointing because it is more transportable, widely understood and can, like sign language for the deaf, be used to form simple sentences and to hold a simple conversation. (Williams 1996, pp.157–8)

'Tactile language'

If visual, auditory and kinaesthetic systems do not work for a child, *tactile language* could be tried. For some children (those with severe sensory-perceptual problems and who are usually non-verbal) touch is often the most reliable sense. They often find it easier to recognize objects through 'feel'. In this case a tactile system should be favoured. Children can be taught to read by giving them plastic or wooden letters to feel. They can learn about many activities by feeling objects involved in these activities. To make their life more predictable, you may give them some objects to feel in advance to prepare them for future events; for example, a spoon or a plate before a meal, a towel before bath time, etc.

If you teach the child the names of some objects, give him these objects to feel (or smell, or tap to produce a sound). Use his language to translate the meaning of the word.

Even those with dominant visual or auditory systems often benefit from having tactile messages introduced during stressful or unfamiliar situations. Many parents intuitively use this method. While going for a trip they give their child something she likes (a toy, a piece of cloth). It gives the child the feeling of home, security and reliability.

What they say

Even though the sense of touch is often compromised by excessive sensitivity, it can sometimes provide the most reliable information about the environment for people with autism. (Grandin 1996a, p.65)

What we can do to help

Whatever language the child 'speaks', comment on what your child is doing, feeling, seeing, hearing. It will help the child to connect the word with his internal image, to 'wrap up' the sensory-based word into a 'verbal envelope'.

Written communication

'And the moral of that is – "Be what you would seem to be" – or if you'd like to put more simply – "Never imagine yourself not to be otherwise than what it might appear to others that what you were or might have been was not otherwise than what you had been would have appeared to them to be otherwise".'

'I think I should understand that better,' Alice said very politely, 'if I had it written down: but I can't follow it as you say it.' (Lewis Carroll, *Alice in Wonderland*, p.66)

A study of an epileptic patient who had undergone a commissurotomy – a procedure that severs all connections between the two hemispheres (Strauss 1998) has shown that speech and writing 'can reside in different hemispheres', suggesting that written and spoken language can develop independently of one another.

Sometimes teaching individuals with autism to read and write can bring a real breakthrough in communicating with them. Many autistic individuals find their voices in their writings.

Written communication (handwritten or typed) is indirect and that is why it can reduce information-processing overload. Making the connection between feelings and expression is easier through written than spoken language:

> With typing one doesn't have to take in a simultaneous sense of self and other, so the three channels of self, other, and topic become two channels: self and topic. Furthermore, the visual overload of keeping visual contact with a moving face and body in front of you is gone, leaving you far more processing time for retrieval. It also takes far less energy to waggle your fingers out in front of you than to connect to ever changing patterns in your mouth with the feedback bombarding back at you in your ears… (Williams 2003a, p.80)

> I write fast with neat, tiny letters, or I type to communicate. This way, I can reach into my depths, and my silent words are much more expressive than a weirdly-echoing voice could be. (O'Neill 2000)

However, a warning should be made. Quite often the main strategy used to teach autistic children to write is to make them copy written words and texts. The activity becomes really meaningless as in this case they copy not texts but meaningless patterns; it is sort of 'written echolalia':

> When I copied, somehow my meaningful language switched off, and my typing became equivalent of my nonsense speech. My finger movements changed to a frantic swooping that looked to an observer as if I were typing competently. However, the person touching me would note a complete self-absorption, and I did not notice if the original were nonsensical. It became a pattern of shapes in my mind's eye. The letters went from sight to hand, as if I had never learned to read. (Blackman 2001, p.141)

Facilitated communication

> My beginning to learn and express myself is a turning point in my life. (Mukhopadhyay 2000, p.17)

Facilitated communication (FC) is a type of augmentative and alternative communication for people who do not speak or whose speech is highly limited and disordered and who cannot point reliably (Biklen 1990; Crossley 1992). This method of communication is not new. It was discovered independently in several countries: Sweden, Canada, Denmark, Australia and the USA.

The FC technique has become widely known thanks to the work of Rosemary Crossley in Australia and Douglas Biklen in the USA. Rosemary Crossley, educator and founder of the DEAL Communication Centre in Melbourne, Australia, formulated the main principles of facilitation in communication. She believes that for many people with communication/ language impairments the problem of communication is not so much a cognitive or receptive one as a difficulty with expression. These ideas are illustrated and explained in the book (Crossley and McDonald 1980) about the use of FC with Anne McDonald, a woman with cerebral palsy and (diagnosed) intellectual disability. Anne had been institutionalized since the age of three. She was literally speechless and seemed uncommunicative until the age of 16 when Crossley started working with her, using FC. For Anne, it was a real breakthrough that allowed her to express herself and make decisions about her life. For Crossley, it was a discovery of a new method that could give a chance for many speechless individuals to make their voices heard.

In 1990, Douglas Biklen, Professor of Special Education at Syracuse University, introduced FC in the USA. Since then, FC has been used with people with Down syndrome, cerebral palsy, autism and other developmental disabilities.

FC is a very controversial method that has brought a huge amount of both positive and negative responses in the field of autism. Here we will consider this method very briefly; more detailed discussions of the pros and cons can be read elsewhere (see, for example, Biklen 1990, advocating FC, and Jacobson, Mulick and Schwartz 1995, criticizing it). I will try not to take sides but rather provide the reader with the main arguments from both camps and some quotations from those who have experienced it, i.e. those autistic individuals who can type *independently* and whose 'authorship' cannot be questioned.

The main arguments of proponents of FC

The theoretical foundation of FC is based on the following assumptions:

- There are people who cannot communicate because of their apraxia or developmental dyspraxia: they experience problems with initiating and stopping action (perseveration), modulating the pace of action, impulsiveness, an inability to speak or automatic echolalic speech, articulation and prosody (pitch, volume, rhythm) (see, for example, Biklen 1990; Crossley and Remington-Gurney 1992). Other problems may be poor hand–eye coordination, low or high muscle tone, tremor, proprioception problems and difficulty extending the index finger.

- Many people with autism and other developmental disabilities have literacy skills without other people knowing they can read or spell. They just have no way to demonstrate them.

What they say

The reading tests I had previously been given had relied on speaking words or small groups of words, or on card matching. Now I had the opportunity to glance quickly at a paragraph. Then, still tracking my hand against the light grip of my teacher [facilitator], I would point at one of several sentences randomly listed below to indicate which of them most accurately reflected what I understood to be the gist of the whole passage. Whereas slowly working word-by-word confused me and robbed me of the meaning, in this method I could not only show the other people in the room that I could read, but I could also prove it to myself for the first time. Because I had learnt by observation with no feedback, I was not sure until now that I was really literate in the sense of continuous reading of texts. (Blackman 2001, p.87)

According to the proponents of FC, FC overcomes dyspraxic difficulties through physical and emotional support where a facilitator helps a person with communication disabilities to point at pictures, symbols or letters in order to let them communicate. The physical support may include:

- assistance in isolating the index finger

- stabilizing the arm to overcome tremor

- backward resistance on the arm and pulling it back to overcome impulsiveness and prevent the person from striking the same key repetitively

- a touch of the arm or shoulder to help the person to initiate
  pointing/typing.

The amount of physical support provided in FC is different for different
people: it may be support of the hand, wrist or elbow, or just a touch on the
shoulder. Emotional support gives the person encouragement and confidence
in his abilities to communicate.

The FC proponents emphasize that FC is not a cure from a disability but a
means of communicating, and its long-term goal is independent typing.

Although successful stories of people who have got the chance to
communicate through FC have been documented and some of them have
achieved complete independence in typing, there has been and still is a lot of
controversy about FC.

The main arguments of the critics of FC

One of the main arguments of the critics of FC is that there is no evidence
that all individuals with autism have motor problems (Allen 1992). However,
there is increasing evidence that autistic individuals do experience motor
problems (Prizant 1996), especially those with proprioceptive and vestibular
difficulties.

What they say

Coming back to my learning to write, I shall say that it would be a lie, if I said
that it came to me in a day. I did not know how to imitate. Although I did
recognise the basic figures like squares and triangles and numbers and
alphabet, I could not draw them even if they were meant to be copied out from
somewhere. I needed to learn how to imitate… At first she [mother] held my
hands and made me run the pencil… At first it looked as if the pencil was
pushing my hand which was being pushed by mother… Slowly I began to
understand what the pencil was doing. I started to help the pencil as it trav-
elled around the square and circles and rectangles and star shapes with which
mother had filled the page. (Mukhopadhyay 2000, p.21)

The main questions asked by the critics of FC

WHAT IS IT ABOUT THE ACT OF HOLDING SOMEONE'S HAND THAT UNLOCKS PREVIOUSLY UNDEMONSTRATED LITERACY AND COGNITIVE SKILLS? WHY WOULD THE INDIVIDUAL NEED TO BE TOUCHED TO PRODUCE TYPED OUTPUT? WHAT IS NECESSARY TO MAKE IT WORK?

'There is no support in the research literature for the need to touch a person with autism in order for skill acquisition or maintenance to occur' (Smith and Belcher 1993, p.177).

What they say

In stabilising my hand Rosie [facilitator] had given me another gift. My hand and my mind were connected… The steady touch on my own hand and forearm somehow made me bring it into focus, and at the same time feeling the point of contact gave me an accurate measurement as to the distance between my fingertip and my sensation of that touch… I…registered in my own mind that it was easier to see and track my own finger movements when my arm was held. I was also more aware of exactly what point in time my finger was likely to touch the key of the computer. Here was part of the solution to why touch and typing had gone together. (Blackman 2001, pp.83, 277)

WHY IS THERE A NEED TO PROVIDE EMOTIONAL SUPPORT TO THE INDIVIDUAL WITHOUT WHICH THE INDIVIDUAL IS INCAPABLE OF LITERATE OUTPUT?

'There has been no demonstrated need of ongoing emotional support in the form of touch for individuals with autism to maintain other skills' (Smith and Belcher 1993, p.177).

What they say

Also I was reacting better because I was trying to live up to those people's perception that I was an intelligent person. (Blackman 2001, p.114)

WHY IS THE PERSON ABLE TO COMMUNICATE FLUENTLY WITH ONE FACILITATOR WHILE WITH ANOTHER FACILITATOR THE SAME PERSON PRODUCES GIBBERISH? WHY IS IT NECESSARY FOR A FACILITATOR TO BELIEVE THAT THE INDIVIDUAL IS LITERATE FOR THE INDIVIDUAL TO ACT LITERATE?

The literature demonstrates that individuals with autism may achieve substantial gains through the implementation of a variety of educational, vocational and behavioural procedures without reference to the beliefs or attitudes of trainers (Smith *et al.* 1994).

What they say

I see now that people who worked with me successfully were those who developed a real skill in monitoring and controlling their own interactions. This allowed me to get excited enough by their interest to create some kind of language, without giving me any cues to act as I thought the other person expected me to. (Blackman 2001, p.97)

★ ★ ★

It is interesting that the same might be true for an autistic child who has just started speaking – the child reacts only to somebody he knows and ignores any attempt at conversation from 'strangers':

> *Alex was sitting in the living room when a visitor came to talk to his mother.*
>> *Visitor: 'Hello, Alex. How are you today?'*
>> *Alex did not seem to hear the question, when his mother 'intervened': 'Alex, how are you today?'*
>> *Alex reacted immediately, though he used a learned phrase: 'Fine. Thank you.'*
>> *The whole 'conversation' went on via Alex's mother who, instead of 'interpreting', just repeated the questions. It seemed to make the whole difference.*

WHY DO INDIVIDUALS WITH AUTISM FAIL TO GIVE CORRECT ANSWERS TO SIMPLE, VERIFIABLE QUESTIONS, IN CONTRAST TO HIGHER LEVEL, OPEN-ENDED, NON-VERIFIABLE COMMUNICATIONS?

There is no evidence that individuals with autism resent the intrusion or the testing, or that they have a need to displease the facilitator under testing conditions. It has been demonstrated that individuals with autism have been motivated in many cases by the use of social praise alone (Smith 1990).

What they say

Some have progressed to independent typing, but this is a long hard battle with their own Exposure Anxiety in daring the eventual ownership of this ability to communicate. Others, perhaps because they have been watched, manoeuvred, been the object of too much external hope or need, forced to prove ownership of their communication, or gave up or failed to progress from fully-supported typed communication. Perhaps the understanding of the mechanics of Exposure Anxiety and the need to attribute expression to the control or volition of something non-self, will help to change this state of things for non-verbal people with the potential to communicate through other media. (Williams 2003a, p.129)

WHY DOES FC APPEAR TO WORK?

Some individuals with autism have literacy skills (Smith and Belcher 1993). However, these individuals can write and type unassisted. It is possible that some individuals who are being facilitated in fact could type without touch, but the facilitation procedure is given credit for what could be done independently.

What they say

In a world of proof, those who merely demonstrate insight in an indirectly-confrontational way, to the directly-confrontational observer, are not considered to have it. Those who use typed communication are perhaps some of the best examples here. If able to attribute responsibility for their communication to the assistance of someone else, some functionally 'non-verbal' people can communicate. In fact what drew such criticism to this technique [FC] was that some such people had, in spite of their social-emotional retardation being mistaken for mental retardation, not only picked up how the written word corresponds to concepts, but sometimes expressed profound and moving observations and experiences. Often their typed communications were cast aside either because it was considered impossible that they indicated a normal intelligence or because the person's own surprise at what emerged through typing gave the impression that the communication was done without any real selfawareness. (Williams 2003a, pp.140–1)

★　　★　　★

The main argument used to 'ban' FC is that there have been several cases of autistic children accusing their relatives or staff via FC of physical or sexual abuse. Although the majority of cases of abuse have been ruled as false, some have been proved true. (Unfortunately, we do know about abuse of disabled people that occur without 'official notice'.)

What they say

It is important to point out the role of stereotypes in contributing to some of the problems confronting facilitation. The residue of assumptions by facilitators that 'autistic people do not joke' or 'autistic people do not understand lies' can have its effect on the validity of what comes out in FC. Where an autistic person has written something as a private joke or for its shock value, to test a reaction or even in response to a perceived expectation to have experienced something, some facilitators may take these communications to be facts and truths and act upon them with unfortunate consequences. This is not to say that people with 'autism' lie or joke or attempt to shock or manipulate or meet expectations any more than any non-'autistic' person does. What it means is that many people with 'autism' are capable of these things as non-'autistic' people are and that even if they don't express them verbally or through their actions, they may do so in their thoughts (if only subconsciously) and this, in the case of FC, just might come out on paper. (Williams 1996, p.58)

Conclusion of the FC debate

The conclusion made by the critics of FC may be summarized by the following statement:

> Controlled research using single and double blind procedures in laboratory and natural settings with a range of clinical populations with which FC is used have determined that, not only are the people with disabilities unable to respond accurately to label or describe stimuli unseen by their assistants, but that the responses are controlled by the assistants. (Jacobson *et al.* 1995, p.750)

There arises a very important question: What about those who have learned to communicate via FC and can now type independently? Shall we consider them 'not truly autistic'? Or just ignore their evidence as they are 'in a minority'?

How would we describe, for example, Lucy Blackman, an Australian autistic woman, who has 'found her voice' via FC and whose success was witnessed by Tony Attwood? (Surely Tony Attwood, PhD, a recognized expert in the field of autism, would have detected a 'fraud'?) Having met Lucy and having read her book (2001), Tony Attwood encourages professionals to learn from Lucy's experiences and 'her response to specific programs and how to adapt strategies to other children and adults with a similar expression of autism' (Attwood 2001, p.vii).

What would we say about people like Sharisa Kochmeister who has both cerebral palsy and autism and does not speak? Once, when she could not express herself because of her 'dispraxic inertia', people believed she was 'hopelessly retarded'. When Sharisa started to type, she needed her hand held and index finger supported. Over time, she moved to wrist support, elbow support, a hand on her shoulder, and just having someone's hand 'shadowing' hers. All these helped her to overcome her inertia. Now she types independently.

Dr Bernard Rimland (1993), although he believes that FC may work for some individuals with autism, gives a warning that the percentage may not be as high as we would hope. He might be right. As we know that each person is unique in his/her sensory-perceptual, cognitive and communication profile, what works for one does not work for another. This is quite common in autism: some treatments (for instance, the Irlen method or Auditory Integration Training) are beneficial for some children while having no effect on or even harming others. The issue must be about finding a communication system that works for each particular individual, and not 'banning' one particular method because it does not work for all.

FC may be useful, for example, for those with impulse-control problems or for those with intense exposure anxiety for whom typing is far less directly confrontational (Williams 1996).

Even if it does not work for all (and it will not), it is important to recognize that FC does give a 'voice' to a group of autistic (functionally non-verbal) people who otherwise might never get a chance to be heard:

> I have found so much strength from being able to communicate my thoughts and feelings to people via typing. In fact, being able to communicate has changed my life. Although as you most probably realize communicating via typing is a form of indirect communication, when I communicate via typing I know I can respond. I can ask questions, I can relate my feelings and just in fact be myself with no pressure to speak. (Attfield 1998, p.2)

Chapter 14

Teaching Communication

I was sent by my teacher to fetch a tube of glue from another class, which was full. I walked in, asked for, and received the object. 'Kevin, what's the magic word?' I was asked upon receiving it... I replied straight-faced 'Abracadabra'. (Phillips 2002)

There are many different approaches to addressing the communication problems experienced by autistic people. Here we will briefly discuss the most widely used ones.

A social skills approach

Aarons and Gittens (2000) suggest an eclectic approach to developing social skills, which takes into account the different needs of autistic children with severe learning difficulties and those who are cognitively able. They assume that while a behavioural approach should be useful for the former group, more able and verbal autistic children and adults will benefit from a *social skills approach*. The overall aim of a social skills programme is to teach basic strategies for social communication, not merely as rote-learned responses, but as meaningful interactions which require reflection and help autistic individuals to interpret 'non-autistic culture'. The authors emphasize the importance of understanding 'the culture of autism' and appreciating the efforts autistic individuals have to make in order to be accepted in society. A social skills programme takes into account the underlying cognitive deficits in autism, such as the Triad of Impairments, lack of Theory of Mind and weak central coherence. All social skills programmes should be developmentally based and start as soon as possible. The aims of these programmes for pre-school children include developing attention control, awareness of other children in the group and the social use of language. Older children are taught to consider other people's needs and different social behaviours through discussing different topics, sharing their experiences, role playing and having their awareness raised of alternative ways of coping with everyday situations. Providing a set of social rules is not sufficient unless understanding of what these rules mean is also developed. Aaron and Gittens (2000) state that it is possible to effect real changes and improvements in autistic children with good cognitive abilities because they have the capacity to acquire through learning the social skills other people absorb naturally.

Drama, role play and social skills groups are useful for developing the art of conversation (turn-taking, topic maintenance, language pragmatics).

Social stories

The *social stories approach* was developed by Carol Gray (1994) and has been proven successful in enabling autistic children to understand the cues and actions for specific situations (Attwood 1998). Social stories are written for each child in response to her particular needs, to describe social situations which she finds difficult. Each story begins with the information as to where the chosen situation occurs and describes who is involved and what happens. Gray (1994) suggests using three types of sentences for the stories: descriptive, perspective and directive, with a ratio of between two and five descriptive and perspective sentences to every one directive sentence in each story. The vocabulary and grammatical structure of sentences are adapted to a child's age and ability.

Another useful technique introduced by Carol Gray is *comic strip conversations*. A comic strip conversation is a drawing representing an interaction between two or more people. These drawings illustrate an ongoing communication, identifying what people say, do and think in certain situations. Autistic children (whose preferred mode is visual) find it easier to follow the conversation and understand intentions and feelings of others when the 'communication' is visually displayed.

Rules

Another approach that has been found beneficial is introducing *rules of behaviours* in different situations. Autistic individuals will find following the rules very useful as the rules will help them 'act normally' in situations they might not fully understand. Some autistic individuals, in the absence of conventional rules may create their own and demand others to adhere to them:

> I have rules for everything. If there are no rules specified, for example: only cross a road at a crossing, then I invent my own rules. I do this so that I have guidelines enabling me to navigate my way through the process of daily living. (Lawson 1999, p.3)

> I live a rule-based life and, I have a rule system I still use today.

> *Really Bad Things* – Examples: murder, arson, stealing, destroying property, injuring or hitting other people…

> *Courtesy Rules* – Examples: not cutting in on a line at the movie theatre or airports, table manners, saying thank you, and keeping oneself clean. These things are important because they make other people around you more comfortable. I don't like it when somebody else has sloppy table manners, so I try to have decent table manners. It annoys me when other people cut in front of me in a line, so I don't do this to other people.

> *Illegal But Not Bad* – Examples: slight speeding on the highway and illegal parking…

> *Sins of the System (SOS)* – Examples: smoking pot and being thrown in jail for ten years and sexual misbehaviour. (Grandin 1999a, p.6)

What they say

It was only three years ago…that I learnt the rule that people are allowed to change their minds! This new rule really helped me to cope with the fickleness of human nature. It also gave me an escape route for times when things happened, usually things beyond my control that meant I had to change my plans. For years and years I lived with guilt and extreme anxiety just because things changed all the time. One of the best tools that we can equip our youngsters with is that of teaching them strategies to cope with change. One of those being that it is OK if things don't go exactly to plan. (Lawson 1999, p.5)

Since people with autism and Asperger's are emotionally immature, they must have basic morality pounded into their heads when they are small children… Some Asperger's children and adults have done some bad deeds because the basic rules were not taught to them. (Grandin 1999a, p.6)

This [learning rules] can be a good mechanical way to get around not transferring information properly from one situation to the next. There is no point telling people 'silly girl' or 'you'll get hurt'. Things like that don't tell you what to do or what not to do. Things like 'don't ask people how old they are' or 'no playing on the stairs' are good because the cues of seeing signs of age and the urge to comment on it can fire the replay of the rule, 'don't ask people how old they are'. Being on the stairs and starting to mess about can trigger the replay of 'no playing on the stairs'. These work like 'have tos' and they usually work for me in stopping me from doing a lot of things that might have caused me some trouble. It wasn't that I'd learned about these things, it was that I'd stored rules about these things and I paid attention not so much to the content of these stored rules, but to the 'not' command within them.

Behaviour modification isn't usually about teaching rules, it is about making people take account of consequences. This teaching of consequences usually didn't work so well for me because part of my information processing problems involved the transfer of lessons learnt to new situations. This was why, in spite of constantly being sworn at and physically abused for my unintentional but compulsively addictive and manic repetitive door-bell ringing, I never seemed to get the message. If I'd simply been firmly ordered, 'no ringing', the cue of approaching the doorbell might have triggered the rule, 'no ringing' and I might have knocked instead.

...I have seen so many professionals training people out of useful 'have tos' that are causing no harm, just because they don't look 'sensical' or 'normal'. Some of these 'have tos' have led to me putting other people's dishes away, picking up laundry in other people's houses, turning lights off in other people's houses ('no wasting electricity'). (Williams 1996, pp.175–7)

Other approaches

Traditional approaches to teaching autistic children to speak focus on eye contact, imitation of sounds, pointing and signing. These methods are very slow and often meaningless to the child as they do not lead to functional communication:

> Speech therapy was just a lot of meaningless drills in repeating mean-ingless sounds for incomprehensive reasons. I had no idea that this could be a way to exchange meaning with other minds. (Sinclair 1992, p.296)

Lovaas method / Applied Behaviour Analysis (ABA) / behaviour modification therapy

To teach language to autistic children, Lovaas (1966) employed a *behaviour modification* procedure based on reinforcement learning theory and shaping techniques to develop a 'program for the establishment of speech in psychotic children' (Lovaas 1966). The methods of this programme include discrete-trial training, incidental teaching, the natural language paradigm, and time delay. The Lovaas approach (also known as Applied Behaviour Analysis or ABA) is very well documented (both favourably and unfavourably). Here we just briefly describe the methods used.

- *A discrete trial* is a traditional language-training method. It consists of four parts and is conducted in a structured sit-down session.

- *Incidental teaching* (also called natural language teaching) is teaching the language in natural environments, using naturally occurring interactions.

- *Time delay* procedure involves the trainer presenting a target stimulus (for example, a ball) to the child and prompting the appropriate response – 'I want a ball'. Once the child can imitate the trainer's phrase, the delay between the presentation of the stimulus and the prompt is gradually increased until the child requests the item spontaneously.

Other important techniques in ABA are reinforcing (rewarding) the target behaviours and stopping the unwanted behaviours. The target behaviour (for instance, speech) is broken down into many simple steps which are eventually 'chained' together to form a desired response.

The first three drills children have to learn on a Lovaas programme are 'come here', 'sit down' and 'look at me' (Watkins 2001), i.e. directly confrontational approach.

As with any other method, the ABA approach works with some children (those who do not experience severe sensory problems, for example), while may be damaging for others (especially those with severe anxiety).

What they say

Almost half of all very young children with autism respond well to gently intrusive programs in which they are constantly encouraged to look at the teacher and interact ... The popular Lovaas program is being used success-fully...to mainstream...young autistic children into a normal kindergarten or first grade ... While this program is wonderful for some kids, it is certain to be confusing and possibly painful for children with severe jumbling and mixing problems. (Grandin 1996a, pp.53–4)

Now consider the force-feeding praise as part of the educational system ... How many people...have played down or lost their abilities because the praise itself feels like a gut-wrenching imposition or because the constant reinforced awareness it triggers feeds Exposure Anxiety responses until the demonstration of anything which could lead to being joined, applauded or celebrated becomes taboo? Yet Applied Behavioural Analysis (Behavioural Modification Approach) is said, by its supporters, to 'work' with fifty per cent of people with autism. Compliance is co-opted by Exposure Anxiety and this is not the same as *self*-expression. What if what works is merely the sense of pattern and structure, rather than the invasion of praise – yet we attribute success, perhaps to our later detriment, to the misassumption that praise works?...

If someone with Exposure Anxiety is playing down or losing skills after six months of ABA and directly-confrontational praise or 'reward', then the environment should listen. Six months of damage is not too much to undo and some children without severe Exposure Anxiety respond well to conventional Behaviour Modification approaches such as ABA. (Williams 2003a, pp.111, 118)

The Options Approach. Floor-time

Both the *Options Approach* and the *Floor-time Approach*, though differing somewhat in their underlying philosophies, emphasize early intensive inter-vention, and establishing interaction with a child by 'entering the child's world' (imitating the child's activities and following his lead) in order to grad-ually introduce the child to 'our world'. There exists extensive literature describing these methods (see, for example, Greenspan, Wieder and Simons 1998; Kaufman 1976).

What they say

The Option Technique works almost in antithesis to conventional behaviour modification techniques. Yet I see it as almost equally problematic... The

Option Approach involves, while being very non-intrusive toward the child, mirroring the child's movements, interests, sounds in order to 'break into the child's own world' and bring the child 'into theirs'... Some children...with autism don't have very high Exposure Anxiety and their main problem is information-processing problems or impulse control. They may very much intend their own actions. [However, for others, with Exposure Anxiety, these actions] are not voluntary, they are compulsions and most often self-defensive ones... When the environment assumes that these are expressions and mirrors them back, trying to join someone through what they didn't intend in the first place, the most likely result is a confused social dialogue... The person with Exposure Anxiety can develop a heightened alienation and a sense that the environment doesn't understand. (Williams 2003a, pp.292–3).

The Miller Method

The main assumptions of the *Miller Method* (see www.millermethod.org and Cook 1998) are:

- Children learn far more effectively when their entire bodies are actively involved in the process. They learn by pushing, pulling, lifting and carrying things, climbing on elevated structures that focus their attention. Teachers, meantime, narrate and sign what the children are doing so they become more conscious of themselves and how words and signs relate to their actions.

- Disruptive behaviours are worked upon to transform them into functional behaviours.

- Sign and spoken language and their related objects or events are presented and taught simultaneously. Following such simultaneous presentations, children may begin to respond to spoken words without requiring a sign or an object.

The Symbol Accentuation Reading Program (a part of the Miller Method) is designed for children who are unable to find meaning in the conventional forms of printed words. The programme introduces sequences that show a picture morphing into a printed word in a way that provides a transition from pictures which look like their objects to printed words that do not.

What they say

A visualized-reading method developed by Miller and Miller (1971) would also have been helpful. To learn verbs, each word has letters drawn to look like the action. For example, 'fall' would have letters falling over, and 'run' would have letters that look like runners. This method needs to be further developed for learning speech sounds. Learning the sounds would have been much easier if I had a picture of a choo-choo train for 'ch' and a cat for hard 'c' sound. For long and short vowels, long 'a' could be represented by a picture of somebody praying. This card could be used for both 'pr' and long 'a' by having a circle around 'pr' on one card and the 'a' on another. (Grandin undated)

Computer-assisted teaching

Nowadays computers are often used effectively in educational settings with autistic children.

The advantages of using computers to teach language and communication skills include:

- The computer may be used as a tool for communication for those autistic individuals who find written language easier to understand and produce than spoken language.

- Teaching via a computer is a sort of indirectly confrontational approach that may be useful with those for whom directly confrontational styles of teaching lead to challenging behaviours and/or withdrawal.

- A computer can be used to increase problem-solving demands in a controlled way, where each step is explored and learnt before the next one is added (Jordan 1995).

However, contrary to popular belief, not *all* autistic individuals are interested in computers. Some people with severe visual distortions and hypersensitivities can cope only with short sessions in front of the screen because they can see flicker on TV-type computer monitors. They can sometimes see better on laptops and flat panel displays that have less flicker (Grandin 2001). The majority, on the other hand, find communicating via computers liberating and use it as a bridge to reach other autistic individuals on the Web, in order to share ideas and find support. In recent years, websites have emerged both by and for autistic individuals and their carers that have given voices to hundreds of autistic persons who used to be silent for so long.

What they say

Computers do not present with social demands. They don't require you to smile at them or listen to their opinion. They do not offer distracting stimuli to invade your concentration and interrupt your thinking!... As an aid to education, leisure activities and communication with others, the computer is an asset that should not be overlooked. Being given the opportunity to use a computer as a tool for everyday life, both at home and at school, can mean the difference between feeling able to succeed and failure... Giving us appropriate forms of communication and a medium to express ourselves through, can aid healthy development and instil confidence along the rocky outcrops of life's stormy road. (Lawson 2001, pp.165, 166)

Computers! Autistics love computers. They can tap in to learn about things they're interested in, and can even create their own programmes and contact other autistic people through the Internet. (O'Neill 1999, p.113)

As for the best intervention (therapy) for teaching communication to autistic people, one should remember there are no two autistic persons who are completely alike. What is good for one person can be harmful or of no use for the other. The right intervention for each person should be based on her strengths and abilities.

Teaching 'accessories' of communication

Eye contact

In Chapter 3 we discussed one of the perceptual styles which is quite common in autism – avoidance of direct perception (peripheral perception). For many people with autism, eye contact does not come naturally. It often brings overload and stress. This is true for those who experience visual hypersensitivity, fragmentation and distortion. It is these people who have acquired the strategy to 'work in mono', using one channel at a time. No matter how unusual it may seem to non-autistics, not looking the interlocutor in the eye does not mean an autistic person is not listening. Quite the contrary:

I can concentrate better not having to keep eye contact at the same time. I tell people, 'You have a choice. Do you want a conversation or do you want eye contact?' You will not get both unless I am comfortable with you and I do not have to concentrate so much on eye contact. (Bovee undated)

What they say

Eye contact is something that I have always had trouble with... All of the stress that is put on doing it makes me more nervous, tense, and scared. Doing it also assumes that I can read the messages in another person's eyes. Don't count on it! I can look at person's eyes and not be able to tell what he or she is saying to me. (Bovee undated)

I did not know that eye movements had meaning until I read *Mind Blindness* by Simon Baron-Cohen. I had no idea that people communicate feelings with their eyes. I also did not know that people get all kinds of little emotional signals which transmit feelings. (Grandin 1999b)

Teaching eye contact should be very gradual, never forced. When an autistic person becomes comfortable with you, he will glance at you from time to time, and eventually will learn to keep his eyes on your face. Autistic children have to learn how and why to give eye contact.

Gestures

Gestures can be described as a referential form of communication. The first gesture to develop is reaching, then showing, giving, and the last, pointing. Gestures can be classified into deictic gestures and representative gestures. Deictic gestures are used to gain something, have something moved, call somebody's attention to something in order to share the interest. Representational gestures too serve to call somebody's attention to something of shared interest and also carry some extra meaning, for instance, waving bye-bye. The development of both types of gestures is an important indicator of communication development.

Autistic children are reported to lack the use of many conventional gestures, such as waving, showing, pointing, nodding the head and other symbolic gestures (Stone and Caro-Martinez 1990; Wetherby, Prizant and

Hutchinson 1998). Important gestures for developing joint attention such as pointing are not used spontaneously by children with autism and need formal teaching. Instead, they use a primitive contact gesture (hand-leading) when they take an adult by the hand and throw the hand in the direction of the desired object (instrumental use). Although this gesture is communicative, it is atypical and functionally very limited.

Emotions, facial expressions, body language

It has been estimated that 90 per cent of emotions are communicated via facial expressions, tone of voice and body language, and only 10 per cent via words. Bearing in mind sensory-perceptual differences and lack of shared experiences, we may distinguish the problems autistic people experience with both recognition and expression of emotions.

It has been noticed (Ricks and Wing 1975) that in their facial expressions, autistic children tend to show only the extremes of emotion, often in ways that are inappropriate for their age and the social situation:

> Some of my non-verbal social clues I consciously produce. Though I may grin widely, or shriek impulsively, for various stimuli, with far less conscious control than most people, and giggle uncontrollably when I am amused, I am often expressionless. Most of my social signals are honest but artificial – I give friendly smiles only to be friendly or show affection, but I may over-do it, do it at the wrong time, or may forget to smile when I should... Add to this fact that I often have to pause to process when responding to a statement or question, makes me look like an 'idiot' or 'lunatic' to many people. (Blackburn 1999, p.6)

Understanding emotional expressions in others is another difficulty in autism:

> I had such difficulties in even remotely understanding what other people meant when their faces curved, wrinkled up and smoothed out, or when their bodies turned away, let alone all the other social signals. (Blackman 2001, p.24)

> Sometimes I'm not aware of social cues because of the same perceptual problems that affect my understanding of other aspects of environment. My visual processing problems are no more the result of indifference that blindness is – are blind people considered insensitive if they fail to recognize people or to respond to others' facial expressions? Sometimes I notice the cues but I don't know what they mean. I have to develop a separate translation code for every person I meet – does it

indicate an uncooperative attitude if someone doesn't understand information conveyed in a foreign language? (Sinclair 1992, p.300)

Because of the perceptual problems many autistic children (with visual-
perceptual problems and who are monoprocessing) find facial expressions
and body language meaningless, overwhelming or even threatening. If they
have auditory perceptual difficulties, they find it difficult to interpret the tone
of the voice as 'emotionally coloured'. Instead of intuitively 'extracting' the
emotional load from non-verbal communication, even adults with high-functioning autism struggle to cope with extra information they cannot interpret:

> Emotive body language and intonation may not only be visually and
> auditory distracting, superfluous and overloading but may also provoke
> emotional responses that someone may be unable to process or cope
> with. (Williams 1996, p.117)

Another difficulty we encounter is that, as autistic people have problems with
abstract concepts, they can have problems with the *meaning* of emotional
words. (How could you describe in sensory language the meaning of 'fear',
'anger', 'love', 'kindness'?) One of the solutions to teaching these concepts
seems to be metaphors (Gibbs 1994; Lakoff 1987; Lakoff and Johnson
1980). For example, Lakoff and Johnson (1980) suggest that the abstract
concept of 'anger' can be represented by 'liquid exploding from a container'.
Some autistic people use this strategy. For instance, for one autistic adult
'kindness' was represented by his grandfather patting the dog.

It is important to remember that the difficulty to understand and express
emotions does not mean that autistic people lack emotions! They do have
emotions but, first, they often cannot 'label' and understand them and,
second, they do not know how (and why) to translate their experiences to
other people. They have to learn explicitly to recognize, name and understand
the meaning of emotions and what to do about them. It is important to teach
that emotions can have particular facial and bodily expressions and to explain
what they are (Lawson 1998):

> And through all this condenscending concern about feelings and
> emotional issues, no one ever bothered to explain to me what the words
> meant! No one ever told me that they expected to *see* feelings on my
> face, or that it confused them when I used words without showing cor-
> responding expressions. No one explained what the signals were or
> how to use them. They simply assumed that if *they* could not *see* my
> feelings, *I* could not *feel* them. I think this shows a serious lack of
> perspective-taking! (Sinclair 1992, p.298)

Do not expect someone with autism automatically to recognize from your facial expression or body language what you are feeling. Instead, it might be helpful to explain what you are feeling, how your body feels when you have this feeling, what signs and clues on your face and body could tell you are feeling this way (Rand undated). It means some autistic people can be formally taught to read facial expressions and body language in a rote, mechanical way. They can be taught to recognize simple and individual signs of anger, boredom or sexual harassment (Williams 1996). However, they will still make mistakes from time to time, because there are several 'readings' of tears, for example, that can bring misperception of the emotion that inspires them.

What they say

Even with verbal autistics, it can be hard to communicate feelings effectively. Feeling the deep emotion in a private inside place is quite different from finding an explanation for it that other people will comprehend... They often also don't feel the same emotions during a particular event that someone else feels... They may laugh at a certain sound or amuse themselves by repeating an action. They have an inner part that isn't seen by outsiders. It's like a private joke that you keep hearing in your head, and it makes you giggle to yourself. Using recorded, stored sensory bits in the brain, you can relive instances vividly, be they positive or negative. (O'Neill 1999, pp.35, 36)

I think that these problems [difficulty in understanding one's own emotions] require overt explanations of emotion-related terms and the overt naming of expressions (factually and unemotionally...so as not to detract from the lesson in definition) and their related inner sensations. If someone is unable to tolerate directly-confrontational interaction, a carer could make a brief, concise, home-made video that explains some of these things simply and in a logical way that takes account of the 'autistic' person's ability.

There is also a game which involves drawing one's hand over one's face to produce a different facial expression each time and naming them. Although this only explains the outward appearance of certain emotion-caricatures, and does not explain their connection to inner sensations or what one can socially do about feelings, this may be better than nothing for some people. This may help to work out the contrasts between different facial expressions, some of their theoretical labels and how to express and comprehend very basic emotion-related facial expressions in others. Later, however, one could help such a person to link and name some of the INNER sensations that go with some of these facial expressions or even draw up charts or diagrams or lists, showing different things that appear to cause these sorts of feelings and expressions in the person with 'autism' (being careful not to impose an assumed non-autistic emotional reality upon this person). (Williams 1996, p.289)

When someone says something vague like 'You're not paying attention to my feeling', I feel inadequate, and I am also frustrated because I don't know what to do about it... If instead the person says, 'These are some signals I use to express my feelings, and this is what they mean, and this is how I'd like you to respond when you notice them', this gives me information I can use to improve my understanding and responsiveness. (Sinclair 1989)

Use of interpersonal space

Autistic children use their interpersonal space differently from other people; they may get too close to strangers or they may prefer greater distance between themselves and people they interact with.

Autistic children with sensory distortions and hypersensitivities (whether they are visual, auditory, tactile or olfactory) often find it too threatening, even painful, if they are approached by others, especially if the approach is unexpected and direct. They should always feel in control of their environment in order to feel safe:

> Occasionally I lost all sense of perspective. Something would seem monstrously large if coming towards me at speed, or if I was unprepared. Someone suddenly leaning over me could frighten me enormously. I felt something was falling onto me and that I'd be crushed underneath it. (Gerland 1997, p.12)

If they want to approach somebody, people with autism usually do it indirectly to avoid overload. Thus, they may circle or pace around someone. It is important not to threaten them by sudden movements or direct confrontation. It is better to sit side by side with an autistic child than to face him directly.

It is necessary to teach them when certain physical contact is appropriate:

> I found it very hard to understand that certain physical contact was appropriate and some was not. It was also hard to understand the concept of 'personal space'. I always wanted my cuddles, irrespective of how the other person was feeling! I can only ask for understanding in this matter. (Lawson 1998, p.113)

To teach or not to teach?

As we recognize that autistic people have different cognitive mechanisms, it means that they probably will never be able to understand communication as we do. For autistic people social skills is another academic class, a foreign language that they have to study, research and observe (Willey 1999).

> I took the social life as seriously as I took my [university] course but unfortunately, I found that the social chemistry was quite a lot harder [than] the study of biomolecular forces when applied to enzyme kinetics. (Segar undated, p.8)

Some researchers consider it pointless to remediate communication difficulties experienced by autistic individuals and suggest to teach them compensatory skills instead, while others insist on teaching understanding (whether it is achievable or not).

Individuals with high-functioning autism and those with Asperger syndrome develop strategies they use to hide their inability to understand social situations, for example:

> If I couldn't hear with meaning, I could always comment on the things around me or create my own topic. If I couldn't make social chit-chat, I could always talk shop, flick through books, act busy, and appear super-conscientious. I could focus on picking out key words and play word association games with them in a way that passed for agreement and conversation. If I didn't understand someone's behaviour or feelings, I could hide my anxiety at being confused and lost, express nothing, and appear calm and unaffected. If I read a story and had no idea what it was about, I could assume an air of authority and secrecy and meet every question with another question, deflect everything... There were many things I couldn't combat but I had a bag full of strategies that made me look good trying. (Williams 1999c, pp.67–8)

> Over time, I have built up a tremendous library of memories of my past experiences, TV movies, and newspapers to spare me social embarrassments caused by my autism; and I use these to guide the decision process in a totally logical way. I have learned from experience that certain behaviors make people mad. Earlier in my life, my logical decisions were often wrong because they were based on insufficient data. Today they are much better, because my memory contains more information. Using my visualization ability, I observe myself from a distance. I call this my little scientist in the corner, as if I'm a little bird watching my own behavior from up high. (Grandin 1999b)

So, the question is: to teach or not to teach understanding of communication itself?

Pros

1. Although it seems immoral to 'train' people to act 'normal', especially when it is only on the surface without much inner understanding, it nevertheless can bring about their acceptance in society. We live in a real world where, unfortunately, many people are unaware of differences of autistic people, and any bizarre behaviours may cause cruel comments, or worse, insistence on the isolation (even locking up) of the person exhibiting these behaviours.

    > In my experience, being socially accepted in some way (whether I could efficiently process the experience, meaning or significance of that social acceptance consciously and *in context* or not) still meant that I was exposed to a greater range of information than I otherwise might have been and, even if I couldn't process this information at the time, I could still accumulate it for eventual pre-conscious or subconscious processing. The knowledge arising from that processing could then sometimes later, albeit haphazardly, be triggered or cued. (Williams 1996, p.102)

2. Being exposed to 'mainstream life' gives autistic children the opportunity to learn (even by rote) and get at least theoretical information about the way the majority of people experience life:

    > Being in mainstream schools meant that I accumulated lots of information about how people moved and spoke and what they liked or wanted or thought and how they responded to certain things. I accumulated information about people seeming like other people in certain ways when they said or did things in the same way someone else had. (Williams 1996, p.102)

3. Being unable to control themselves may be helped by introducing 'external control'. Quite a few people with autism express gratitude to their parents and teachers who have never made excuses for autism and have taught autistic children to function in the 'real world' while providing adjustments and compensatory strategies to help them cope with their difficulties:

> Probably the most important and biggest reason, why I have done as well as I have done, is that no excuses whatsoever were made for autism. Making excuses for autism is so futile, so damaging and above all, so wasteful of learning opportunities... If I am to exist and get along in the real world, I will have to learn and obey the ways and conventions of the real world, whether I understand them or not. This may seem rather harsh and unfair on the person with autism but reality is harsh and quite often unfair. Surely it is even more unfair if parents, teachers, support workers, etc. do not prepare the person with autism for reality, but shelter them from it. (Blackburn 2000, pp.3–4)

Cons

There are risks to pushing children with autism too hard, when the constant stress of 'autism-unfriendly' situations may lead to nervous breakdowns. Besides, it is important to let them not only 'appear' but also 'be' what they are. It is vital that they have their individuality and identity unaltered during the process and are allowed to remain autistic.

And another important thing to remember. The process of socialization should not be one way. The other side – non-autistic people – should make an effort to understand, accept and *respect* the differences.

Now we can answer the question put in the title of this section 'To teach or not to teach?'

The answer is: 'To teach and to learn'. Only then could we bring communication between two different 'cultures' into harmony.

Conclusion

One day I dream that we can grow in a matured society where
nobody would be 'normal or abnormal' but just human beings,
accepting any other human being – ready to grow together.
(Mukhopadhyay 1999)

Given all the differences in perception and thinking styles in autism, it is very
difficult for autistic people to respond to the world as we (non-autistics)
expect them to. We can teach them to see the world our way and monitor their
behaviour accordingly. It will take time and effort to help them learn things
they have no equipment to learn spontaneously and intuitively. They can be
taught to perform if they are given the right cues and triggers. But. (There is a
very important 'but'.) To make the process easier for them (and for us), we
have to begin to learn to see and understand things from their perspective
(even if it seems very unconventional – we often call it 'idiosyncratic'). We
have to use all our imagination to place ourselves in their shoes. Only then we
can make the process of acculturalization easier and mutually beneficial. It
should be a two-way process. If we are ready to grow together, we can bring
our two cultures, our two worlds into harmony.

   This book is to help professionals and parents understand autistic
perspective and communication systems autistic individuals use. It gives some
clues where to look and what to do.

   We have to respect autistic culture. We have to adapt to them as they have
to adapt to us. We have to learn their ways to perceive, interpret, communicate
as they learn our ways. We could live together if only we accept our
differences. This world is still autism-unfriendly, no matter how much we talk
about the support of autistic people. All this talk is empty because we often use

empty words that bring a lot of misunderstanding in our communication with autistic people.

And one more thing. Why do we always think that it is us who have to teach autistic people? If we want to 'grow together', we have to learn from them.

What they say

The role of professionals should be to help people use their natural processes to learn and grow. This might mean helping people develop strategies for dealing with sensory oversensitivities… It might mean teaching self-monitoring and self-management of behavior and emotions. Probably it always means learning and teaching translation skills to enable people with different communication systems to communicate with each other. (Sinclair 1998)

Glossary

Agnosia – the loss of the ability to interpret sensations.

Ambidextrous – able to use the right and left hands equally well.

Aphasia – partial or total loss of speech; loss of ability to understand or produce speech as a result of damage to the brain.

Attention Deficit Hyperactivity Disorder (ADHD) – a disorder of attentional mechanisms which is reflected in the three major categories of symptoms: inattention, hyperactivity and impairments in social, academic and occupational functioning.

Cognition – knowing, perceiving or conceiving as an act or faculty distinct from emotion and volition; mental operations such as thinking, conceiving, reasoning, symbolizing, problem-solving, imagery, belief, intention, etc.

Communication – transmission and reception of information.

Concept – a general notion; an abstract idea; an idea or mental picture of a group or class of objects formed by combining all their aspects.

Culture – a particular form or type of intellectual development comprising patterns of learnt behaviour, shared knowledge and beliefs that are integrated in accordance with some learnt dominant value systems.

Delayed echolalia – repetition of words and phrases heard in the past.

Dyspraxia – a condition in which voluntary but not reflexive control of muscles is impaired.

Echolalia – a parrot-like repetition of another person's spoken words.

Generalization – (forming of) general notion or proposition obtained by induction.

Gestalt perception – (here) inability to filter background and foreground information; perception (at the level of sensation) of the whole scene as a single entity with all the details perceived simultaneously.

Gustation – the sense of taste; faculty of perceiving the sensation of a soluble substance caused in the mouth and throat through contact with that substance.

Hearing – the faculty of perceiving sounds.

Imagination – mental faculty for forming images of external objects not present to the senses; creative faculty of the mind.

Immediate echolalia – repetition of words and phrases just heard.

Kinaesthesia – the brain's awareness of the position and movement of the body, limbs, etc. by means of sensory nerves in the muscles and joints.

Language – a system of symbols (words) and methods (rules) of combining these symbols used by a section or group of people (as a nation, community, etc.); a structured symbolic form of communication.

Literal perception – the first stage of perception when sensation is experienced without interpretation and meaning being attached to it.

Meme – a cultural or behavioural element passed on by imitation or other non-genetic means.

Memory – the faculty by which things are recalled to or kept in the mind.

Metaphor – the application of a name or descriptive term or phrase to an object or action to which it is imaginatively but not literally applicable.

Mitigated echolalia – speech consisted of learnt phrases of various lengths which are manipulated so that they result in new utterances.

Monotropism – the ability to focus on one aspect at a time, or processing information in one modality only.

Morpheme – a meaningful morphological unit of a language that cannot be further divided, for example *come*, *-ing*, forming *coming*.

Morphology – the system of forms in a language.

Mutism – an inability to talk.

Neologism – a made-up word not belonging to any conventional vocabulary, but not meaningless.

Olfaction – the sense of smell; faculty of perceiving odours or scents.

Onomatopoeia – formation of names or words from sounds resembling those associated with the object or action to be named, or seemingly naturally suggestive of its qualities, for example *cuckoo, rustle*.

Percept – a mental concept resulting from perceiving.

Perception – the ability of the mind to refer sensory information to an external object as its cause; the process by which an organism collects, interprets and comprehends information.

Phoneme – any of the units of sound in a specified language that distinguish one word from another, for example *p, b, d, t* in the English words *pad, bad, pat, bat*.

Phonology – a rule-governed speech sound system.

Pidgin – a simplified language containing vocabulary from two or more languages, used for communication between people who do not have a common language.

Pragmatics – an individual's choice and use of language; rules of conversation that enable the person to use language in ways that are appropriate to the social context.

Proprioception – faculty of perceiving stimuli produced within an organism, especially relating to the position and movement of the body; body awareness.

Semantics – the actual meaning of the words used.

Sensation – the consciousness of perceiving or seeming to perceive some state or condition of one's body or its parts or of the senses; an instance of such consciousness.

Sign language – a linguistic system of communication through visual gestures.

Speech – vocal production of words; faculty or art of speaking.

Synonym – a word or phrase that means exactly or nearly the same as another in the same language, for example *shut* and *close*.

Syntax – grammatical arrangement of words showing their connection and relation.

Tactility – faculty of perceiving touch, pressure, pain, temperature.

Tourette syndrome – a developmental disorder characterized by motor and verbal tics, beginning in early childhood, often accompanied by obsessive-compulsive behaviours.

Transformational grammar – a grammar that describes a language by means of transformation.

Vestibular system – structures within the inner ear that detect movement and changes in the position of the head.

Vision – the faculty of seeing.

References

Aarons, M. and Gittens, T. (2000) 'Autism – a social skills approach. Speech and language therapy for able children.' *Communication*, Spring, 18–19.

Aitchison, J. (1976) *The Articulate Mammal*. New York: McGraw-Hill.

Allen, D. (1992) 'CSAAC interview.' *Community News: The Newsletter of Community Services for Autistic Adults and Children, Inc.*, VI, 1–4.

Allen, D.A. and Rapin, I. (1993) 'Autistic children are also dysphasic.' In H. Naruse and E.M. Ornitz (eds) *Neurobiology of Autism*. Burlington, MA: Elsevier Science Publishers.

APA (1994) *Diagnostic and Statistical Manual of Mental Disorders, Fourth Edition.* (DSM-IV) Washington, DC: American Psychiatric Association.

Attfield, R. (1998) 'My half of the tide.' *Facilitated Communication Digest*, 6, 2, March, 2.

Attwood, T. (1998) *Asperger's Syndrome: A Guide for Parents and Professionals*. London: Jessica Kingsley Publishers.

Attwood, T. (2001) 'Foreword', *Lucy's Story*. London: Jessica Kingsley Publishers.

Banich, M.T. (1997) *Neuropsychology: The Neural Bases of Mental Function*. Boston, MA: Houghton-Mifflin.

Baron-Cohen, S. (1993) 'Are children with autism acultural?' *Behavioral and Brain Sciences*, 16, 512–13.

Baron-Cohen, S. (1998) 'Autism and "theory of mind": An introduction and review.' *Communication*, Summer, 9–12.

Baron-Cohen, S., Leslie, A.M. and Frith, U. (1985) 'Does the child with autism have a theory of mind: A case specific developmental delay?' *Cognition*, 21, 37–46.

Bartolucci, G., Pierce, S.J., Streiner, D. and Eppel, P.T. (1976) 'Phonological investigation of verbal autistic and mentally retarded subjects.' *Journal of Autism and Childhood Schizophrenia*, 6, 303–16.

Bates, E. (1976) *Language and Context: The Acquisition of Pragmatics*. New York: Academic Press.

Bates, E. (1979) *The Emergence of Symbols: Cognition and Communication in Infancy*. New York: Academic Press.

Bates, E., Benigni, T., Bretherton, I., Camaioni, L. and Voltera, V. (eds) (1979) *The Emergence of Symbols: Cognition and Communication in Infancy*. New York: Academic Press.

Bates, E. and Dick, F. (2000) 'Beyond phrenology: Brain and language in the next millennium.' *Brain and Language*, 71, 18–21.

Bates, E. and Goodman, J. (1997) 'On the inseparability of grammar and the lexicon.' *Language and Cognitive Processes*, 12, 507–86.

Battison, R. (1978) *Lexical Borrowing in American Sign Language*. Silver Spring, MD: Linstok Press.

Benson, D.F. and Zaidel, E. (1985) *The Dual Brain: Hemispheric Specialization in Humans*. New York: The Guilford Press.

Berlin, B. and Kay, P. (1969) *Basic Color Terms: Their Universality and Evolution*. Berkeley, CA: University of California Press.

Bickerton, D. (1981) *Roots of Language*. Ann Arbor, MI: Karoma Publishers.

Biklen, D. (1990) 'Communication unbound: Autism and praxis.' *Harvard Educational Review*, 60, 291–314.

Bion, W.R. (1963) *Elements of Psycho-Analysis*. London: Heinemann.

Bjorklund, D.F. (1997) 'The role of immaturity in human development.' *Psychological Bulletin*, 122, 2, 153–69.

Blackburn, J. (1999) *My Inside View of Autism*. www.planetc.com/urers/blackjar/aisub (Site no longer active.)

Blackburn, R. (2000) 'Within and without autism.' *Good Autism Practice*, 1, 1, 2–8.

Blackman, L. (2001) *Lucy's Story: Autism and Other Adventures*. London: Jessica Kingsley Publishers.

Bloom, L., Hood, L. and Lightbown, P. (1974) 'Imitation in language development: If, when and why.' *Cognitive Psychology*, 6, 380–420.

Bloom, L. and Lahey, M. (1978) *Language Development and Language Disorders*. New York: John Wiley.

Bogdashina, O. (2003) *Sensory Perceptual Issues in Autism and Asperger Syndrome: Different Sensory Experiences – Different Perceptual Worlds*. London: Jessica Kingsley Publishers.

Bondy, A. and Frost, L. (1994) 'The picture exchange communication system.' *Focus on Autistic Behavior*, 9, 1–19.

Bonvillian, J.D. and Nelson, K.E. (1978) 'Development of sign language in autistic children and other language-handicapped individuals.' In P. Siple (ed.) *Understanding Language Through Sign Language Research*. New York: Academic Press.

Bornstein, M.H. (1987) 'Perceptual categories in vision and audition.' In S. Harnad (ed.) *Categorical Perception: The Groundwork of Cognition*. New York: Cambridge University Press.

Bosch, G. (1970) *Infantile Autism*. (Translated by D. Jordan and I. Jordan). New York: Springer-Verlag.

Boucher, J. (1976) 'Is autism primarily a language disorder?' *British Journal of Disorders of Communication*, 11, 135–43.

Bovee, J.P. (undated) 'My experiences with autism and how it relates to Theory of Mind.' Geneva Centre for Autism publication. www.autism.net/infoparent

Brooks, T. (1999) *Star Wars. Episode 1: The Phantom Menance.* London: Century Random House.

Brown, R. (1958) *Words and Things.* Glencoe, IL: Free Press.

Brown, R. and Hanlon, C. (1970) 'Derivational complexity and order of acquisition in child speech.' In J.R. Hayes (ed.) *Cognition and the Development of Language.* New York: John Wiley.

Bryson, S. (1996) 'Brief report: Epidemiology of autism.' *Journal of Autism and Developmental Disorders, 26,* 165–7.

Bucci, W. (1997) 'Symptoms and symbols: A multiple code theory of somatization.' *Psychoanalytic Inquiry, 2,* 151–72.

Burack, J.A. and Enns, J.T. (eds) (1997) *Attention, Development, and Psychopathology.* New York: The Guilford Press.

Burt, C.L. (1955) 'The evidence for the concept of intelligence.' *British Journal of Educational Psychology, 25,* 158–77.

Carr, E.G. and Durand, V.M. (1985) 'The social-communicative basis of severe behavior problems in children.' In S. Reiss and R. Bootzin (eds) *Theoretical Issues in Behavior Therapy.* New York: Academy Press.

Carroll, L. (1964) *Alice in Wonderland.* London: Andrew Dakers Limited.

Carruthers, P. (1996) *Language, Thought and Consciousness: An Essay in Philosophical Psychology.* Cambridge: Cambridge University Press.

Carter, R. (1998) *Mapping the Mind.* London: Weidenfeld and Nicolson.

Charles, M. (1999) 'Patterns: Unconscious shaping of self and experience', *J. M. Klein and Object Relations, 17,* 367–88.

Charles, M. (2001) 'A "confusion of tongues": Difficulties in conceptualizing development in psychoanalytic theories.' *Human Nature Review,* 28 March, www.human-nature.com/ksej/charles.htm

Chomsky, N. (1957) *Syntactic Structures.* The Hague: Mouton Publishers.

Christie, A. (2000) *The Mysterious Affair at Styles.* London: Planet Three Publishing.

Churchill, D. (1972) 'The relation of infantile autism and early childhood schizophrenia to developmental language disorders of childhood.' *Journal of Autism and Childhood Schizophrenia, 2,* 182–97.

Code, C. (1987) *Language, Aphasia, and the Right Hemisphere.* New York: John Wiley & Sons.

Condon, W. and Sander, L. (1974) 'Neonate movement is synchronized with adult speech.' *Science,* 183, 99–101.

Cook, C.E. (1998) 'The Miller Method: A case study illustrating use of the approach with children with autism in an interdisciplinary setting.' *Journal of Developmental and Learning Disorders 2,* 2, 231–64.

Courchesne, E., Townsend, J., Akshoomoff, N.A., Saitoh, O., Yeung-Courchesne, R., Lincoln, A.J., James, H.E., Haas, R.H., Schreibman, L. and Lau, L. (1994) 'Impairment in shifting attention in autistic and cerebellar patients.' *Behavioral Neuroscience*, 108, 848–65.

Craig, J. and Baron-Cohen, S. (1999) 'Creativity and imagination in autism and Asperger syndrome.' *Journal of Autism and Developmental Disorders*, 29, 4, 319–26.

Crary, M.A. (1993) *Developmental Motor Speech Disorders*. San Diego, CA: Singular Publishing Group.

Crossley, R. (1992) 'Getting the words out: Case studies in facilitated communication training.' *Topics in Language Disorders*, 12, 4, 46–59.

Crossley, R. and McDonald, A. (1980) *Annie's Coming Out*. Middlesex: Penguin Books.

Crossley, R. and Remington-Gurney, J. (1992) 'Getting the words out: Facilitated communication training.' *Topics in Language Disorders*, 12, 4, 29–45.

Curcio, F. (1978) 'Sensorimotor functioning and communication in mute autistic children.' *Journal of Autism and Childhood Schizophrenia*, 8, 3, 281–92.

Dale, P. (1976) *Language Development: Structure and Function*. Hinsdale, IL: The Dryden Press.

Damasio, A.R. and Damasio, H. (1992) 'Brain and language.' *Scientific American*, 267, 88–109.

Dawson, G., Finley, C., Phillips, S. and Galpert, L. (1986) 'Hemispheric specialization and the language abilities of autistic children.' *Child Development*, 57, 1440–53.

DeCasper, A.J. and Fifer, W.P. (1980) 'Of human bonding: Newborns prefer their mother's voices.' *Science*, 208, 1174–6.

Dekker, M. (undated) 'On our terms: Emerging autistic culture.' Autism99 Internet Conference Papers. www.autism99.org

Demetras, M.J., Post, K.N. and Snow, C.E. (1986) 'Feedback to first language learners: The role of repetitions and clarification questions.' *Journal of Child Language*, 13, 275–92.

DePaolo, S. (1995) 'The ups and downs of silence.' *The Advocate*, May–June, 9.

DeVilliers, J.G. and DeVilliers, P.A. (1978) *Language Acquisition*. Cambridge, MA: Harvard University Press.

Doman, R. Jr. (1987) 'Learning disabilities.' *Journal of the National Academy for Child Development*, 7, 1, 4–6.

Donald, M. (1991) *Origins of the Modern Mind: Three Stages in the Evolution of Culture and Cognition*. Cambridge, MA: Harvard University Press.

Dore, J. (1974) 'A pragmatic description of early language development.' *Journal of Psycholinguistic Research*, 3, 343–50.

Duchan, J. (1984) 'Clinical interactions with autistic children: The role of theory.' *Topics in Language Disorders*, 4, 62–71.

Eimas, P.D., Miller, J.L. and Jusczyk, P.W. (1987) 'On infant speech perception and the acquisition of language.' In S. Harnad (ed.) *Categorical Perception.* New York: Cambridge University Press.

Elman, J., Bates, E.A., Johnson, M., Karmiloff-Smith, A., Parisi, D. and Plunkett, K. (1997) *Rethinking Innateness: A Connectionist Perspective on Development.* Cambridge, MA: MIT Press.

Eriksen, C.W. and Yeh, Y. (1985) 'Allocation of attention in visual field.' *Journal of Experimental Psychology,* 11, 583–97.

Farah, M.J. (1989) 'The neural basis of mental imagery.' *Trends in Neuroscience,* 12, 395–9.

Fay, W. and Schuler, A. (1980) *Emerging Language in Children with Autism.* Baltimore MD: University Park Press.

Flege, J.E. (1981) 'The phonologic basis of foreign accent: A hypothesis.' *TESOL Quarterly,* 15, 4, 443–55.

Fodor, J. (1975) *The Language of Thought.* Cambridge, MA: Harvard University Press.

Frith, U. (1989) *Autism: Explaining the Enigma.* Oxford: Basil Blackwell.

Frith, U. (2003) Questions for Dr Uta Frith, Discussion, 25 November, www.autismconnect.org

Furrow, D. (1984) 'Young children's use of prosody.' *Journal of Child Language,* 3, 203–13.

Gardner, H. (1983) *Frames of Mind: The Theory of Multiple Intelligences.* New York: Basic Books.

Garfinkel, H. (1967) *Studies in Ethnomethodology.* Englewood, NJ: Prentice Hall.

Garner, I. and Hamilton, D. (2001) 'Evidence for central coherence: Children with autism do experience visual illusions.' In J. Richer and S. Coates (eds) *Autism: The Search for Coherence.* London: Jessica Kingsley Publishers.

Gerland, G. (1997) *A Real Person – Life on the Outside.* (Translated from the Swedish by J. Tate.) London: Souvenir Press.

Gerland, G. (1998) 'Now is the time! Autism and psychoanalysis.' *Code of Good Practice on Prevention of Violence against Persons with Autism.* Brussels: Autism-Europe publication.

Gibbs, R.W. Jr. (1994) *The Poetics of Mind: Figurative Thought, Language, and Understanding.* New York: Cambridge University Press.

Gibson, E.J. (1969) *Principles of Perceptual Learning and Perceptual Development.* New York: Appleton Century Croft.

Grandin, T. (1988) 'Teaching tips from a recovered autistic.' *Focus on Autistic Behavior,* 3, 1, 1–8.

Grandin, T. (1996a) *Thinking in Pictures and Other Reports from My Life with Autism.* New York: Vintage Books.

Grandin, T. (1996b) 'My experiences with visual thinking, sensory problems and communication difficulties.' Centre for the Study of Autism. www.autism.org/temple/visual.html

Grandin, T. (1998) 'Consciousness in animals and people with autism.' www.grandin.com

Grandin, T. (1999a) 'Genius may be an abnormality: Educating students with Asperger's Syndrome or high functioning autism.' Autism99 Internet Conference Papers. www.autism99.org

Grandin, T. (1999b) 'Social problems: Understanding emotions and developing talents.' www.autism.org/temple/social.html

Grandin, T. (2000) 'My mind is a web browser: How people with autism think.' *Cerebrum*, 2, 1, Winter, 14–22.

Grandin, T. (2001) 'Teaching tips for children and adults with autism.' Centre for the Study of Autism. www.autism.org/temple/tips.html

Grandin, T. (2002) 'My experiences with visual thinking, sensory problems and communication difficulties (Part 2).' *Link*, 34, 6–10.

Grandin, T. (undated) 'Deficits and Abilities.' www.autismtoday.com/articles/An_Inside_View_of_Autism.html

Grant, K. (2000) 'My five senses.' *The Autism Society of America Colorado Chapter Newsletter*, 3, 10–11.

Gray, C. (1994) *The New Social Story Book*. Arlington, TX: Future Horizons.

Greenspan, S., Wieder, S. and Simons, R. (1998) *The Child with Special Needs: Encouraging Intellectual and Emotional Growth*. New York: Perseus Publishing.

Hall, E.T. (1989) 'Deaf culture, tacit culture and ethnic relations.' *Sign Language Studies*, 65, 291–303.

Halliday, M. (1975) *Learning How to Mean: Exploration in the Development of Language*. London: Edward Arnold.

Happé, F.G.E. (1994) *Autism: An Introduction to Psychological Theory*. London: UCL Press.

Happé, F.G.E. (1997) 'Central coherence and theory of mind in autism: Reading homographs in context.' *British Journal of Developmental Psychology*, 15, 1–12.

Harding, C. (1984) 'Acting with intention: A framework for examining the development of the intention to communicate.' In L. Feagans, C. Garvey and R. Golinkoff (eds) *The Origins and Growth of Communication*. Norwood, NJ: Ablex.

Hawthorne, D. (2002) 'My common sense approach to autism.' *Autism Today*, www.autismtoday.com/articles/commonsense.htm

Hendrickson, L. (1996) 'Phenomenal talent – the autistic kind.' www.nexus.edu.au/TeachStud/gut/hendric1.htm

Hermelin, B. (2001) *Bright Splinters of the Mind*. London: Jessica Kingsley Publishers.

Hill, A.A. (1958) *Introduction to Linguistic Structures*. New York: Harcourt.

Hirsh-Pasek, K., Treiman, R. and Schneiderman, M. (1984) 'Brown and Hanlon revisited: Mothers' sensitivity to ungrammatical forms.' *Journal of Child Language,* 11, 81–8.

Hjelmslev, L. (1961) *Prolegomena to a Theory of Language.* (Translated by F. J. Whitfield.) Madison, WI: University of Wisconsin Press.

Hogan, K. (2001) 'Nonverbal thinking, communication, imitation, and play skills from a developmental perspective.' www.teacch.com/develop.htm

Holowka, S. and Petitto, L.A. (2002) 'Left hemisphere cerebral specialization for babies while babbling.' *Science,* 297, 1515.

Humphrey, N. (2002) 'Thinking about feeling.' In R.L. Gregory (ed.) *Oxford Companion to the Mind.* Second edition. Oxford: Oxford University Press.

Huxley, A. (1954) *The Doors of Perception.* New York: Harper and Row.

Innes-Smith, M. (1987) 'Pre-Oedipal identification and the cathexis of autistic object in the aetiology of adult psychopathology.' *International Journal of Psycho-Analysis,* 68, 405–13.

Jacobson, J.W., Mulick, J.A. and Schwartz, A.A. (1995) 'A history of Facilitated Communication: Science, pseudoscience, and antiscience: Science working group on Facilitated Communication.' *American Psychologist,* 50, 9, 750–65.

James, A.L. and Barry, R.J. (1983) 'A review of psychophisiology in early onset psychosis.' *Schizophrenia Bulletin,* 6, 506–25.

Jaynes, J. (1976) *Origin of Consciousness in the Breakdown of the Bicameral Mind.* Boston, MA: Houghton Mifflin.

Joan and Rich (1999) 'What is autism?' www.ani.autistics.org/joan_rich.html

Johnson-Laird, P.N. (1989) 'Analogy and the exercise of creativity.' In S. Vosniadou and A. Ortony (eds) *Similarity and Analogical Reasoning.* Cambridge: Cambridge University Press.

Jolliffe, T., Lakesdown, R. and Robinson, C. (1992) 'Autism, a personal account.' *Communication,* 26, 3, 12–19.

Jordan, R. (1989) 'An experimental comparison of the understanding and use of speaker–addressee personal pronouns in autistic children.' *British Journal of Disorders of Communication,* 24, 169–79.

Jordan, R. (1995) 'Computer assisted education for individuals with autism.' Paper presented to the Autisme-France Third International Conference, 'Autism and Computer Applications', Nice, 27–29 January.

Jordan, R. and Powell, S. (1995) *Understanding and Teaching Children with Autism.* Chichester: John Wiley & Sons.

Kanner, L. (1943) 'Autistic disturbances of affective contact.' *Nervous Child,* 2, 217–50.

Kanner, L. (1971) 'Follow-up study of eleven autistic children, originally reported in 1943.' *Journal of Autism and Childhood Schizophrenia,* 2, 119–45.

Kaufman, B.N. (1976) *Son-Rise.* New York: Harper and Row.

Kaye, L. (1995) 'The language of thought.' *Philosophy of Science*, 62, 92–110.

Kess, J. (1976) *Psycholinguistics: Introductory Perspectives.* New York: Academic Press.

Kochmeister, S. (1995) 'Excerpts from "Shattering Walls".' *Facilitated Communication Digest*, 5, 3, 9–11.

Krystal, H. (1988) *Integration and Self-Healing: Affect, Trauma, Alexithymia.* Hillsdale, NJ: Analytic.

Lakoff, G. (1987) *Women, Fire, and Dangerous Things: What Categories Reveal about the Mind.* Chicago: University of Chicago Press.

Lakoff, J. and Johnson, M. (1980) *Metaphors We Live By.* Chicago, IL: University of Chicago Press.

Lawrence, D.H. (1950) 'Acquired distinctiveness of cues: II. Selective association in a constant stimulus situation.' *Journal of Experimental Psychology*, 40, 175–88.

Lawson, W. (1998) *Life Behind Glass: A Personal Account of Autism Spectrum Disorder.* London: Jessica Kingsley Publishers.

Lawson, W. (1999) 'Reflection on autism and communication: A personal account.' Autism99 Internet Conference Papers. www.autism99.org

Lawson, W. (2001) *Understanding and Working with the Spectrum of Autism: An Insider's View.* London: Jessica Kingsley Publishers.

Lenneberg, E.H. (1967) *Biological Foundation of Language.* New York: John Wiley & Sons.

Lester, B.M. and Zeskind, P.S. (1978) 'Brazelton scale and physical size correlates of neonatal cry features.' *Infant Behavioral Development*, 1, 393–402.

Lewis, M.M. (1957) *How Children Learn to Speak.* London: G. Harrap Co.

Lord, C. and Paul, R. (1997) 'Language and communication in autism.' In D. Cohen and F. Volkmar (eds) *Handbook of Autism and Pervasive Developmental Disorders.* New York: John Wiley & Sons.

Lovaas, O.I. (1966) 'A program for the establishment of speech in psychotic children.' In J.K. Wing (ed.) *Early Childhood Autism.* New York: Pergamon Press.

Lovaas, O.I. (1977) *The Autistic Child: Language Development Through Behavior Modification.* New York: Irvington Press.

McKean, T. (1999) Articles. www.geocites.com/-soonlight/SWCTL/ARTICLES

Marmor, G.S. and Petitto, L.A. (1979) 'Simultaneous communication in the classroom: How well is English grammar represented?' *Sign Language Studies*, 3, 99, 136.

Matte-Blanco, I. (1975) *The Unconscious as Infinite Sets: An Essay in Bi-Logic.* London: Duckworth.

Mehler, J., Jusczyk, P., Lambertz, G., Halsted, N., Bertoncini, J. and Amiel-Tison, C. (1988) 'A precursor of language acquisition in young infants.' *Cognition*, 29, 143–78.

Menn, L. (1976) 'Pattern, control, and contrast in beginning speech: A case study in the acquisition of word form and function.' Unpublished doctoral dissertation, University of Illinois.

Merzenich, M.M., Jenkins, W.W., Johnson, P., Schreiner, C., Miller, S.L., Tallal, P. (1996) 'Temporal processing deficits of language-learning impaired children ameliorated by training.' *Science,* 271, 77–81.

Mesibov, G.B. (1992) 'A comprehensive program for serving people with autism and their families: The TEACCH Model.' In J.L. Matson (ed.) *Autism in Children and Adults: Etiology, Assessment, and Intervention.* Pacific Grove, CA: Brooks Cole.

Mesibov, G.B. and Shea, V. (1996) *The Culture of Autism: From Theoretical Understanding to Educational Practice.* Division TEACCH, Department of Psychiatry: University of North Carolina at Chapel Hill Press.

Meyerding, J. (undated) 'Thoughts on finding myself differently brained.' www.inlv.demon.nl/subm-brain.jane.eng.html

Miller, G.A. (1951) *Language and Communication.* New York: McGraw-Hill Book Co.

Mirenda, P. and Donnellan, A. (1986) 'Effects of adult interactions style on conversational behavior in students with severe communication problems.' *Language, Speech and Hearing Services in the Schools,* 17, 126–41.

Morgan, J.L. (1996) 'Prosody and the roots of parsing.' *Language and Cognitive Processes,* 11, 69–106.

Morris, B. (1999) 'New light and insight, on an old matter.' Autism99 Internet Conference Papers. www.autism99.org

Moulton, W. (1970) *The Nature of Language.* Chicago, IL: University of Chicago Press.

Mowrer, O.H. (1960) *Learning Theory and the Symbolic Processes.* New York: John Wiley & Sons.

Mukhopadhyay, R. (1999) 'When silence speaks: The way my mother taught me.' Autism99 Internet Conference Papers. www.autism99.org

Mukhopadhyay, R. (2000) 'My memory.' www.cureautismnow.org/tito/memories/my_memory.pdf

Mundy, P., Sigman, M. and Ungerer, J.A. (1989) 'Specifying the nature of social impairment in autism.' In G. Dawson (ed.) *Autism: Nature, Diagnosis and Treatment.* New York: The Guilford Press.

Murray, D.K.C. (1992) 'Attention tunnelling and autism.' In P. Shattock and G. Linfoot (eds) *Living with Autism: The Individual, the Family, and the Professional.* Sunderland: Autism Research Unit, University of Sunderland.

Myers, F.L. and Myers, R.W. (1983) 'Perception of stress contrasts in semantic and nonsemantic contexts by children.' *Journal of Psycholinguistic Research,* 12, 227–38.

Nelson, K.E. (1973) *Monographs of the Society for Research in Child Development 38. Structure and strategy in learning to talk.* Chicago: University of Chicago Press.

Ojemann, G.A. (1991) 'Cortical organisation of language.' *Journal of Neuroscience,* 11, 2281–7.

Oller, D.K. (1980) 'The emergence of the sounds of speech in infancy.' In G.H. Yeni-Komshian, J.F. Kavanagh and C.A. Furguson (eds) *Child Phonology: Vol. 1: Production.* New York: Academic Press.

O'Neill, J.L. (1999) *Through the Eyes of Aliens: A Book about Autistic People.* London: Jessica Kingsley Publishers.

O'Neill, J.L. (2000) 'I live in a home within myself.' The National Autistic Society. www.nas.org.uk/nas/jsp/polopoly.jsp?d=120&a=2204

Ornitz, E.M. (1989) 'Autism at the interface between sensory and information processing.' In G. Dawson (ed.) *Autism: Nature, Diagnosis and Treatment.* New York: The Guilford Press.

Ornitz, E.M. and Ritvo, E.R. (1976) 'The syndrome of autism: A critical review.' *American Journal of Psychiatry,* 133, 609–22.

Osgood, C.E. (1962) 'Studies on generality of affective meaning systems.' *American Psychologist,* XVII, January, 10–28.

Padden, C. and Humphries, T. (1988) *Deaf in America: Voices from a Culture.* Cambridge, MA: Harvard University Press.

Park, D.C. and Youderian, P. (1974) 'Light and number: Ordering principles in the world of an autistic child.' *Journal of Autism and Childhood Schizophrenia,* 4, 313–23.

Peacocke, C. (1992) *A Study of Concepts.* Cambridge, MA: MIT Press.

Peeters, T. (2000) 'The language of objects.' In S. Powell (ed.) *Helping Children with Autism to Learn.* London: David Fulton Publishers.

Peters, A.M. (1983) *The Units of Language Acquisition.* Cambridge: Cambridge University Press.

Petitto, L.A. (1994) 'Are signed languages "real" languages? Evidence from American Sign Language and Langue des Signes Québecoise.' *Signpost (International Quarterly of the Sign Linguistics Association),* 7, 3, 1–10.

Petitto, L.A. and Marentette, P.F. (1991) 'Babbling in the manual code: Evidence for the ontogeny of language.' *Science,* 251, 1493–6.

Petitto, L.A., Katerelos, M., Levy, B., Gauna, K., Tétrault, K. and Ferraro, V. (2001) 'Bilingual signed and spoken language acquisition from birth: Implications for mechanisms underlying bilingual language acquisition.' *Journal of Child Language,* 28, 2, 1–44.

Petitto, L.A., Zatorre, R., Gauna, K., Nikelski, E.J., Dostie, D. and Evans, A. (2000) 'Speech-like cerebral activity in profoundly deaf people while processing signed languages: Implications for the neural basis of human language.' Proceedings of the National Academy of Sciences, December 2000, 97, 25, 13961–6.

Phillips, K. (2002) 'KJP's Asperger's Syndrome site and many other things.' www.angelfire.com/amiga/aut

Piaget, J. (1926) *The Language and Thought of the Child.* New York: Routledge and Kegan Paul.

Posner, M.I. (1980) 'Orienting of attention.' *Quarterly Journal of Experimental Psychology*, 32, 3–25.

Potter, C. and Whittaker, C. (2001) *Enabling Communication in Children with Autism*. London: Jessica Kingsley Publishers.

Powell, S. (2000) 'Learning about life asocially: The autistic perspective on education.' In S. Powell (ed.) *Helping Children with Autism to Learn*. London: David Fulton Publishers.

Prizant, B.M. (1982) 'Gestalt processing and gestalt language acquisition in autism.' *Topics in Language Disorders*, 3, 16–23.

Prizant, B.M. (1983a) 'Echolalia in autism: Assessment and intervention.' *Seminar in Speech and Language*, 4, 63–78.

Prizant, B.M. (1983b) 'Language acquisition and communicative behavior in autism: Toward an understanding of the "whole" of it.' *Journal of Speech and Hearing Disorders*, 48, 296–307.

Prizant, B.M. (1996) 'Brief report: Communication, language, social and emotional development.' *Journal of Autism and Developmental Disorders*, 26, 2, 173–8.

Prizant, B.M. and Duchan, J.F. (1981) 'The function of immediate echolalia in autistic children.' *Journal of Speech and Hearing Disorders*, 46, 241–9.

Prizant, B.M. and Rydell, P.J. (1993) 'Assessment and intervention considerations for unconventional verbal behavior.' In J. Reichle and D. Wacker (eds) *Communicative Alternatives of Challanging Behavior: Integrating Functional Assessment and Intervention Strategies*. Baltimore, MD: Paul H. Brookes Publishing.

Prizant, B.M. and Wetherby, A.M. (1985) 'Intentional communicative behavior of children with autism: Theoretical and practical issues.' *Australian Journal of Human Communication Disorders*, 13, 21–59.

Prizant, B.M. and Wetherby, A.M. (1989) 'Enhancing language and communication in autism: From theory to practice.' In G. Dawson (ed.) *Autism: Nature, Diagnosis, and Treatment*. New York: The Guilford Press.

Purves, D. (1994) *Neural Activity and the Growth of the Brain*. New York: Cambridge University Press.

Rand, B. (undated) 'How to understand people who are different.' www.hunnybee.com/autism/bradrand.html

Ratey, J. (2001) *A User's Guide to the Brain*. London: Little, Brown and Company.

Reber, S. (1995) *Dictionary of Psychology*. Second edition. London: Penguin Books.

Richer, J. (2001) 'The insufficient integration of self and other in autism.' In J. Richer and S. Coates (eds) *Autism: The Search for Coherence*. London: Jessica Kingsley Publishers.

Ricks, D. (1979) 'Making sense of experience to make sensible sounds.' In M. Bullowa (ed.) *Before Speech: The Beginning of Interpersonal Communication*. New York: Cambridge University Press.

Ricks, D. and Wing, L. (1975) 'Language, communication and the use of symbols in normal and autistic children.' *Journal of Autism and Childhood Schizophrenia*, 5, 3, 191–221.

Rimland, B. (1993) 'Facilitated Communication: Now the bad news.' *Autism Reasearch Review International*, 6, 3.

Rizzolatti, G. and Arbib, M.A. (1998) 'Language within our grasp.' *Trends in Neurosciences*, 21, 5, 188–94.

Roberts, J. (1989) 'Echolalia and comprehension in autistic children.' *Journal of Autism and Developmental Disorders*, 19, 2.

Rutherford, S. (1988) 'The culture of American Deaf people.' *Sign Language Studies*, 59, 129–47.

Rutter, M., Bartak, L. and Newman, S. (1971) 'Autism – a central disorder of cognition and language?' In M. Rutter (ed.) *Autism: Concepts, Characteristics, and Treatment*. London: Churchill Livingstone.

Sacks, O. (1995) *An Anthropologist on Mars*. London: Picador.

Sainsbury, C. (2000) *The Martian in the Playground: Understanding the Schoolchild with Asperger's Syndrome*. Bristol: Lucky Duck Publishing.

Sapir, E. (1929) 'The status of linguistics as a science.' *Language*, 5, 207–14.

Schuler, A.L. and Prizant, B.M. (1985) 'Echolalia.' In E. Schopler and G. Mesibov (eds) *Communication Problems in Autism*. New York: Plenum Press.

Schutz, A. (1962) 'Common sense and scientific interpretations of human action.' *Collected Papers, Vol. 1*. The Hague: Martinus Nijhoff.

Segar, M. (undated) 'The battles of the autistic thinker.' *A Survival Guide for People with Asperger's Syndrome*. www.shifth.mistral.co.uk/autism/marc1.htm

Sejnowski, T. (2003) 'How Does the Autistic Brain Work?' www.pbs.org/kcet/closertotruth/explore/show_03.html

Selfe, L. (1977) *Nadia: A Case of Extraordinary Drawing Ability in an Autistic Child*. London: Academic Press.

Selfe, L. (1985) 'Anomalous drawing development: Some clinical studies.' In N.H. Freeman and M.V. Cox (eds) *Visual Order: The Nature and Development of Pictoral Representation*. Cambridge: Cambridge University Press.

Seliger, H. (1978) 'Implications of a multiple critical period hypothesis for second language learning.' In W. Ritchie (ed.) *Second Language Acquisition Research*. New York: Academic Press.

Shore, S. (2003) 'Life on and slightly to the right of the Autism Spectrum.' *Exceptional Parent Magazine*, October, 85–90.

Shore, S. (undated) 'My life with autism: Implications for educators.' www.behaviorstore.com/behavior/default.asp?pgC=article2

Siegel, B. (1996) *The World of the Autistic Child*. New York: Oxford University Press.

Silverman, F. (1996) *Communication for the Speechless.* Third edition. Boston, MA: Allyn & Bacon.

Simmons, J.Q. and Baltaxe, C.A.M. (1975) 'Language patterns of adolescent autistics.' *Journal of Autism and Childhood Schizophrenia,* 5, 333–51.

Sinclair, J. (1989) *Thoughts about empathy.* http://web.syr.edu/%7Ejisincla/empathy.htm

Sinclair, J. (1992) 'Bridging the gaps: An inside-out view of autism.' In E. Schopler and G.B. Mesibov (eds) *High-Functioning Individuals with Autism.* New York: Plenum Press.

Sinclair, J. (1993) 'Don't mourn for us.' *Our Voice,* 1, 3, 1–4.

Sinclair, J. (1998) 'Is cure a goal?' www.members.xoom.com/JimSinclair

Siple, P. (1978) 'Visual constraints for sign language communication.' *Sign Language Studies,* 7, 19, 95–110.

Skinner, B.F. (1957) *Science and Human Behavior.* New York: Macmillan.

Smith, M.D. (1990) *Autism and Life in the Community: Successful Interventions for Behavioral Challenges.* Baltimore, MD: Paul H. Brookes.

Smith, M.D. and Belcher, R.G. (1993) 'Facilitated Communication and autism: Separating facts from fiction.' *Journal of Autism and Developmental Disorders,* 23, 1, 175–83. www.csaac.org/pub-fac.htm

Smith, M.D., Belcher, R.G., Juhrs, P.D. and Nabors, K. (1994) 'Where people with autism work.' *Journal of Vocational Rehabilitation,* 4, 10–17.

Snyder, A.W. (1996a) 'Breaking mindset.' Keynote address 'The Mind's New Science' Cognitive Science Miniconference, Macquarie University, 14 November. www.centreforthemind.com/publications/Breaking_Mindset.htm

Snyder, A.W. (1996b) 'Shedding light on creativity.' *Australian and New Zealand Journal of Medicine,* 26, 709–11.

Snyder, A.W. and Barlow, H. (1988) 'Human vision: Revealing the artist's touch.' *Nature,* 331, 117–18.

Snyder, A.W. and Mitchell, J.D. (1999) 'Is integer arithmetic fundamental to mental proceeding? The mind's secret arithmetic.' *Proceedings of the Royal Society of London,* 2666, 587–92.

Snyder, A.W. and Thomas, M. (1997) 'Autistic child artists give clues to cognition.' *Perception,* 26, 93–6.

Spicer, D. (1998) 'Self-awareness in living with Asperger syndrome.' Asperger Syndrome Conference Papers, Vasteras, Sweden, March 12–13.

Stark, R.E. (1986) 'Prespeech segmental feature development.' In P. Fletcher and M. Garman (eds) *Language Acquisition.* Second edition. New York: Cambridge University Press.

Stern, D.N. (1994) 'One way to build a clinically relevant baby.' *Infant Mental Health Journal,* 15, 9–25.

Stone, W. and Caro-Martinez, L. (1990) 'Naturalistic observations of spontaneous communication in autistic children.' *Journal of Autism and Developmental Disorders*, 20, 437–54.

Strauss, E. (1998) 'Writing, speech separated in split brain.' *Science*, 8 May, 280, 827.

Streeter, L.A. (1976) 'Language perception of 2-month-old infants shows effects of both innate mechanisms and experience.' *Nature*, 259, 39–41.

Sullivan, R. (1980) 'Why do autistic children...?' *Journal of Autism and Developmental Disorders*, 10, 2, 231–38.

Tager-Flusberg, H. (1981) 'On the nature of linguistic functioning in early infantile autism.' *Journal of Autism and Developmental Disorders*, 11, 45–54.

Tager-Flusberg, H. (1988) 'On the nature of a language acquisition disorder: The example of autism.' In F. Kessel (ed.) *The Development of Language and Language Researchers: Essays presented to Roger Brown*. Hillsdale, NJ: Lawrence Erlbaum.

Tager-Flusberg, H. (1989) 'A psycholinguistic perspective on language development in the autistic child.' In G. Dawson (ed.) *Autism: Nature, Diagnosis, and Treatment*. New York: The Guilford Press.

Tanguay, P.E. and Edwards, R.M. (1982) 'Electrophysiological studies of autism: The whisper of the bang.' *Journal of Autism and Developmental Disabilities*, 12, 177–84.

Thiong'o, N. wa (1984) 'The tension between national and imperialistic culture.' *World Literature Written in English*, 24, 3–9.

Tikhomirov, O.K. (1959) 'Review of B.F. Skinner's "Verbal Behavior".' *Word*, XV, 2, 362–7.

Travers, J.F. (1982) *The Growing Child*. Second edition. Glenview, IL: Scott, Foresman & Co.

Trehub, S.E. (1976) 'The discrimination of foreign speech contrasts by infants and children.' *Child Development*, 47, 466–72.

VanDalen, J.G.T. (1995) 'Autism from within: Looking through the eyes of a mildly afflicted autistic person.' *Link*, 17, 11–16.

Vaneechoutte, M. and Skoyles, J.R. (1998) 'The memetic origin of language: Modern humans as musical primates.' *Journal of Memetics – Evolutionary Models of Information Transmission*, 2, 84–117.

Virostek, S. and Cutting, J. (1979) 'Asymmetries for ameslan and other forms in signers and nonsigners.' *Perception and Psychophysics*, 26, 6, 505–8.

Waterhouse, L. and Fein, D. (1982) 'Language skills in developmentally disabled children.' *Brain and Language*, 15, 307–33.

Watkins, A. (2001) 'A home-based Applied Behavioural Analysis Programme: A personal view.' In J. Richer and S. Coates (eds) *Autism: The Search for Coherence*. London: Jessica Kingsley Publishers.

Wechsler, D. (1958) *The Measurement and Appraisal of Adult Intelligence*. Baltimore, MD: Williams & Wilkins.

West, T. (1991) *In the Mind's Eye*. New York: Prometheus Press.

Wetherby, A.M. (1986) 'Ontogeny of communicative functions in autism.' *Journal of Autism and Developmental Disorders*, 15, 295–315.

Wetherby, A., Cain, D., Yonclus, D. and Walker, V. (1988) 'Analysis of intentional communication of normal children from prelinguistic to the multiword stage.' *Journal of Speech and Hearing Research*, 31, 240–52.

Wetherby, A.M. and Prizant, B.M. (1992) 'Facilitating language and communication development in autism: Assessment and intervention guidelines.' In D.E. Berkell (ed.) *Autism: Identification, Education and Treatment*. Hillsdale, NJ: Lawrence Erlbaum Publishers.

Wetherby, A., Prizant, B.M. and Hutchinson, T. (1998) 'Communicative, social-affective, and symbolic profiles of young children with autism and pervasive developmental disorder.' *American Journal of Speech-Language Pathology*, 7, 79–91.

White, B.B. and White, M.S. (1987) 'Autism from the inside.' *Medical Hypothesis*, 24, 223–9.

WHO (1992) *International Statistical Classification of Diseases and Related Health Problems, Tenth Revision*. (ICD-10). Geneva: World Health Organization.

Whorf, B. (1956) *Language, Thought, and Reality*. Cambridge, MA: MIT Press.

Willey, L.H. (1999) *Pretending to Be Normal*. London: Jessica Kingsley Publishers.

Williams, D. (1996) *Autism. An Inside-Out Approach*. London: Jessica Kingsley Publishers.

Williams, D. (1998) *Autism and Sensing. The Unlost Instinct*. London: Jessica Kingsley Publishers.

Williams, D. (1999a) *Like Colour to the Blind: Soul Searching and Soul Finding*. London: Jessica Kingsley Publishers.

Williams, D. (1999b) *Nobody Nowhere*. London: Jessica Kinglsey Publishers.

Williams, D. (1999c) *Somebody Somewhere*. London: Jessica Kingsley Publishers.

Williams, D. (2003a) *Exposure Anxiety – The Invisible Cage: An Exploration of Self-Protection Responses in the Autism Spectrum and Beyond*. London: Jessica Kingsley Publishers.

Williams, D. (2003b) 'Tinted lenses.' *Autism Today Online Magazine*, www.autismtoday.com/articles/tinted_lenses.htm

Williams, R. (1983) *Culture and Society*. New York: MIT Press.

Wing, L. (1992) *The Triad of Impairments of Social Interaction: An Aid to Diagnosis*. London: National Autistic Society.

Winnicott, D.W. (1960) 'Ego distortion in terms of true and false self.' In D.W. Winnicott (ed.) (1965) *The Maturational Processes and the Facilitating Environment*. New York: International Universities Press.

Woodward, J. (1976) 'Sign of change: Historical variation in American sign language.' *Sign Language Studies*, 10, 81–94.

Zeki, S. (1992) 'The visual image in the mind and brain.' *Scientific American*, September, 69–76.

Subject Index

Author Index